CATCH THE WAVE

Customizing OS X Mavericks

Fantastic Tricks, Tweaks, Hacks, Secret Commands, & Hidden Features to Customize Your OS X User Experience

2ND EDITION

Tom Magrini

2nd Edition
© 2014 Tom Magrini

Cover photo: EpicStockMedia/Shutterstock.com

Created & Printed in the United States of America.

ISBN-13: 978-1505423266
ISBN-10: 1505423260

Terms & Conditions of Use

Some of the customizations contained in this book allow access to hidden preference settings not visible in the OS X System Preferences application. These customizations do not add to or change any part of the OS X operating system. The customization settings described in this book are additional preference settings defined by Apple and built into OS X. All of the customizations are reversable and can be reset to the OS X defaults. The customizations were tested in OS X Mavericks (Version 10.9). There is always the possibility that future updates to OS X could cause some of the customizations to no longer work as expected.

While the author has taken every precaution in the preparation of this book, the author assumes no responsibility whatsoever for errors or omissions, or for damages resulting from the use of the information contained herein. The information contained in this book is used at your own risk. Any use of the information contained in this book constitutes your agreement to be bound by these terms and conditions.

IN LOVING MEMORY OF CORBIN (2004 – 2013)

While writing this book I had to put my best friend to sleep. My beloved black lab Corbin lost his five-month battle against osteosarcoma. Corbin was my best friend and faithful companion of 9½ years, spending many hours at my feet while I worked. I would give anything for one more swim in the pool or walk around the neighborhood with him. The moments we spent together were precious and far too few. I think Corbin somehow understood the neverending demands on my time and appreciated the time we spent together as much as I did. Corbin was my best friend and I was his.

Table of Contents

1

Customize Your Mac

Why customize your Mac? Well, because you can. It's that simple.

The default OS X settings that come out of the box make your Mac incredibly easy and efficient to use. And for most people the defaults are all they'll ever need. But if you are reading this book, then you aren't like most people. Like me, you want to tinker and tweak OS X to personalize it to the way we use our Macs, squeezing out every last drop of performance. Besides, who wants their Mac to look, feel, and operate just like every one else's? And of course, its always cool to impress your friends when they notice your Mac does things that theirs doesn't. This book will turn you into an OS X geek, showing you how to bend OS X to your every will.

OS X Mavericks is the world's most powerful desktop operating system. OS X allows you to completely customize your user experience until your Mac has a look and feel different from anyone else's. You can completely personalize your Mac, fine-tuning various aspects of the operating system to transform how you interact with OS X. No two Mac users use their Macs the same way. Besides changing the look and feel, the customizations and tweaks I'll show you will allow you to be more productive and efficient by making OS X more closely match your personal style and the way you work.

You don't need to be a computer geek to customize your user experience. The customizations in this book fall into two categories – basic and advanced. Anyone with a little bit of familiarity with OS X can safely customize their user experience using the basic customizations. And don't let the word "advanced" scare you. These customizations require the use of an application called **Terminal** to enter commands. I'll teach you enough about Terminal in the next few pages to become truly dangerous (just kidding). My goal is not to turn you into a Terminal expert, but to give you a solid foundation. Once you have learned the basics of Terminal, you will be able to configure all of the OS X customizations, hacks, and tweaks in this book to unlock the OS X "hidden" features. So let's satisfy your inner geek

Each chapter focuses on customizing a particular aspect of OS X Mavericks. We'll start first with the basics of OS X customization and move quickly to the advanced level. You'll get an in depth lesson on the command line interface of Terminal to give you the confidence of the nerdiest computer geek.

Once you've mastered these skills, we'll cover the customization of each aspect of OS X starting first with gestures in Chapter 2. In this second edition of *Catch the Wave: Customizing OS X Mavericks,* I'll show you how to go above and beyond the standard sixteen trackpad and 6 mouse gestures offered by OS X. I'll teach you how to create your own personal custom trackpad and mouse gestures that are guaranteed to increase your efficiency and productivity.

Next we'll customize the Desktop in Chapter 3. You'll learn how to customize the Desktop, personalize it, and make it more efficient.

In Chapter 4, we'll tweak Mission Control, which provides a view of everything on your Mac – application windows, full-screen apps, desktop spaces, and the Dashboard. You'll learn how to increase your desktop workspace and efficiently manage window clutter.

We'll customize the various options available in the Menu Bar, a component of the OS X Desktop in Chapter 5.

Next up in Chapter 6 is the Dock, one of the most recognizable features of OS X, where I'll teach you how to fine-tune the default OS X Dock to make it your own personal Dock.

Then we move on to Chapter 7 where you'll learn about Stacks, a cool feature of the Dock. You'll learn more than a dozen different tweaks guaranteed to increase your productivity.

Better searching is the topic of Chapter 8, where we will customize Spotlight, the OS X system-wide search function that allows you to quickly find almost anything on your Mac. I'll show you how the fine tune Spotlight to improve your search results and how to search like a pro. I'll also show you a low-cost app from the Mac App Store that saves time when searching the web.

Then in Chapter 9, we'll check out Notification Center, a one-stop shop that consolidates alerts from a variety of sources.

I'll show you a number of customizations for the Dashboard in Chapter 10 to make this OS X feature a little more useful. I'll even show you how to completely remove the Dashboard if you desire.

In Chapter 11, we'll explore some tweaks to Launchpad, an OS X feature that blurs the line between OS X and iOS.

Chapter 12 focuses on Finder, the OS X file manager application, which provides a user interface to manage files, disk drives, and network drives and to launch applications. We will focus on customizations to make Finder more useful.

Window Snapping and management is the focus of Chapter 13. In this brand new 2nd edition of *Customizing OS X Mavericks*, I'll help those former Microsoft Windows users who miss Windows' snapping feature. Everything is better on a Mac including window snapping. I'll show you how to get the same functionality with the addition of a low cost utility found in the Mac App Store that offers over 20 different window resizing and snapping options.

Next, we'll focus on customizing applications starting with Safari in Chapter 14 and move on to Mail in Chapter 15. I'll show you how to customize Safari and Mail to make both perform more efficiently and add to your productivity. Then I'll show you a bunch of tweaks for various OS X apps in Chapter 16.

Security is the focus of Chapter 17, where I'll show you how to use the Keychain Access application as well as some other useful tweaks to make your Mac a little more secure.

Chapter 18 finishes up with a few final tweaks that I thought you may find handy.

So let's get started first with some basic customizations using the System Preferences application.

Basic Customization

 Apple offers a number of basic customizations to tune OS X and its behavior to fit your personal preferences. Most of these customizations can be accomplished using the OS X graphical user interface through the **System Preferences** application. System Preferences allows users to modify system-wide OS X settings. With lots of colorful icons, the System Preferences application can be a little overwhelming at first. These colorful icons are called preference panes and they contain a tremendous amount of customization power to safely tweak your OS X user experience. Other basic customization is accomplished using the preferences of specific applications, like **Finder** or **Safari**.

Click on the **System Preferences** icon found in the default OS X Dock, launch the app using **Launchpad**, or select > **System Preferences...** from the Apple menu in the upper left corner of the Menu Bar to bring up the System Preferences application.

By default, the preference panes are organized into four categories from top to bottom: Personal, Hardware, Internet & Wireless, and System. A fifth category, called Other, is used for third party preference panes and is only visible if you have a third party application installed (i.e., Adobe Flash). Clicking on an icon brings up a preference pane with various customization options.

Organize the Preference Panes Alphabetically

The organization of the preference panes in System Preferences is our very first customization. By default, the panes are organized by categories. OS X allows you to change the display to alphabetical order. Select **View > Organize Alphabetically**. There are two advantages to organizing alphabetically. The System Preferences window takes up less room on the desktop and you no longer have to know in which category a particular pane is located.

Select **View > Organize by Categories** to return to the default display. The **View** menu also provides a drop down list of all the preference panes in alphabetical order, allowing you to quickly select one. A secondary click on the **System Preferences** icon in the Dock will also display the preference panes in alphabetical order. If neither of these options work for you, clicking and holding the **Show All** button will display an alphabetical list of the preference panes. If you know what preference pane you want, any of these options will get you there quickly.

At the very top of the System Preferences window is a toolbar with three controls: navigation buttons, **Show All**, and a search field. The back button will be grayed out until you click on a preference pane. When in a preference pane, clicking the back button returns you to the main System Preferences display as does clicking **Show All**. The forward button is grayed out until you click on a preference pane and then return to the main display. Essentially these navigation buttons serve the same purpose as they do in a browser, allowing you to navigate backward and forward through the panes.

Search System Preferences

Sometimes finding the preference pane containing the specific setting you want to modify is not always intuitive. The search field comes in handy when you know which particular OS X setting you want to modify, but don't know in which pane to find it.

As you type in the search field, OS X will highlight the panes related to your search and display a list of suggested items in the Spotlight menu below the search field. Eventually, OS X will zero in on the applicable preference panes.

Even if you don't know exactly what the OS X setting is called, the Spotlight menu under the search field will offer suggestions to help you find the right preference pane. Click the highlighted preference pane or one of the spotlighted items listed under the search field to navigate to the appropriate preference pane. Any OS X setting controlled by the System Preferences application can be found using the search field.

Hide Preference Panes

Clicking and holding the **Show All** button not only brings up an alphabetical list of the preference panes, it also offers a **Customize...** option at the very bottom of the menu. Selecting it causes little check boxes to appear at the lower right of each preference pane icon. Unchecking a check box hides a preference pane.

Why would you hide a pane? There are a few preference panes that you will never use or you've made changes in one or more and have no desire to make additional changes. For example, I replaced the optical drive from my MacBook Pro with a second Solid State Drive (SSD). I have absolutely no need for the **CDs & DVDs** preference pane. Hiding preference panes removes superfluous clutter that distracts you from the panes you actually need.

When you are done unchecking or checking preference panes, click the **Done** button, which is located where the **Show All** button was. Note that unchecking a preference pane simply hides it from view. It does not delete the pane. We'll cover how to delete preference panes next. And don't worry, a hidden preference pane can always be unhidden by selecting **Show All > Customize...** and checking its check box.

Delete Preference Panes

As you use your Mac, you'll likely install and try software and then uninstall it if it doesn't fit your needs. Often third-party software comes with its own preference pane to modify various application preferences. Third-party preference panes are shown at the very bottom of System Preferences in the Other category. If you want to delete a preference pane for third-party software you no longer use, secondary click on the preference pane icon to bring up an option to remove it.

OS X will not only remove the preference pane icon from System Preferences, it will locate the preference pane file and move it to the trash.

Note that OS X only allows you to remove third-party preference panes. OS X does not allow you to remove a standard preference pane that is needed by OS X.

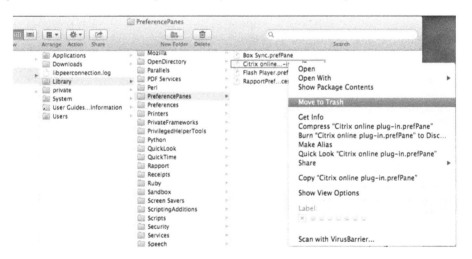

Another option to delete an unwanted preference pane is to open **Finder** and navigate to the **Library > PreferencePanes** folder. Select the unwanted pane and drag it to the trash. The **Library** folder can be found in the root directory of your startup disk.

Sometimes you will not find the preference pane in the **PreferencePanes** folder. For this reason it is better to utilize the secondary click method in System Preferences to remove unwanted preference panes.

The OS X System Preferences application is extremely powerful, giving the average user the power to customize a multitude of systemwide settings. In each of the basic customization sections of the coming chapters, we'll focus on a specific aspect of the OS X user experience, checking out options available to tweak. Even if you find System Preferences a little intimidating, I'll show you just how easy it is to customize your OS X user experience. It's your Mac, so feel free to customize, hack, and tweak it.

Advanced Customization

Apple offers a number of advanced customizations to turn numerous features on or off or to change the behavior of OS X to fit your personal preferences. Often these features are described as "hidden" or "secret" on various websites. There is nothing really hidden or secret about these features other than the fact they are not directly accessible from the OS X graphical user interface. Each feature requires the use of the **Terminal** application to enter specific commands in its command line interface. Terminal provides a text-based method for Mac users to directly interact with the OS X operating system, allowing customization far beyond what is possible using only System Preferences.

If entering commands into a command line interface sounds intimidating, it isn't. Don't let the word "advanced" scare you. First, I'll show you how to use the Terminal application. Once you have learned the basics of Terminal, you will be able to configure all of the OS X customizations, hacks, and tweaks in this book and unlock OS X's so-called "hidden" or "secret" features. The advanced customizations in this book take OS X customization to an entirely different level not achievable using System Preferences alone. Each of the commands listed in the advanced customizations have been tested on my own personal Early 2011 MacBook Pro. Many represent my personal favorites.

Introduction to Terminal

 The average Mac user may never know the existence of the **Terminal** application. Everything the average Mac user needs to do can be accomplished through the graphical user interface of OS X. Those who know of Terminal's existence tend to avoid it because they find its archaic command line interface strange and intimidating. The modern computer user sees Terminal as a throwback to the old days of computing before graphical user interfaces became the norm. Terminal reminds us of a time when geeky computer scientists with thick birth control glasses sat hunched over their keyboards, pounding away in a strange language more familiar to the computer than human.

Why bother using Terminal in the first place? While Terminal appears at first glance to be a relic more appropriate for a museum then your modern, beautiful, and elegant OS X graphical user interface, Terminal is one of the most powerful, versatile, and useful features of OS X. It has many uses beyond just customization of your OS X user experience. And as you'll see in the next few pages, Terminal may seem archaic, but it certainly isn't intimidating.

Terminal can be used by users of all skill levels, even a novice Mac user who is learning about Terminal for the first time. We'll take some baby steps to build your confidence and learn the basics of Terminal, enough so that you will be able to configure all of the OS X customizations, hacks, and tweaks to unlock the OS X "hidden" or "secret" features.

Before You Begin

The legal folks tell me I have to give you a standard warning here. You will use Terminal to change preference settings which are not visible in the OS X System Preferences. These preference settings do not add or change any part of the OS X operating system. The preference settings described in this book are defined by Apple as part of OS X. All of the customizations are reversible.

While the Terminal commands in this book are safe to use and I have tested them on my MacBook Pro in OS X Mavericks (version 10.9), you must enter the commands exactly as shown. I cannot be there to correct you when you fat finger a command, so I assume no responsibility for any damages resulting from the use of the information contained in this book. You are using the information contained in this book at your own risk.

Terminal is a powerful application that allows you to do amazing things with your Mac, however, you can also use it to royally screw up your Mac. So the warning is to **make sure you have a current Time Machine backup in case you have to restore your Mac**. While I recommend backing up before running any of the advanced customizations, having a current Time Machine backup is just good practice. To create a Time Machine backup, select **Back Up Now** from the **Time Machine Menu Extra** in the Menu Bar.

Terminal Basics

Let's open the **Terminal** application. By default, Terminal is not in the Dock. Use **Launchpad** to open it. You'll find it in the **Utilities** folder. You can also search for it using **Spotlight**. It will show up under Top Hit or under Applications at the top of the Spotlight menu. You can also open Terminal by navigating to the **Applications** folder. You'll find it in the **Utilities** folder.

Once open, Terminal displays a text-based user interface showing the name of the computer and your location in the file system (normally your Home directory) followed by a

$ sign. A gray rectangular cursor, called a **prompt**, patiently awaits your command. The default view is shown in the picture.

Terminal Preferences

This is a good time to introduce the topic of application preferences before we learn more about Terminal. While the System Preferences application controls systemwide OS X preferences, each application has its own unique preference pane. Application preference panes control various settings within the application itself. These settings are not systemwide nor do they affect other applications.

Application preferences can be found under the application menu, the menu immediately to the right of the (Apple) menu in the Menu Bar. First, open Terminal if you haven't opened it already. If it's open,

click on the Terminal window to bring it to the front. Select **Preferences...** from the **Terminal** menu in the Menu Bar. You can also access the application preference pane by entering ⌘, (command+comma). Once the Terminal preference pane appears, make sure **Settings** is selected from the icons on the toolbar and **Text** is selected from the five choices at the top of the pane.

The first setting I normally change is the font as I find Menlo Regular 11 point a little too small for me to read. Click change to bring up the font dialog box to select a font and font size that is more readable.

Profiles are listed on the side bar on the left of the Settings preference pane. By default, Terminal will open for the first time using the **Basic** profile, the profile highlighted at the top of the profile settings. If you find the default color scheme rather boring, you can change it by selecting one of the profiles on the left. To preview a color scheme, simply double-click on it and it will open a new window in your chosen profile.

Once you are satisfied with a **Profile**, click on the **Default** button at the bottom right of the Profiles sidebar. The word Default will appear under your desired Profile selection after you click the Default button. This will ensure Terminal uses your desired settings the next time you open the application.

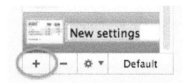

If you would like to create your own profile click the **+** sign at the lower left and rename the **New Settings** profile to anything you desire. Once you're done, be sure to click the Default button to make your new settings the Default profile.

You can also select your own color scheme. Select the colors from the color palette at the center of the pane and drag them to the rectangles next to **Text**, **Bold Text**, **Selection**, and **Cursor**. If you want to create your own colors, click one of the colors on the color palette to bring up a dialog box. When finished, close the dialog box and drag your newly created color to its desired location.

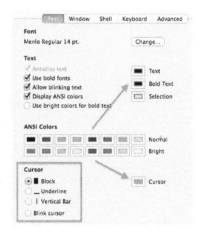

If you don't like the block style cursor, you have two other choices – **Underline** or a **Vertical Bar**. You can also make the cursor blink by checking the check box next to **Blink cursor**. Color and cursor changes take place immediately and are saved to the currently active profile.

We won't go into the settings available in the other three tabs on the toolbar as this is only a basic introduction to the Terminal application. Other settings are more appropriate for more advanced uses of Terminal which are beyond the scope of this book. We've covered enough that we can move onto some basic Terminal commands.

Basic Terminal Commands

The first thing you'll notice about Terminal is the **prompt**. The prompt is where we will enter all of the commands shown in this book. When you open Terminal, the first two lines will look something like this.

```
Last login: Thu Sep 5 11:29:21 on ttys000
Toms-MacBook-Pro:~ Tom$ |
```

The first line tells you when you last logged in via the Terminal application. The second line is the prompt. The beginning of the prompt tells you the machine you're logged into and your location in the file system. The cursor appears after the $ sign. Depending on your selections in the Terminal preferences the cursor may or may not be blinking and could appear as a block, an underline, or a vertical bar.

Commands will be entered at the prompt. You do not have to use your mouse or trackpad as anything you type will appear at the prompt. Once a command has been completely entered, you will hit the **return** key to execute it.

A behavior first time users often find odd is that Terminal will provide no feedback when a command is entered correctly. Feedback is only provided when an invalid command has been entered. And don't worry, OS X will not make any changes if the command is mistyped or invalid. If a command is entered correctly, a new prompt line will appear with the cursor awaiting your next command.

So far it sounds pretty simple doesn't it? The advanced customizations in this book simply require you to type a couple of commands exactly as you see them into Terminal, hitting the return key after each command.

If you purchased an e-book edition, I strongly recommend that you copy and paste the commands into the text editor. Once in text editor, check the command to make sure you copied the entire command, then copy and paste it over to Terminal. Remember that you will enter one command at a time into Terminal. You will hit the return key after each command to execute it. Note that some commands shown in this book are case sensitive, therefore you must enter each one exactly as shown.

Let's try a couple of commands. First, I need you to empty your Trash. If your Trash is not already empty, secondary click on the Trash icon in the Dock and then select **Empty Trash**. Click **Empty Trash** again when the dialog box appears asking for confirmation.

Next, open the Terminal application if it is not open already. Type the following command at the prompt.

`defaults write com.apple.dock trash-full -bool TRUE`

Check the command to make sure that you entered it exactly as shown above. If it is not correct, backspace over it and then correct any mistakes. If the command is correct, press the **return** key. If Terminal gave you an error, enter the command again, but this time check it twice to make sure you entered it correctly.

Nothing happened. Nothing should have happened because there is one more command to enter before you can see the change.

Next, enter the following command at the Terminal prompt. This command will restart your Dock. The Dock will disappear momentarily and then reappear with the change you configured with the first command. Note that this command is case sensitive, so be sure to capitalize the **D** in Dock.

`killall Dock`

Like before, check the command to make sure that you entered it correctly. Correct any mistakes. Then hit the **return** key.

Take a look at the trash in the Dock. It should be full. Wait a minute, didn't we just empty the Trash? Double-click on it to bring up Finder. The Trash is empty but the trash can looks full. That was the "hidden" or "secret" OS X setting. The Trash icon will no longer change from full to empty. Give it a try. Find an unwanted file and drag it to the Trash. After emptying the Trash, you'll see the Trash icon stays full.

What if you don't like this customization and want to go back to the default behavior? Like all the customizations in this book, this one is reversible. To go back to the OS X default behavior, enter the following command.

`defaults write com.apple.dock trash-full -bool FALSE`

Check the command to make sure that you entered it correctly. Correct any mistakes. Then hit the **return** key.

Next we'll restart the Dock like we did before with the following command.

`killall Dock`

Check it for errors and if correct, hit the **return** key.

After your Dock restarts, you'll notice the Trash icon shows that it is empty. The Trash icon will now behave as it did before since the last two commands reverted the change back to the default OS X behavior.

Congratulations! You just completed your first advanced customization and reverted back to the default behavior. Yes, the advanced customizations in this book are that simple to configure and reverse.

Some Handy Terminal Commands

Before we finish our basic lesson on Terminal, let me show you some additional commands that will come in handy as you configure the advanced customizations. The first command will provide a history of all the commands you have entered in your Terminal session. History comes in handy when you want to see what you did or you want to reuse a command.

From the Terminal session you used to enter the four commands in the last section, enter the following command at the prompt and hit the **return** key.

`history`

The output should look something like this.

```
Toms-MacBook-Pro:~ Tom$ history
    1  defaults write com.apple.dock trash-full -bool TRUE
    2  killall Dock
    3  defaults write com.apple.dock trash-full -bool FALSE
    4  killall Dock
    5  history
Toms-MacBook-Pro:~ Tom$
```

12

The four commands you entered to change the behavior of the Trash icon and revert back to the default will be shown in the order you executed them. The last command shown will be the **history** command.

Now is probably a good time to mention the typeface. All Terminal commands will be shown in the bold typeface on the previous page. When you see this typeface, it is your signal that these are commands you will enter into Terminal.

Now that you can get a history of the commands you entered, I bet you're wondering if you can use the copy and paste command. Yes you can. Highlight one of the **killall Dock** commands in the history then copy and paste it to the prompt. Now hit the **return** key and watch the Dock restart.

Next, try hitting the **up** arrow key. Terminal will display the **killall Dock** command at the prompt. Hit the **up** arrow again and Terminal displays the **history** command. Note that Terminal lists each command in reverse order, essentially going backwards through your history. Keep hitting the **up** arrow until you reach the first command you entered. Terminal will beep to let you know you reached the end of your history.

Now try the **down** arrow. The **down** arrow will move you forward through your history of commands. The up and down arrows come in handy when you need to enter a previous command again.

After entering a number of commands, the prompt will be at the bottom of the window. If you want to clear the window, enter this command. Don't forget to hit the **return** key.

```
clear
```

The terminal window will clear and the prompt will now be at the top of the window. Let's try entering the **history** command again. Your output should look something like this.

```
Toms-MacBook-Pro:~ Tom$ history
    1   defaults write com.apple.dock trash-full -bool TRUE
    2   killall Dock
    3   defaults write com.apple.dock trash-full -bool FALSE
    4   killall Dock
    5   history
    6   killall Dock
    7   clear
    8   history
Toms-MacBook-Pro:~ Tom$
```

Entering Long Commands

Some of the commands in this book are too long to fit on a single line in **Terminal**. That's okay. A long command will simply flow onto the next line in Terminal. In fact, a really long command can take two, three, or even four lines. Even though the command appears on multiple lines, it is still a single command and will not be executed until you press the **return** key.

For example, note that the following command would appear on one line in the book as:

defaults write com.apple.dock workspaces-edge-delay-float 0.25

However when it is typed into **Terminal** it appears on two lines as shown below. Remember, the command is not executed until you press the **return** key.

```
 ⊖ ○ ○              ⌂ tmagrini — bash — 80×24
Last login: Mon Sep 23 13:48:43 on ttys000
Toms-MacBook-Pro:~ tmagrini$ defaults write com.apple.dock workspaces-edge-delay
 -float 0.25
```

Congratulations! You have now finished your basic Terminal lesson. You are now more powerful than the run-of-the-mill Mac user and can configure any of the advanced customizations in this book. You now have access to features the average user doesn't even know exist. Using your new Terminal skills, you can directly interact with the OS X operating system and customize it far beyond what is possible in System Preferences.

One Last Command

Occasionally I hear Mac users (usually the ones who recently switched from a Windows PC) pronounce OS X as OS "ex," like the letter "X." I hate to nitpick here, but the X is actually the Roman numeral ten. So unless you want to get a funny look from more seasoned Mac users, OS X should be pronounced as OS "ten."

If you don't believe me, just ask your Mac. First, make sure your sound is on and turned up so you can hear it. Next, open Terminal and enter the following command. Don't forget to hit the **return** key. Note that this command is case sensitive, so be sure to capitalize **OS X**.

say OS X

Well that settles it, doesn't it?

2

Gestures

When I'm teaching someone who has never used a Mac before, the first thing I show them is how to set up trackpad gestures. Hands down, Apple has the best multitouch trackpad in the industry and once you have mastered trackpad gestures, it's hard to go back to using a mouse. While I will cover both trackpad and mouse gestures, the trackpad gestures allow you to be far more productive.

If you're an experienced MacUser you may be thinking about skipping this chapter because you are already quite familiar with trackpad and mouse gestures. If that's the case, I suggest you skip directly to the advanced customization section where you'll find a few customizations you may not be familiar with. I'll also show you how to create your own custom trackpad and mouse gestures in the Advanced section of this chapter.

A built-in trackpad is standard on the MacBook Air and MacBook Pro series of laptops. If you have an iMac, Mac Mini, or Mac Pro desktop computer and are using an Apple Magic Mouse, you only have access to a limited number of gestures. In Mavericks, a Magic Mouse supports only six gestures while the Magic Trackpad supports sixteen. I highly recommend that you indulge yourself and spend $69 for an Apple Magic Trackpad so you can take advantage of the full set of gestures in OS X. It will look great next to your Apple Wireless Keyboard.

Users switching from a Windows PC typically find gestures to be strange and foreign. Where is the right mouse button? Nevermind that, where is the left one?! However, with just a little practice, gestures become completely natural. In fact, gestures become so natural that eventually you'll no longer need to think about what gesture does what. You'll rely completely on muscle memory, performing all sixteen gestures without any conscious effort. Once you have mastered the OS X gestures, it is difficult to go back to a Windows PC and mouse.

Let's first start with trackpad gestures then move onto mouse gestures.

Trackpad Gestures

Apple turns on several OS X trackpad gestures by default. However, there are an equal number that are disabled. My guess is that Apple doesn't want to overwhelm users unfamiliar with gestures, therefore it limits the number that are enabled by default. My suggestion is to spend about a half an hour to an hour in the Trackpad preference pane learning all the gestures and turn them all on. After a few days of practice, you'll find all of the gestures will become completely natural and you will no longer have to think which gesture you need to accomplish a specific task.

Besides turning the gestures on, the Trackpad preference pane also allows you to customize five of the gestures. OS X allows you to decide how many fingers you will use for certain gestures.

To configure tackpad gestures, open the **Trackpad** preference pane by launching the **System Preferences** application from the Dock or **Launchpad** and selecting the **Trackpad** icon. You can also launch from the Apple menu by selecting > **System Preferences... > Trackpad**. The **Trackpad** preference pane is located under **Hardware** if you still have the preference panes organized by category.

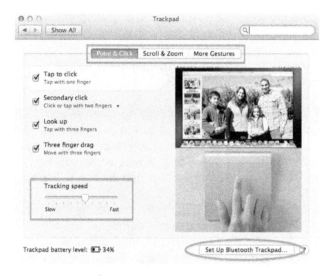

At the top of the trackpad preference pane are three tabs for the three categories of gestures – **Point & Click**, **Scroll & Zoom**, and **More Gestures**. Towards the bottom of the pane is a slider allowing you to adjust the tracking speed of the pointer as it moves across the desktop. If you need to set up a new Apple Magic Trackpad, click the **Set Up Bluetooth Trackpad...** button at the lower left. If you need to see the battery status of an external trackpad, it will be displayed at the lower left.

The left hand side of the pane lists various trackpad gestures with check boxes next to them. To turn on a gesture, simply check the check box. In the right hand pane, Apple included a video demonstrating what the highlighted gesture does and how to perform the gesture. Slide your pointer and hover over any of the gestures and the video in the right pane will automatically change to demonstrate the highlighted gesture.

The best way to learn the gestures in OS X is to watch the video in the Trackpad preference pane and try it for yourself. In no time at all, you'll learn all of the gestures and will wonder how you could have used a computer without them.

Tap To Click

By default, this option is disabled which forces you to press down on the trackpad in order to click. Selecting this option will allow you to tap the trackpad with one finger to click. Tapping the trackpad does not replace pressing down on it as both options are supported. Pressing down on the trackpad is still required to click and hold in order to drag, move, or lasso a bunch of files in Finder.

Secondary Click

A secondary click is used to reveal context sensitive menus and is similar to a right button mouse click in the Windows PC world. Secondary click has three options – **Click or tap with two fingers**, **Click in the bottom right corner**, or **Click in the bottom left corner**. Personally, I prefer tapping with two fingers over using one of the corners. This allows me to execute a secondary click regardless of where my fingers are on the trackpad. The corner options are too restrictive for me and remind me of a Windows PC.

Look Up

Selecting this option will allow you to use a three finger tap on a word to look it up in the dictionary, thesaurus, and Wikipedia. This is an extremely handy feature of OS X.

Three Finger Drag

The three finger drag is by far one of the most useful gestures, essentially accomplishing what a click, hold, and drag does in a single gesture. When you position the pointer over the title bar of a window, you can use the three finger drag to move the window anywhere on the desktop or to another desktop space. This gesture can also be used to copy or move files within Finder. Position the pointer over a file or folder and use the three finger drag to copy it or move it to a new location. You can also use it to drag a file to the Trash.

If you happen to see an image on a webpage that you want to download, position your pointer over the picture and use the three finger drag to copy it to a Finder window or to the desktop.

The three finger drag is also handy for selecting text. Position the cursor in a sentence and use the three finger drag gesture either forward or backward to select the text. You can also use the gesture to select files in Finder or a group of emails in Mail.

Place the pointer on a window title bar and use the three finger drag to move it a little. Leaving two fingers on the trackpad, flick your third finger left or right. The window will coast for a little while and slowly come to a stop. Coasting can also be used to select files, text, or any items in a list, although coasting requires some practice.

Scroll Direction: Natural

Natural scrolling was much derided when it first appeared in OS X Lion. This is because the gesture is opposite how most of us learned how to scroll using scroll bars. Using a scrollbar, you scroll up to move your content down and scroll down to move your content up. OS X's natural scrolling works in the opposite direction. Your content moves in the same direction as your fingers, which is how scrolling works on an iPhone or iPad.

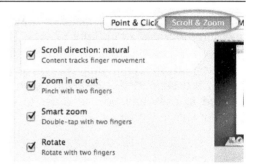

With natural scrolling, you swipe in the direction you want to move your content. If you want to move your content up, you swipe up with two fingers. Similarly, if you want to move your content down, you swipe down with two fingers. While I'll admit that I was turned off initially, once I got my head around the fact that natural scrolling works exactly the same on my iPhone and iPad, it made perfect sense. Despite all the complaining in the news media. OS X's natural scrolling is natural and makes far better sense than how scrollbars work. The way scrollbars work is backwards, not OS X's natural scrolling.

Scrollbars only appear along the right edge of a window when you are scrolling. This is configurable. See the chapter on Finder to see how to configure the options.

If you flick your fingers at the end of your swipe, you will generate momentum and scroll farther and faster than you would without flicking.

Rubberband scrolling lets you scroll a little further past the end of a file or webpage, and then bounces back to the end of the content. The rubberband animation lets you know you've reached the end. This is the same animation used by iOS on the iPhone and iPad.

Zoom In or Out

Similar to the two-finger pinch zoom of an iPhone or iPad, OS X allows you to spread two fingers to zoom in. Be sure to maintain continuous contact with the trackpad while spreading your fingers apart. To stop zooming, stop moving your fingers. Rubberband animation will let you know when you have reached the maximum limit of the zoom.

When you have multiple tabs open in Safari, a two-finger pinch zoom can display the content as a strip of tabs. Swipe left or right with two fingers to navigate through the tabs. To take a tab back to full size, either click on it or zoom in by spreading two fingers apart.

To zoom out, pinch your two fingers together and stop when you have reached the desired zoom. Rubberband animation will let you know when you have fully zoomed out.

Smart Zoom

Smart Zoom is another feature OS X adds from iOS on the iPhone and iPad. When you want to zoom in on an area of a webpage, double tap with two fingers and Safari will zoom in. Double tap again to zoom out.

Rotate

Rotate is another handy feature I use often in iPhoto and when working with PDF documents. Using two fingers you can rotate a picture or a page in a clockwise or counterclockwise direction.

Swipe Between Pages

Swipe to navigate is very much like thumbing through pages in a book. This gesture can be used to move forward and backward through webpages in Safari by swiping right and left, respectively. The gesture is also used to scroll horizontally in documents. There are three options – two fingers, three fingers, or an option to use either two or three fingers.

Swipe Between Full-Screen Apps

If you use fullscreen apps or desktop spaces, this gesture will allow you to swipe between them. The gesture can be set up to work with either three or four fingers. Swiping to the left moves the current desktop space left and reveals its neighboring space 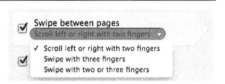 located to the right. Similarly, swiping to the right moves the current desktop right, revealing its neighboring space located to the left. A rubberband animation signifies that you have reached the last space or full screen app.

Notification Center

This gesture seems a little odd at first because you actually start at the very edge of your trackpad. Starting at the right edge, swipe left with two fingers to reveal the Notification Center. Swiping in the opposite direction hides Notification Center.

Mission Control

 Mission Control is a handy tool that provides a view of every application window running on every desktop space as well as all full screen applications. It allows you to quickly jump to another desktop space, full screen app, or an app window running in another space. Mission Control also allows you to move application windows from one desktop space to another by clicking and dragging or using the three finger drag gesture. Desktop spaces can be created, deleted, or rearranged using Mission Control.

The gesture to access Mission Control is to swipe up with either three or four fingers. The Mission Control gesture does the same thing as hitting the **F3** key, **^up** (control+up arrow), or clicking the Mission Control icon in Launchpad or the Dock.

For more information about desktop spaces, see the chapter on Mission Control.

App Exposé

App Exposé is an OS X feature that allows you to see all the windows of an open application regardless in which space the window resides. It differs from Mission Control which allows you to see all windows of every open application active within a desktop space. The gesture to access App Exposé is to swipe down with the either three or four fingers.

Launchpad

 Launchpad is another feature OS X brings over from the iPhone and iPad. Launchpad allows you to see, launch, and organize all of the applications on your Mac in a very iOS-looking screen. The gesture to access Launchpad is to pinch with your thumb and three fingers. You can also access Launchpad by clicking the Launchpad icon in the Dock. To exit Launchpad, press the the **esc** key or use the **Show Desktop** gesture.

Show Desktop

The Show Desktop gesture has two functions. It can be used to exit Launchpad or to completely clear all application windows from your desktop so you can see your desktop wallpaper.

Mouse Gestures

The Magic Mouse supports six gestures, but due to its limited surface space, it can only support one or two finger gestures. Similar to the trackpad gestures, it takes only a short amount of time before the mouse gestures become completely natural.

To configure mouse gestures, open the **Mouse** preference pane by launching the **System Preferences** application from the Dock or **Launchpad** and selecting the **Mouse** icon. You can also launch from the Apple menu by selecting > **System Preferences... > Mouse**.

The **Mouse** preference pane is located under **Hardware** if you still have the preference panes organized by category.

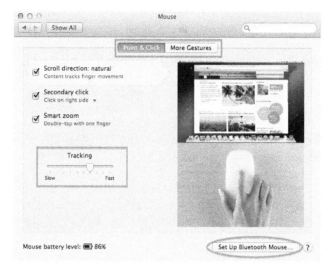

At the top of the mouse preference pane are two tabs for the two categories of gestures – **Point & Click** and **More Gestures**. Towards the bottom of the pane is a slider to adjust the tracking speed of the pointer as it moves across the desktop. If you need to set up a new Apple Magic Mouse, click the **Set Up Bluetooth Mouse...** button at the lower left. The round **?** button at the lower right brings up the Magic Mouse page from the Apple Help Center. If you need to see the battery status of your mouse, it is displayed at the lower left.

The left hand side of the pane lists various mouse gestures with check boxes next to them. To turn on a gesture, simply check the check box. In the right hand pane, Apple included a video demonstrating what the highlighted gesture does and how to do it. Slide your pointer and hover over any of the gestures and the video in the right pane will automatically change to demonstrate the highlighted gesture.

The best way to learn the gestures in OS X is to watch the video in the Mouse preference pane and try it for yourself. In no time at all, you'll learn all of the gestures and will wonder how you could have used a computer without them.

Scroll Direction: Natural

Natural scrolling was much derided when it first appeared in OS X Lion. This is because the gesture is opposite how most of us learned how to scroll using scroll bars. Using a scrollbar, you scroll up to move your content down and scroll down to move your content up. OS X's natural scrolling works in the opposite direction. Your content moves in the same direction as your fingers, which is how scrolling works on an iPhone or iPad.

With natural scrolling, you swipe in the direction you want to move your content. If you want to move your content up, you swipe up with one finger. Similarly, if you want to move your content down, you swipe down with one finger. While I'll admit I was turned off initially, once I got my head around the fact that natural scrolling works exactly the same on my iPhone and iPad, it made perfect sense. Despite all the complaining in the news media. OS X's natural scrolling is natural and makes far better sense than how scrollbars work. The way scrollbars work is backwards, not OS X's natural scrolling.

Scrollbars only appear along the right edge of a window when you are scrolling. This is configurable. See the chapter on Finder to see how to configure the options.

If you flick your fingers at the end of your swipe, you will generate momentum and scroll farther and faster than you would without flicking.

Rubberband scrolling lets you scroll a little further past the end of a file or webpage and then bounces back to the end of the content. The rubberband animation lets you know you've reached the end. This is the same animation used by iOS on the iPhone and iPad.

Secondary Click

A secondary click is used to reveal context sensitive menus and is similar to a right button mouse click in the Windows PC world. On the Magic Mouse, secondary click has two options – **Click on right side** or **Click on left side**.

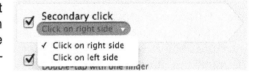

Smart Zoom

Smart Zoom is another feature OS X adds from iOS on the iPhone and iPad. When you want to zoom in on an area of a webpage double tap your Magic Mouse with one finger and Safari will zoom in. Double tap again to zoom out.

Swipe Between Pages

Swipe to navigate is very much like thumbing through pages in a book. This gesture can be used to move forward and backward through webpages in Safari by swiping right or left, respectively. The gesture is also used to scroll horizontally in documents.

There are three options – swipe with one finger, swipe with two fingers, or an option to use either one or two fingers.

Note that if you configure swiping between pages to use two fingers, the swipe between full screen apps check box will uncheck itself and be disabled. So if you want to use both gestures, using one finger to swipe between pages is the only option that will allow you to turn on swiping between full screen apps.

Swipe Between Full Screen Apps

If you use fullscreen apps or desktop spaces, this gesture will allow you to swipe between them. Swiping to the left with two fingers moves the current desktop space left and reveals its neighboring space located to the right. Similarly, swiping to the right moves the current desktop right, revealing its neighboring space located to the left. A rubberband animation signifies that you have reached the last space or full screen app.

Note that if you configure swiping between pages to use two fingers, turning on swipe between full screen apps will disable swiping between pages. The only valid option that allows both gestures is to configure swiping between pages with one finger.

Mission Control

 Mission Control is a handy tool that provides a view of every application window running on every desktop space as well as all full screen applications. It allows you to quickly jump to another desktop space, full screen app, or a particular app window running in another space. Mission Control also allows you to move application windows from one desktop space to another by clicking and dragging. Desktop spaces can be created, deleted, or rearranged using Mission Control.

The gesture to access Mission Control is to double tap with two fingers. This gesture does the same thing as hitting the **F3** key, **^up** (control+up arrow), or clicking the Mission Control icon in Launchpad or the Dock.

For more information about desktop spaces, see the chapter on Mission Control.

Advanced Customization

If you're already familiar with gestures, I hope to show you a few features you may not know existed. One of these customizations utilizes System Preferences. Normally I would have classified it as a basic customization. However, I've included it under this section for those of you who are already familiar with gestures and skipped directly to this part of the chapter.

Ignore the Built-in Trackpad

I often use my external Bluetooth trackpad when I'm using my MacBook Pro. However, I find it annoying that accidentally brushing against my MacBook Pro's built-in trackpad will often send my pointer flying off into left field. OS X has a solution for this annoyance.

To ignore the built-in trackpad, open the **Accessibility** preference pane by launching the System Preferences application and selecting the **Accessibility** icon or from the Apple menu by selecting **> System Preferences... > Accessibility**. Next, click **Mouse & Trackpad** in the left-hand pane. Check the check box next to **Ignore built-in trackpad when mouse or wireless trackpad is present**.

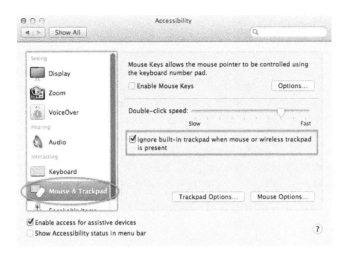

When this check box is checked, OS X will ignore the built-in trackpad on your MacBook Pro or MacBook Air when it sees an external Bluetooth mouse or trackpad. To turn this feature off, uncheck the box in the **Accessibility** preference pane. A quicker option is to turn off Bluetooth in the menu bar. Turn Bluetooth back on to utilize your external mouse or trackpad and ignore your built-in trackpad.

Turn Rubberband Scrolling Off in iTunes

This tweak turns off rubberband scrolling in iTunes. First, quit iTunes. Open **Terminal** and enter the following command. You must log out and log back in for the change to take effect.

```
defaults write com.apple.iTunes disable-elastic-scroll -bool YES
```

To turn rubberband scrolling back on for iTunes, first quit iTunes if it is open. Then enter the following command in **Terminal**.

```
defaults delete com.apple.iTunes disable-elastic-scroll
```

Log out and log back in for the change to take effect.

Adjust the Double-Click Speed

If you find the default double-click speed either too slow or too fast for your liking, OS X allows you to adjust it.

To change the double-click speed, open the **Accessibility** preference pane by launching the System Preferences application and selecting the **Accessibility** icon or from the Apple menu by selecting **> System Preferences... > Accessibility**. Next, select **Mouse & Trackpad** in the left-hand pane. Use the slider in the middle of the right-hand pane to adjust the **Double-click speed**. The slider adjusts double-click speed for both the mouse and trackpad.

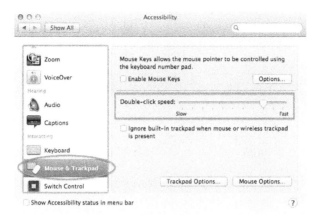

Enable Trackpad Drag Lock

By default, when dragging an item from one location to another the drag ends when you remove your fingers from the trackpad. If you were dragging a file from one folder to another, the drag ends the moment you remove your fingers from the trackpad and the file will be moved to its new location.

The **Drag Lock** feature changes this default behavior so that the drag ends only when you tap the trackpad once when reaching the destination. This means that if you accidentally lift your fingers off the trackpad the drag will not end nor will the item be copied by mistake into the wrong folder. Drag Lock comes in handy when you're dragging an item from one side of the screen to another as you often run out of trackpad space before completing the drag.

To enable Drag Lock, open the **Accessibility** preference pane by launching the System Preferences application and selecting the **Accessibility** icon or from the Apple menu by selecting **> System Preferences... > Accessibility**. Next, select **Mouse & Trackpad** in the left-hand pane. Click the **Trackpad Options...** button.

An added benefit of enabling Drag Lock is that it makes using the spring-loaded folders feature easier. For more information on spring-loaded folders, see the chapter on Finder.

Create Custom Gestures

OS X features a set of 16 standard trackpad gestures and another 6 for your Magic Mouse. Allowing you to execute various common tasks. But what if you want to squeeze every drop of productivity from your trackpad or mouse? Several utilities exist that allow you to create custom gestures, but my favorite application is **BetterTouchTool** by Andreas Hegenberg.

BetterTouchTool lets you assign various actions to trackpad and mouse gestures that you create. You can create custom gestures using one, two, three, four, or five fingers combined with a tap or with one or more of the following modifier keys: ⇧ **fn** ^ ⌥ ⌘ (shift, function, control, option, and command). You can assign your own gesture to an existing or custom keyboard shortcut or to any one of nearly 125 predefined actions.

BetterTouchTool also includes some window snapping capabilities available in Andreas' other application, BetterSnapTool. Note there is one word of caution. BetterTouchTool is not available in the App Store. In fact, as of the time of this writing BetterTouchTool is still in alpha. Essentially, that means it can be a little buggy at times (there is a bug reporting function), some features may not work as you expect (although I have not run into any roadblocks), and you are using it at your own risk. Despite this, I consider BetterTouchTool to be the best application available to create customized gestures. BetterTouchTool is available for free, although a donation is requested, at: http://www.boastr.de.

Getting Started

After downloading and installing BetterTouchTool, you'll notice a new Menu Extra in the Menu Bar. Click the BetterTouchTool Menu Extra to reveal the menu. Select **Preferences** to open the main window.

BetterTouchTool's main window offers a choice of a **Basic** or **Advanced** toolbar with additional tools. Click **Advanced** if not already highlighted. Next click **Settings** to display BetterTouchTool's settings preference pane.

The settings preferences allow you to enable or disable BetterTouchTool's Menu Extra and whether you want BetterTouchTool's icon to appear in the Dock while it is running. You can choose to launch BetterTouchTool on startup and search for crash reports on startup. You can configure one or a combination of the following modifier keys to temporarily disable BetterTouchTool: ⇧ **fn** ^ ⌥ ⌘ (shift, function, control, option, and command).

BetterTouchTool will automatically check for updates when the box next to **Enable automatic** checking is checked. You can decide whether you want to update alpha versions, which warns you that you are updating at your own risk. I suggest disabling automatic updates as BetterTouchTool is still in alpha.

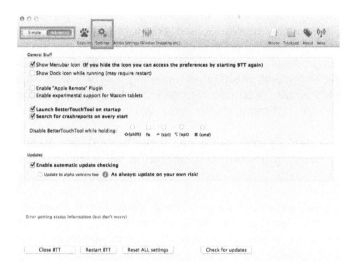

Two additional options allow you to enable the Apple Remote plug-in and to enable experimental support for Wacom tablets.

Create a Custom Trackpad Gesture

To create a custom trackpad gesture, first click **Gestures** in the BetterTouchTool toolbar. Next, click **Trackpads**, if not already highlighted, to display the trackpad gesture palette where you will create, modify, and delete your custom gestures.

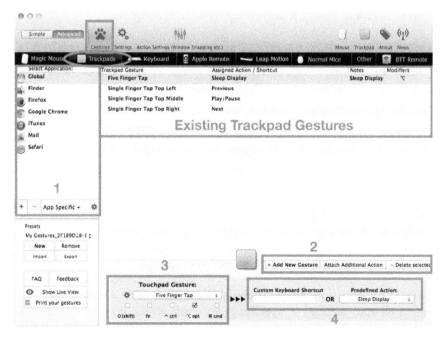

The main window displays any gestures that currently exist. Here you can see I have created 4 custom trackpad gestures. My first custom gesture is a 5-finger tap using the ⌥ (option) key as a modifier to lock my Mac. This gesture allows me to quickly lock my Mac when I want to take a break. The next 3 gestures use both a finger, tap, and location. I often play music from my iTunes library when writing. These 3 gestures allow me to play the previous song, toggle play or pause, and skip to the next song. The gestures are location aware, meaning I have to do a single-finger tap along the top of my trackpad to execute them. A single-finger tap anywhere else on the trackpad works like a normal single-finger tap. All 4 gestures are **Global**, meaning they will work regardless of which application is currently active. You can also see that I have created application specific gestures for Finder, Firefox, Chrome, iTunes, Mail, Word, and Safari.

To modify an existing gesture, highlight it and make the desired changes in (3) and (4) above. To delete an existing gesture, first highlight it and click **- Delete selected** in (2) above.

Creating a new trackpad gesture is simple. First, determine if your new gesture will be global (works in all applications) or specific to an application. If global, click on **Global** at the top of the column in (1). If application specific, click the **+** button at the bottom of (1) to open your Applications folder where you will select the application.

Next, click **+ Add New Gesture** from (2) and select your trackpad gesture from the drop-down menu under **Touchpad Gesture** at (3). BetterTouchTool supports 1-, 2-, 3-, 4-, and 5-finger trackpad gestures in combination with single or double taps, swipes up, down, left, or right, click swipes up, down, left or right, and trackpad location with 1-, 2-, and 3-finger gestures. Add one or more modifier keys to your gesture, if desired.

Next, assign a keyboard shortcut by typing it in the field below **Custom Keyboard Shortcut** at (4). Or select from one of 125 pre-defined actions from the drop-down menu under **Pre-Defined Action** at (4). You can add notes to your gesture, if you wish, by entering them in the **Notes** field in the list of existing gestures. Close the BetterTouchTool window when finished and try out your new custom trackpad gesture.

That's how simple it is to create a custom trackpad gesture in BetterTouchTool. Have fun creating your own gestures!

Create a Custom Magic Mouse Gesture

Creating a custom gesture for your Apple Magic Mouse is very similar to creating a trackpad gesture. To create a custom Magic Mouse gesture, first click **Gestures** in the BetterTouchTool toolbar. Next, click **Magic Mouse**, if not already highlighted, to display the Magic Mouse gesture palette where you will create, modify, and delete your custom gestures.

The main window displays any gestures that currently exist. To modify an existing gesture, highlight it and make the desired changes in (3) and (4) above. To delete an existing gesture, first highlight it and click **- Delete selected** in (2).

Creating a new Magic Mouse gesture is simple. First, determine if your new gesture will be global (works in all applications) or specific to an application. If global, click on **Global** at the top of the column in (1). If application specific, click the **+** button at the bottom of (1) to open your Applications folder where you will select the application.

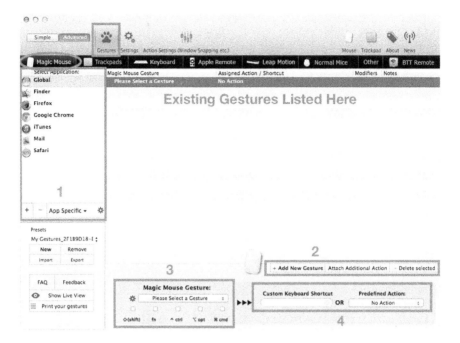

Next, click **+ Add New Gesture** from (2) and select your Magic Mouse gesture from the drop-down menu under **Magic Mouse Gesture** at (3). BetterTouchTool supports 1-, 2-, 3-, and 4-finger Magic Mouse gestures in combination with single or double taps, swipes up, down, left, or right, and location with 1- and 2-finger gestures. Add one or more modifier keys to your gesture, if desired.

Next, assign a keyboard shortcut by typing it in the field below **Custom Keyboard Shortcut** at (4). Or select from one of 125 pre-defined actions from the drop-down menu under **Pre-Defined Action** at (4). You can add notes to your gesture, if you wish, by entering them in the **Notes** field in the list of existing gestures. Close the BetterTouchTool window when finished and try out your new custom Magic Mouse gesture.

Exporting Gestures

If you want to share the gestures you created with friends and family or wish to create a backup file, BetterTouchTool lets you export them.

First, click **Gestures**, then **Magic Mouse** or **Trackpads**, as appropriate. Click **Export** under **Presets** at the lower left. A save dialog will open. Name your file, choose the save location and press **Save**.

Importing Gestures

BetterTouchTool allows you to import gesture files. I first got started with a gesture file located on the website **Tuts+** at:
http://cdn.tutsplus.com/mac/uploads/2014/02/TutsPlusGestures.zip.

To import a gesture file, click **Import** under **Presets** at the lower left. Browse to the file, select it, and click **Open**.

3

Desktop

The **Desktop** is the main component of OS X through which you interface with your Mac and it provides the large portion of your user experience. All folder, file, and application windows appear on the Desktop. Even though you may work within an application, the application is delivered to you on the OS X Desktop. The Desktop has three major components – the **Menu Bar**, the **Dock**, and the **Desktop** itself – as shown in the picture below. The flock of flamingoes is part of the Desktop wallpaper.

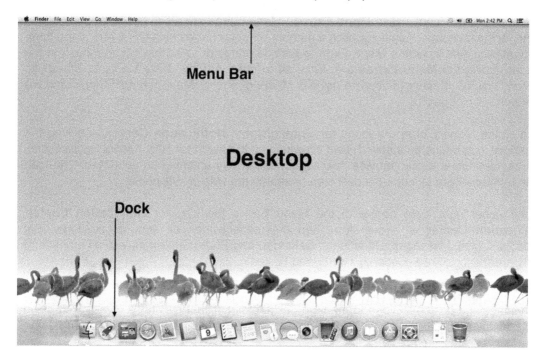

A translucent bar, called the **Menu Bar**, is located across the top of the desktop. There are two halves to the Menu Bar. The left half, shown below, is comprised of two elements, the **Apple** menu and the **Application** menu.

The **Apple** menu, denoted by the , provides access to system-wide OS X commands that allow you to update OS X and application software, see hardware information, configure System Preferences and the Dock, open recent applications and documents, force quit misbehaving apps, and put your Mac to sleep, restart, shutdown, or log out.

Next to the menu is the **Application** menu, which provides drop-down menus filled with commands and tools specific to the currently active application. The name of the currently active application is shown to the right of the menu. In the example shown above, the active application is **Finder** and this menu is called the **Finder** menu. The **Application** menu will change as you open other applications and make them active, however, the drop-down menus for **File**, **Edit**, **View**, **Window**, and **Help** are pretty standard from application to application.

There are three elements on the right side of the Menu Bar, the **Status Menu**, the **Spotlight** icon, and the **Notification Center** icon, from left to right. The OS X Mavericks default Status Menu is shown below. Note that if you upgraded from a previous version of OS X, your status menu may look different.

The **Status Menu** displays the status of and provides quick access to various OS X features via small icons called **Menu Extras**. Menu Extras are also called menulets, menu items, or status items. Apple supplies a number of Menu Extras with OS X and many third-party applications include a Menu Extra to provide status or to access preferences. In the picture above, the **Menu Extras** are, from left to right, AirPlay, Time Machine, Bluetooth, AirPort, Volume, Battery (if you are using a MacBook Pro or MacBook Air), Clock, and the user currently logged in.

Next to the Menu Extras are icons for **Spotlight** and **Notification Center**. Clicking the **Spotlight** icon brings up a search field allowing you to search for files, folders, applications, events, reminders, music, movies, messages, essentially anything on your Mac. You can even use **Spotlight** to look up a definition or search the web or Wikipedia.

In the upper right hand corner of the Menu Bar is the icon for **Notification Center**. **Notification Center** is a one-stop shop that consolidates all your notifications from FaceTime, Mail, Messages, Reminders, Calender, and Photo Stream as well as many third party applications like Facebook, Twitter and LinkedIn.

First I'll show you how to customize your Desktop and then the Menu Bar. We'll check out techniques and customizations to manage desktop clutter that inevitably comes with using any computer. I'll show you techniques to manage application windows and learn how to increase your desktop space.

The **Dock**, although a component of the Desktop, is such a large topic because it is so customizable, I created a separate chapter specifically focusing on Dock customization. Because **Stacks**, which are a component of the Dock, are also extremely customizable, they deserved their own chapter too. After the chapters on the Dock and Stacks, I'll show you how to search more accurately with Spotlight and to customize the Notification Center.

Let's start with your first desktop customization, changing your desktop wallpaper.

Change the Desktop Wallpaper

The most noticeable item on your Desktop is the desktop wallpaper, sometimes called the background. In OS X Mavericks, the default wallpaper is a huge wave. Why a wave? As of OS 10.9, Apple changed its OS X naming convention from big cats to locations in California. The first location Apple chose was Mavericks, a surfing spot just north of Half Moon Bay in Northern California. Mavericks attracts the world's best big wave surfers as waves routinely crest over 25 feet and can top out at over 80 feet.

You don't have to live with the standard desktop wallpaper image Apple selected for OS X. Apple included a number of other desktop images from which you can select. Or you can change your wallpaper to any picture or set of pictures you want.

As you will see, there are always a number of ways to do the same thing in OS X. It is up to you to decide which method is best for you. To change your desktop wallpaper, secondary click anywhere on the Desktop to bring up the Desktop context menu shown to the right. Note that if you do not have any items on your Desktop, you will not see the **Clean Up** and **Clean Up By** options. Select **Change Desktop Background...** to bring up the **Desktop & Screen Saver** preference pane.

Another option is to open the **Desktop & Screen Saver** preference pane by launching the System Preferences application and selecting the **Desktop & Screen Saver** icon or from the Apple menu by selecting > **System Preferences... > Desktop & Screen Saver**.

Once the **Desktop & Screen Saver** preference pane appears, ensure the **Desktop** tab is selected. The current desktop wallpaper is shown in the upper left portion of the pane. The left hand pane allows you to choose to use standard wallpaper offerings from Apple, a picture from your iPhoto library, or a picture located in any folder on your Mac.

Apple provides a number of standard wallpaper images under **Apple > Desktop Pictures**. If you like one of the standard images, click to select it. Apple also offers a set of solid color wallpaper images under **Apple > Solid Colors**.

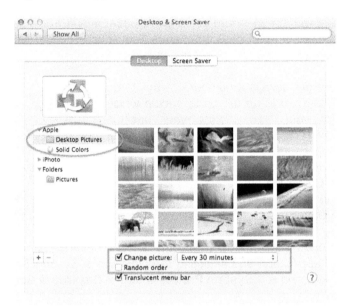

You don't have to settle for one desktop wallpaper, you can select them all and OS X will change your desktop wallpaper at an interval selected by you. Check the check box next to **Change picture** and select how frequently you want OS X to change your desktop wallpaper.

When logging in
When waking from sleep

Every 5 seconds
Every minute
Every 5 minutes
Every 15 minutes
✓ Every 30 minutes
Every hour
Every day

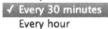

By default, OS X will cycle through the wallpaper sequentially from the first picture to the last. Check the check box next to **Random order** and OS X will cycle through the pictures randomly. When you choose **Random order**, the picture in the upper left of the **Desktop & Screen Saver** preference pane will change to show a set of circular arrows as shown at the left.

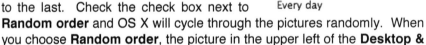

If the thumbnail previews are too small for you, move your pointer over one of the thumbnails and use the pinch zoom gesture to make the thumbnail images bigger.

Now that we know how to change the default desktop wallpaper using the standard set of wallpapers provided by Apple, let's leverage our knowledge to really personalize our desktop using our own pictures from iPhoto or a folder.

Use an iPhoto Album for your Desktop Wallpaper

 Any single picture from iPhoto or a set of pictures from an album, event, or Photo Stream can be used as your desktop wallpaper. There are two methods to configure OS X to use a picture from iPhoto as your desktop background. The first method is to use the **Desktop & Screen Saver** preference pane. The second method is to configure directly from the iPhoto application.

From the **Desktop & Screen Saver** preference pane, click on the gray arrow next to iPhoto in the left pane. This will open a drop-down list of events, photos, albums, imports, or Photo Stream. Click on one of the items in the drop-down list and select the photo you want as your desktop wallpaper. Similar to the standard photos provided by Apple, you can choose a single photo or an entire album of photos from iPhoto.

If you select an iPhoto album, you can choose to display the photos sequentially or in random order. And don't forget to select how often you want OS X to change your desktop wallpaper.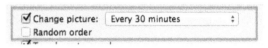

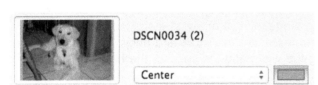 Note that the size of your photos probably doesn't match the screen size of your iMac or MacBook. For example, a photo in portrait mode doesn't fit well. In that case, you can change how the photo(s) will display on your desktop using the drop-down menu to the right of the photo(s) you selected. You have five choices: **Fill Screen**, **Fit to Screen**, **Stretch to Fill Screen**, **Center**, or **Tile**. I never use Stretch to Fill Screen as this selection changes the aspect ratio of the photo, often distorting the image.

For photos in portrait mode, **Fit to Screen** typically works best because the entire photo will be displayed. For photos in landscape mode, **Fill Screen**, **Fit to Screen** or **Center** generally works best. For both the **Fit to Screen** or **Center** options, you'll notice a colored rectangle to the right of the drop-down menu. Clicking on the color brings up a color wheel allowing you to choose the color of the bars that will appear on the left and right of your photo when it doesn't fit the entire desktop.

Configure Desktop Wallpaper Directly from iPhoto

You can configure your desktop wallpaper directly from the **iPhoto** application. From iPhoto, select the photo or photos you want as your desktop wallpaper. A yellow border will appear around the photos selected. Select **Share > Set Desktop**.

If your photos are in different albums or organized in different events, you'll need to create an album for your desktop photos. This will allow you to more easily select multiple photos for your desktop wallpaper.

Once you're done selecting photos in iPhoto, you'll need to go back to the **Desktop & Screen Saver** preference pane to select display options, how frequently the pictures change, and whether you want the pictures displayed in random order. Open the **Desktop & Screen Saver** preference pane from the **System Preferences** application.

You'll notice a new folder underneath the item called **Folders** at the very bottom of the left pane. It is called **iPhoto Selection** and contains the photos you selected from the iPhoto application. Click on it to see your photos. Using the instructions the previous section, configure display, frequency, and order options.

Configure Desktop Wallpaper From a Folder

Another option to configure your desktop wallpaper is to utilize a folder containing picture files. I like to collect desktop wallpaper from the Internet, usually landscape scenes. I have hundreds of pictures in a folder called **Wallpaper** located in the **Pictures** folder of my **Home** directory. If you want to collect wallpaper from the Internet, the first thing you need to do is to understand the resolution of your monitor.

To find the resolution of your monitor, select > **About This Mac**. Click the **More Info...** button at the bottom of the next dialog box. Click on the **Displays** tab at the top of the next screen which is titled **About This Mac** to see your display. The resolution of your monitor is listed on the second line. For example the resolution of my 15-inch MacBook Pro's built-in monitor is 1680 x 1050. The numbers represent the width and height of the screen in pixels with the first number representing the width and the second, the height. The larger the numbers, the higher the resolution.

So when searching Google images (https://images.google.com) or any site with desktop wallpaper, you don't want just any picture, you want pictures that match the native resolution of your display. A picture with a resolution smaller than the native resolution of your display will become pixelated when displayed as wallpaper, distorting the image.

Another important number is the aspect ratio, which is the proportional relationship between a display's width and its height. For my MacBook Pro's built-in display, the aspect ratio is calculated by dividing 1680 (its width) by 1050 (its height). The result is 1.6 which equates to an aspect ratio of 16:10. An image with an incorrect aspect ratio will not fit properly on the desktop. When looking for wallpaper, I look for images with a 16:10 aspect ratio and a minimum resolution of 1680 x 1050 pixels.

Another common aspect ratio is 16:9. If you have an external monitor that you purchased within the past year or so, its aspect ratio is most likely 16:9. For example, I also have an external 27-inch display. Its native resolution is 1920 x 1080. Dividing 1920 by 1080 yields 1.77, which equates to a 16:9 aspect ratio.

To add a folder of images, open the **Desktop & Screen Saver** preference pane by launching the System Preferences application and selecting the **Desktop & Screen Saver** pane or from the Apple menu by selecting > **System Preferences... > Desktop & Screen Saver**.

Click the **+** (plus) sign at the lower left of the preference pane, which will bring up a **Finder** window so you can navigate to and select the folder containing your pictures. You can also drag a folder into the left pane from Finder. To make the folder active, click on it and then choose display, frequency, and randomization options. If the thumbnail previews are too small for you, move your pointer over them and use the pinch zoom gesture to make them bigger.

To remove a folder, highlight it and click the **–** (minus) button.

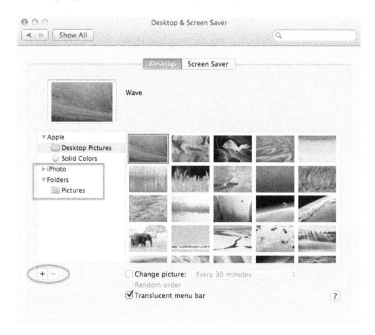

Access Hidden Wallpaper Collections

Apple bundled 44 beautiful high resolution desktop wallpaper images in OS X Mavericks. Mavericks also has an additional 43 high resolution images that can be used as desktop wallpaper. There are 17 gorgeous images from *National Geographic* along with **Aerial** images, pictures of the **Cosmos**, and **Nature Patterns**. Apple intended for you to use these as screensavers, but it only takes a couple of steps to add them to your wallpaper collection.

To use these hidden images as wallpaper, open **Finder** and enter ⇧⌘G (shift+command+G) to bring up the **Go to folder** dialog box. Enter the following path and click **Go**.

/Library/Screen Savers/Default Collections/

Finder will display four folders, numbered from 1 to 4 and labeled *National Geographic*, **Aerial**, **Cosmos**, and **Nature Patterns**, respectively. Each one contains high resolution images you can use as wallpaper.

To use any of these collections as wallpaper, open the **Desktop & Screen Saver** preference pane by launching the **System Preferences** application and selecting the **Desktop & Screen Saver** pane or from the Apple menu by selecting > **System Preferences... > Desktop & Screen Saver**.

Click on the **Desktop** tab at the top of the pane. Drag each of the folders (or just the ones you want) to the bottom of the left-hand pane under **Folders**. You can now select your desktop wallpaper from any of the collections.

If you already have a folder you are using as the source for your desktop wallpaper, another option is to select the images you like from the **Finder** window and copy them into that folder. Just open each of the collections by double-clicking on the folder. Select the images you like and drag them into the source folder for your wallpaper.

Configure a Screensaver

Screensavers are a throwback to the days of ancient cathode ray tube (CRT) monitors. If an image was displayed for too long on a CRT monitor, it would eventually burn a ghost image onto the screen. Screensavers were designed to prevent this phosphor burn in by filling the screen with moving images or patterns when the screen was not in use. Modern computers use Liquid Crystal Display (LCD) or Light Emitting Diode (LED) technology which is not susceptible to burn-in. Therefore, screensavers are primarily used for entertainment purposes today.

If you would like to configure a screensaver, open the **Desktop & Screen Saver** preference pane by launching the **System Preferences** application and selecting the **Desktop & Screen Saver** pane or from the Apple menu by selecting **> System Preferences... > Desktop & Screen Saver**. Click on the **Screen Saver** tab at the top of the pane.

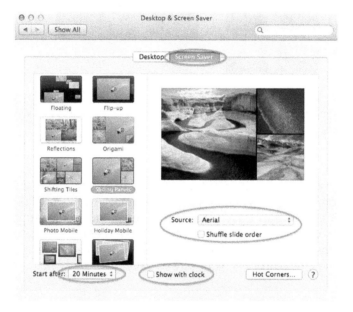

OS X Mavericks offers 21 different screensaver options, which are shown in the list of screen savers on the left side of the **Desktop & Screen Saver** preference pane. Any screensaver chosen in the left-hand side of the pane will be previewed in the right pane. Apple includes four default image collections, **National Geographic**, **Aerial**, **Cosmos**, and **Nature Patterns**, in the right-hand side of the preference pane under **Source**.

Use the drop-down menu to select one or select **Choose Folder** to select your own folder of images for your screensaver.

Select an inactivity time from the drop-down menu next to **Start After**. You can start your screen saver after 1, 2, 5, 10, 20, 30, or 60 minutes of inactivity. If you want the screen saver to display the time, check the check box next to **Show with clock**.

Display Your Own Message as a Screen Saver

OS X allows you to display a message on your computer as your screensaver. To configure a message, first open the **Desktop & Screen Saver** preference pane by launching the **System Preferences** application and selecting the **Desktop & Screen Saver** pane or from the Apple menu by selecting **⌘ > System Preferences... > Desktop & Screen Saver**. Click on the **Screen Saver** tab at the top of the pane.

Choose **Message** towards the bottom of the left-hand pane. By default, OS X will display the name of your computer as the screen saver message. If you would like to display your own message, click the **Screen Saver Options...** button and configure your message on the next dialog box. Click **OK** when done. Don't forget to set the inactivity timer from the drop-down menu under **Start after**. Check the check box next to **Show with clock** if you would like to show the time along with your screen saver message.

Permanently Turn Off the Screen Saver

A screen saver is a throwback to the early days of computing where external monitors were gigantic CRTs. Modern monitors are not susceptible to phosphor burn in, therefore screensavers serve no purpose other than their entertainment value. If you don't want to use a screensaver, OS X offers an option to turn off the display after a period of inactivity in order to save electricity.

To permanently turn off the screen saver, choose the **Never** option from the **Start After** drop-down menu on the **Desktop & Screen Saver** preference pane. To learn how to put the display to sleep after a period of inactivity, see the next section.

Put the Display to Sleep

If you don't want to use a screensaver, another option is to simply put your display to sleep after a period of inactivity. To configure the display sleep timer, open the **Energy Saver** preference pane by launching the **System Preferences** application and selecting the **Energy Saver** pane or from the Apple menu by selecting > **System Preferences... > Energy Saver**.

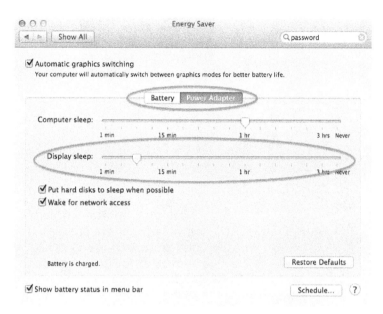

Note that the display sleep timer is configured separately for when your Mac is on battery or AC power. Select **Battery** or **Power Adapter** from the top of the **Energy Saver** preference pane. Next, configure the inactivity timer under **Display sleep** by dragging the slider to the left or right until the desired inactivity time has been selected. Be sure to configure inactivity timers for both **Battery** and **Power Adapter**. When an inactivity timer expires, your computer's display will go to sleep.

Configure Hot Corners

The OS X **Hot Corners** feature allows you to assign a specific action to the four corners of your desktop. A **Hot Corner** is activated by moving your pointer to one of the corners of your desktop to execute the associated command. The supported commands include starting the screen saver, disabling the screen saver, opening Mission Control, application windows (App Exposé), showing the Desktop, Dashboard, Notification Center, Launchpad, or display sleep.

To assign commands to **Hot Corners**, first open the **Desktop & Screen Saver** preference pane by launching the **System Preferences** application and selecting the **Desktop & Screen Saver** pane or from the Apple menu by selecting > **System Preferences... > Desktop & Screen Saver**. Click on the **Screen Saver** tab.

 Next, click the **Hot Corners...** button at the lower right of the preference pane to reveal the drop-down dialog box shown at the left. Assign an action to each of the four **Hot Corners** using the drop-down menu for each of the corners. Click **OK** when finished, then close the **Desktop & Screen Saver** preference pane.

To activate the command assigned to a **Hot Corner**, simply move your pointer to the appropriate corner. To turn off **Hot Corners**, open the **Desktop & Screen Saver** preference pane and select the **Screen Saver** tab. Next, click the **Hot Corners...** button in the lower right corner of the pane. Select the – from the drop-down menu for each corner that you want to turn off.

Hot corners can also be configured from the **Mission Control** preference pane.

Avoid Accidentally Triggering a Hot Corner

Hot Corners are an extremely handy feature, but one problem is that simply moving the pointer near a **Hot Corner** can accidentally trigger the associated command. For example, moving the pointer to the menu often accidentally triggers the command associated with the upper left corner.

To avoid accidentally triggering a Hot Corner, configure the **Hot Corners** feature to utilize a modifier key. For example, you can configure **Hot Corners** so that the ⌥ (option) key must be held down when the pointer is moved to a Hot Corner. Using a modifier key will eliminate the possibility of a pointer movement accidentally triggering a hot corner.

To configure **Hot Corners** to require a modifier key, open the **Desktop & Screen Saver** preference pane by launching the **System Preferences** application and selecting the **Desktop & Screen Saver** pane or from the Apple menu by selecting > **System Preferences... > Desktop & Screen Saver**. Click on the **Screen Saver** tab at the top of the pane. Next click the **Hot Corners...** button at the lower right to bring up the **Hot Corners** configuration drop down.

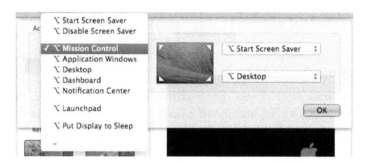

To add a modifier key, hold down the desired modifier key when selecting an action from the drop-down menu. For example, I am holding down the ⌥ (option) key while selecting the **Mission Control** command in the picture. Note that the **Start Screen Saver** and **Desktop** commands also require the ⌥ (option) key. Select any of the supported modifier keys - ⇧ ⌘ ^ ⌥ (shift, command, control, or option). OS X will even allow you to use any combination two, three, or even all four of the modifier keys.

Once you have configured a modifier key, Hot Corners will only work when you're also holding down the modifier keys you specified. This eliminates the possibility of accidentally triggering a Hot Corner.

Clean Up Desktop Clutter

Having too many windows open on the desktop can be a distraction especially if you are trying to concentrate on one particular window. Of course you could always close all the windows or quit the applications entirely to clean up the clutter. But that takes time and what if you don't want to quit applications and want to leave the windows open for later use? In that case quitting or closing windows are not viable options. You could minimize each window, however that could take a lot of time if you have lots of windows open. And minimized windows end up cluttering the right side of the Dock, making each icon smaller and more difficult to differentiate as the Dock expands across the desktop.

A handy feature of OS X that is often overlooked is **Hide**. When you hide an application, all of its windows instantly disappear without crowding the Dock. Because OS X will remember where the windows were located before you hid them, you can restore the windows of any application to their original positions. To hide an application, enter ⌘H (command+H). If you have lots of applications open and want to hide all but the application in which you are working, enter ⌥⌘H (command+option+H). Both of these commands are also available under the application menu, the first menu to the right of the menu.

To unhide any application, simply click on its icon in the Dock and OS X will immediately restore the application's windows to their original locations. Use **App Exposé** to see the windows of any application, whether hidden or not.

How do you know which applications are hidden and which are not? By default, OS X does not differentiate between running applications that are hidden and those that are not. A tweak I will show you in the chapter on customizing the Dock will allow you to clearly differentiate between hidden and unhidden applications.

Remove Devices from the Desktop

OS X displays external hard drives or optical drives on the desktop when they are connected to your computer. To me, these external device icons represent more desktop clutter. I prefer an uncluttered and clean desktop. Therefore the only items on my desktop are typically the handful of documents on which I am currently working or a temporary file like the occasional screenshot that will be dragged to the trash immediately after I'm done with it. One of my hobbies is to collect desktop wallpaper, usually beautiful landscapes (I have hundreds of them), and I don't want desktop clutter to ruin my view.

OS X allows you to turn off the display of external devices on the desktop. There is no need to display external devices on the desktop as they are available in the **Device** list in the **Finder** sidebar. Additionally, turning off the display of external devices is particularly useful when you are using a Volumes Stack, which will display all of your internal and external hard drives and optical drives as a single stack in the Dock. See the chapter on customizing stacks to learn how to create a volumes stack.

To turn off the display of external devices on your desktop open **Finder** and select **Preferences...** from the Finder menu in the menu bar or enter ⌘, (command+comma). By default, OS X will display icons for external hard drives, CDs, DVDs, and iPods, and connected servers on the desktop. To turn this off, uncheck the check boxes next to each of these items in the **Finder** preference pane as shown at the right. Changes take effect immediately and any device icons on your desktop will disappear. Don't worry. Your devices have not been removed. They have been hidden and can still be accessed from the **Device** list in the **Finder** sidebar.

To return to the OS X default, open **Finder** and enter ⌘, (command+comma) to open the Finder Preferences. Then check the boxes next to external disks and CDs, DVDs, and iPods.

Want a Really Clean Desktop?

Unfortunately for most users, the desktop quickly turns out to be the catch-all location for documents and other stuff they're working on. By default, screenshots are saved to the desktop and many downloaded applications save items there too. In the worst case, the desktop clutter can become overwhelming and detract from your ability to get work done.

Items saved to the desktop aren't really saved to the desktop. They are actually saved to the **Desktop** folder located in your **Home** directory. The Desktop folder is easily accessible from your Home directory, the **Finder Sidebar**, or from a document stack in the Dock. See the chapter on customizing stacks to learn how to create a Desktop Stack.

I really hate a messy desktop and often find myself cleaning up the mess I've created. Not only does the mess make the desktop look unsightly, it steals CPU and memory resources from your Mac because each icon must be drawn and its contents previewed. Each icon takes up a little bit of memory and CPU resources, so if you have more desktop icons than wallpaper, OS X has to dedicate more resources to render this clutter.

If you want a really clean desktop sans icons, this OS X tweak will give you a pristine desktop, free of all icon clutter. Essentially this tweak turns off desktop icons, completely preventing them from being displayed in the first place. This tweak will also prevent you from dragging icons onto the desktop. It will also turn off your ability to secondary click on the desktop to create new folders, get info, or change the desktop background..

Open **Terminal** and enter the following commands.

```
defaults write com.apple.finder CreateDesktop -bool FALSE
```

```
killall Finder
```

The icons that normally would have appeared on your desktop are safely tucked away in the **Desktop** folder in your **Home** directory where they belong. This is a handy tweak if you are about to give an important presentation and you are embarrassed by your lack of desktop cleanliness.

To return to the OS X default, enter the following commands.

```
defaults write com.apple.finder CreateDesktop -bool TRUE
```

```
killall Finder
```

Change the Pointer Size

Have you ever lost your pointer on the desktop? You may find the default OS X mouse pointer to be a little bit too small, especially if you're using a larger monitor. For example, the pointer is sized perfectly for my 15-inch MacBook Pro. But when I connect my MacBook Pro to my 27-inch monitor, it is so small I often have trouble finding it on the desktop. OS X allows you to change the size of the pointer from the default size to a gigantic one.

To change the pointer size, open the **Accessibility** preference pane by launching the System Preferences application and selecting the **Accessibility** icon or from the Apple menu by selecting **> System Preferences... > Accessibility**. Next, click **Display** in the left-hand pane if it is not selected already. Slide the **Cursor Size** slider until your pointer is at a comfortable size.

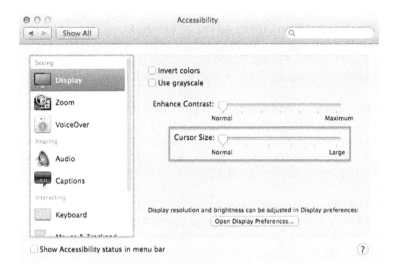

Even a small change in the **Cursor Size** makes a big difference when using a large monitor. Note that changing the pointer size also changes the size of the text input cursor in word processing applications and the crosshairs used to take screenshots.

To return the pointer to its default size, open the **Accessibility** preference pane and slide the **Cursor Size** slider back to **Normal**.

Show the Desktop

Have you ever wanted to look at a pretty wallpaper picture only to find your desktop is way too cluttered with windows? OS X offers a number of methods to quickly clear the clutter to view your desktop wallpaper and put the clutter back when done.

If you configured the **Show Desktop** trackpad gesture I showed you in Chapter 2, the quickest method to show the desktop is by spreading your thumb and three fingers on your trackpad. All open windows will be pushed to the extreme right edge of the screen. Reverse the gesture to return the clutter.

If you didn't turn off the keyboard shortcut I showed you in the **Mission Control** section, pressing the **F11** key also clears the desktop. Note that you may have to hold down the **fn** (function) key while pressing **F11** as this function key is normally used to lower the volume. Press **F11** (or **fn F11**) to return the desktop clutter.

A couple of other options are to use the **^down** (control+down arrow) or to hold down the ⌘ (command) key while pressing **F3,** which is normally used to launch Mission Control. If you use the control down arrow method be sure to click somewhere on the desktop first, otherwise you'll launch App Exposé. Enter **^down** or **⌘F3** to return the windows to the desktop.

Change the Desktop Icon Size

If you want to see icons for devices and files on your desktop, OS X gives you the option of changing the icon size. To change the desktop icon size for devices and files, first open **Finder**. Next, close all **Finder** windows. This last step is important. All Finder windows must be closed to access the Desktop view options panel. Select **Show View Options** from under Finder's **View** menu or enter ⌘ **J**. This will launch the **Desktop** view options panel shown to the left.

There are two sliders at the top of the **Desktop** view options panel. The top one controls the icon size. Use the slider to make the desktop icons appear smaller by dragging the slider to the left. Or, if you want to make the desktop icons appear bigger, drag the slider to the right.

The next slider controls the tightness of the grid separating the desktop icons. For tighter spacing, drag the slider to the left. For more open spacing, drag the slider to the right.

The next section controls the size and location of the text label. OS X places the text label underneath the icon using a 12-point font. OS X will allow you to choose any font size between 10-and 16-point font using 1-point increments. The text label can be located at the bottom, which is the default, or to the right of the icon by selecting the appropriate radio button for the label position.

By default, **Show item info** is off. This option adds the file size or, in the case of a hard drive, the free space to a second line of the text label.

Also by default, the **Show icon preview** check box is checked. Unchecking this check box turns off the preview function of OS X. Only default icons indicating the application in which the file was created will be displayed instead of the file contents preview.

The last option available, **Sort by** allows you to choose a default sort option for your desktop icons. By default, the sort is set to **None**. The available sort options include sorting by Name, Kind, Date Modified, Date Created, Date Last Opened, Date Added, Size, or Tags. The Snap to Grid option will organize your desktop icons into a grid. Once you have finished configuring your options, close the Desktop view panel to save.

Assign Hot Corners for Desktop Functions

The OS X **Hot Corners** feature allows you to assign a specific action to each of the four corners of your desktop. A **Hot Corner** is activated by moving your pointer to one of the corners to execute the associated command. It is often quicker to use a **Hot Corner** than to use a keyboard shortcut or to click on an icon.

To assign a **Hot Corner**, first open the **Mission Control** preference pane by launching the **System Preferences** application and selecting the **Mission Control** preference pane or from the Apple menu by selecting > **System Preferences... > Mission Control**.

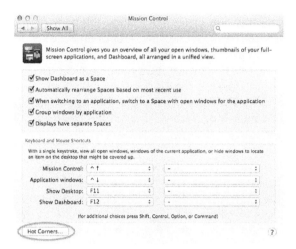

Next, click the **Hot Corners...** button at the lower left of the pane to reveal the drop-down dialog box shown at the right. You can assign a command to each corner. There are multiple desktop functions available. **Desktop** will clear the desktop of all windows. You can also **Start** or **Disable the Screen Saver** or **Put Display to Sleep**. Click **OK** when finished, then close the Mission Control preference pane. Moving your pointer to a Hot Corner executes the assigned command. Moving your pointer back reverses the command.

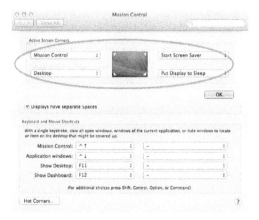

To turn off Hot Corners, open the **Mission Control** preference pane and click the **Hot Corners...** button in the lower left corner. Select the – from the drop-down menu for each corner that you want to turn off.

To learn how to avoid accidentally triggering a Hot Corner, see Avoid Accidentally Triggering a Hot Corner on page 42.

Hot corners can also be configured from the **Desktop & Screen Saver** preference pane.

Increase Settings in Quarter Increments

Sometimes it seems you never can get the volume, display brightness, or keyboard backlighting adjusted to your liking. One segment more is too much. One less is too little. Wouldn't it be great if you could change these settings using smaller increments. OS X has a solution for you!

Hold down the ⇧⌥ keys (shift+option) while adjusting the volume, display brightness, or keyboard backlighting. You are now able to increase or decrease a settings in quarter-segment increments, allowing you to precisely adjust the volume, display brightness, and keyboard backlighting exactly to your liking.

Temporarily Quiet the Volume Adjustment

When you adjust the volume, OS X makes an annoying popping sound each time you press the **F11** or **F12** key. If you're working in a quiet office environment the popping can disturb your concentration or the concentration of others. It is also annoying and loud when listening to music using earbuds.

To temporarily quiet the beeping when adjusting the volume, hold down the ⇧ key (shift) while pressing **F11** or **F12**. Unfortunately, this trick doesn't work when adjusting the volume in quarter segment increments. To turn off the annoying and loud popping sound, check out the next trick.

Permanently Quiet the Volume Adjustment

OS X allows you to permanently turn off the annoying and loud popping sound it makes when you adjust the volume. This is a blessing to anyone who routinely uses earbuds or headphones because this popping is so loud it is ear shattering.

To permanently turn off the annoying popping sound, open the **Sound** preference pane by launching the System Preferences application and selecting the **Sound** icon or from the Apple menu by selecting > **System Preferences... > Sound**. Next, uncheck the check box next to **Play feedback when volume is changed**.

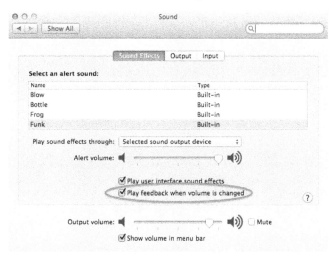

4

Mission Control

 Mission Control is a handy tool that provides a view of everything on your Mac – application windows, full-screen apps, desktop spaces, and the Dashboard. It allows you to quickly jump to another desktop space, full screen app, or an app window running in another space. Mission Control allows you to move application windows to other desktop spaces, rearrange the order of your desktops, and create and delete desktop spaces. For information on desktop spaces, see the next section.

To open **Mission Control** use the trackpad gesture you assigned in Chapter 2, launch it from **Launchpad**, launch it from **Spotlight**, press the **F3** key, or enter **^up** (control+up arrow).

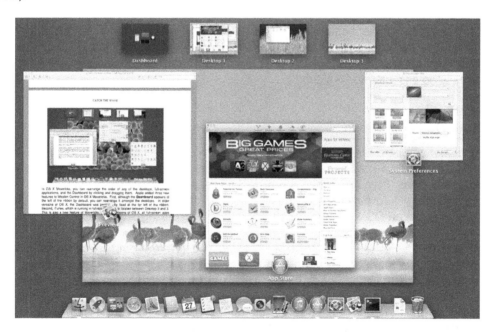

Mission Control and its elements are shown in the picture above. The thumbnails forming a ribbon at the very top of Mission Control are, from left to right, the **Dashboard**, **Desktop 1** (from which Mission Control was launched), **Desktop 2**, iTunes running in full-screen mode, and **Desktop 3**. The three desktops are virtual desktops, called **Spaces** in OS X, and each has one or more application windows assigned to it. Spaces are a way of increasing desktop real estate to accommodate more application windows. Spaces are covered next.

You can rearrange the order of any of the desktops, full-screen applications, and the Dashboard by clicking and dragging them. The only two exceptions are the Dashboard space and Desktop 1, which are permanently fixed at the far left of the ribbon. Other than the Dashboard, no Desktop Space can be moved to the left of Desktop 1. As you rearrange the Desktops, OS X will renumber them accordingly.

Navigating between the desktops, full-screen apps, and the Dashboard is done by clicking on the appropriate thumbnail in the ribbon at the top of Mission Control or by swiping either three or four fingers to the left or right on the trackpad. If you are using a Magic Mouse, swiping left or right with either one or two fingers will navigate between the desktops. See Chapter 2 to learn how to set up trackpad and mouse gestures. You can also hold down the ^ (control) key and press the left or right arrow to navigate left or right.

The large element at the center of Mission Control is a representation of the desktop from which Mission Control was launched. In the picture, I launched Mission Control from Desktop 1, which is running three applications: Preview, App Store, and System Preferences. Previews of the three app windows are shown from left to right, respectively. The Finder appears in Desktop 2 and Desktop 3 does not have an active application.

Mission Control allows you to see all application windows you have open at a glance regardless on which desktop they are assigned. Clicking on any application window makes that window active, bringing it and the desktop to which it is assigned to the front.

The Dock appears at the bottom of Mission Control to allow you to launch additional applications and assign them to specific desktops. For example, if Desktop 3 appears in the main Mission Control window and you launch FaceTime from the Dock, it will automatically be assigned to Desktop 3.

Add More Desktop Space

Desktop clutter can be a real productivity killer. If you have ever opened lots of applications on your Mac, you know how hard it is to sift through all of the application windows looking for a particular one. If you only had more desktop space, your desktop would not be so cluttered and life would be so much easier. OS X granted your wish. You can create desktop space with an OS X feature called **Spaces**.

Spaces is a feature of **Mission Control**, allowing you to create virtual desktops. More desktops equates to more desktop real estate for application windows. Using Spaces, you can create additional desktops each containing a unique application or set of applications. Spaces is so flexible that windows from the same application can be split between different desktops. The multiple desktops remove clutter by allowing you to assign windows to separate desktops instead of all the windows being piled onto your main desktop. For example, let's say you are writing a book on customizing OS X using Microsoft Word, you can run Word in the main desktop space, and create spaces for iTunes, Mail, and Safari – effectively quadrupling your desktop real estate.

Mission Control is the command center for Spaces, allowing you to create new desktops, see and manage all of your desktops, and see which application windows are assigned to each space. To create a new desktop Space, first open Mission Control by using the trackpad gesture you assigned in Chapter 2, launching it from Launchpad, launching it from **Spotlight**, pressing the **F3** key, or entering **^up** (control+up arrow).

If you have never created a desktop space, the very top of Mission Control will show only the **Dashboard** on the left and your main desktop, called **Desktop 1**, on the right. Creating a new desktop space is as simple as moving your pointer to the far right of the existing desktop spaces until the **Add Desktop Button** appears along the right edge as shown below. The Add Desktop Button looks like half a desktop space and contains a plus sign. Clicking the Add Desktop Button creates a new desktop.

OS X Mavericks will allow you to create up to 16 desktop spaces for you to assign application windows. Desktops are numbered sequentially from left to right with the main desktop called **Desktop 1**. The Dashboard space as well as full-screen applications will also appear along the top of Mission Control as each occupies their own space. In the picture below, iTunes is running in full-screen mode.

I utilize four desktop spaces in addition to any applications running in full-screen mode. I do not run the Dashboard as its own space. In the example above, I have Word running in Desktop 1, Safari in Desktop 2, iTunes in Desktop 3, and nothing in Desktop 4. Also note that the currently active desktop space, Desktop 1, is highlighted by a white border.

Did you notice anything about the spaces in the picture? Each desktop can have its own desktop wallpaper. I find that having different wallpaper on each desktop helps me keep track of where I am amongst multiple desktops. It also helps me find applications that I moved to each desktop space.

To assign a different wallpaper to each space, first navigate to the Space. Secondary click anywhere on the desktop to bring up the Desktop contextual menu. Select **Change Desktop Background...** to bring up the **Desktop & Screen Saver** preference pane. Another option is to navigate to the desktop space. Then open the **Desktop & Screen Saver** preference pane by launching the **System Preferences** application and selecting the **Desktop & Screen Saver** icon or from the Apple menu by selecting > **System Preferences... > Desktop & Screen Saver**. To change the desktop wallpaper, follow the instructions in the section Change the Desktop Wallpaper earlier in this chapter.

Remove a Desktop Space

Removing a desktop space is done in **Mission Control**. Hover your pointer over the desktop you want to remove until an **X** appears in the upper left corner of the space. Click the **X** and OS X will remove the space. Any application windows located in the
deleted desktop space will be reassigned to the desktop in the foreground of Mission Control. Any desktop space with the exception of the Dashboard and full-screen applications can be removed in Mission Control.

Another method to remove a desktop space is to first hold down the ⌥ (option) key in Mission Control. An **X** will appear in the upper left hand corner of every desktop space in the ribbon. Remove the desired desktop spaces by clicking on the **X** while keeping the ⌥ (option) key depressed.

Switch Desktop Spaces without Activating Them

If you want to see which windows are assigned to a particular desktop space without making the space active, another method is to hold down the ⌥ (option) key and click on the appropriate desktop space in the ribbon at the top of **Mission Control**. OS X will switch to that desktop space so you can see its application windows without making the space active. When you want to make the space active, simply release the ⌥ (option) key and click on the space.

Moving Windows to Another Desktop Space

An application window can be moved from one desktop space to another in **Mission Control** by clicking and dragging the window to its new destination desktop. Hover your pointer over a window and it will become highlighted in blue. Next, click and drag the window to your desired destination desktop space in the ribbon of desktops at the top of Mission Control.

You can move an application window to any desktop. Multiple application windows can be assigned to the same desktop space. Windows from the same application can be split across multiple desktop spaces. The only restriction is that you cannot assign an application window to the Dashboard space or to a full-screen app.

Move a Window & Create a Space

You can move an application window and create a new desktop to move it to at the same time. Hover your pointer over the application window you intend to move. A blue highlight will appear around it. Click and drag the window to the upper right corner onto the **Add Desktop Button** to simultaneously create a new desktop and assign the application window to it.

In the example shown below, I am moving the App Store application window from Desktop 1 to a brand new desktop by dragging it in the direction of the arrow onto the **Add Desktop Button** in the upper right-hand corner of Mission Control. OS X will create a new desktop space, which it will name Desktop 5, and assign the System Preferences application window to it.

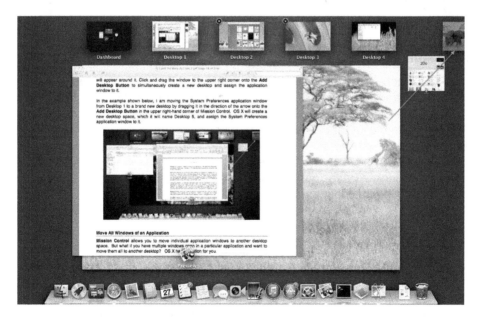

Move All Windows of an Application

Mission Control allows you to move individual application windows to another desktop space. But what if you have multiple windows open in a particular application and want to move them all to another desktop? OS X has a solution for you.

To move all of the windows of an application, click and drag the application's icon (shown below the windows) to the desired desktop space. All the windows will move as a group to their new desktop location.

Toggle Mission Control On & Off

 There are many ways to launch **Mission Control**. You can launch it using a trackpad gesture, launch it from **Launchpad**, launch it from **Spotlight**, press the **F3** key, or enter **^up** (control+up arrow). OS X offers one more alternative that allows you to toggle **Mission Control** on and off. Press and hold the **F3** key to toggle Mission Control on. The moment you release the **F3** key, Mission Control will be toggled off. By the way, this trick also works with the **F4** key to toggle **Dashboard** or **Launchpad** on and off, depending on the age of your Mac and its keyboard configuration.

Disable Mission Control Animation

When opening **Mission Control**, OS X runs an animation that shrinks your current desktop to about 66% of its normal size while revealing the top row of desktop thumbnails along the way. When closing **Mission Control**, the animation runs in reverse. If you prefer to open and close Mission Control immediately without the animation, OS X provides a tweak to turn it off.

To disable the Mission Control opening and closing animations, enter the following commands in **Terminal**. Be sure to press the **return** key after entering each line.

```
defaults write com.apple.dock expose-animation-duration -int 0
```

```
killall Dock
```

The change will take effect immediately and will also turn off the animation when opening and closing **App Exposé**.

To revert back to the OS X default animation for Mission Control and App Exposé, enter the following commands in **Terminal**. The change takes effect immediately.

```
defaults delete com.apple.dock expose-animation-duration
```

```
killall Dock
```

Assign a Hot Corner to Mission Control

The **Hot Corners** feature allows you to assign a specific action to each of the four corners of your desktop. A Hot Corner is activated by moving your pointer to one of the corners to execute the associated command. It is often quicker to use a Hot Corner than to use a keyboard shortcut or to click on an icon.

To assign a **Hot Corner** to **Mission Control**, open the **Mission Control** preference pane by launching the **System Preferences** application and selecting the **Mission Control** preference pane or from the Apple menu by selecting **> System Preferences... > Mission Control**.

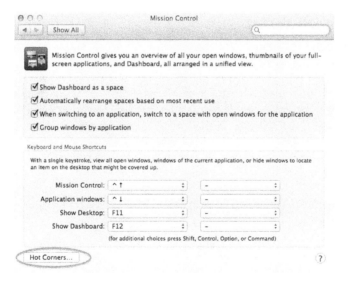

Next, click the **Hot Corners...** button at the lower left of the pane to reveal the drop-down configuration sheet. Choose which corner you want to use to launch Mission Control. Click **OK** when finished, then close the Mission Control preference pane.

Now you can open Mission Control by moving your pointer to the Hot Corner you configured. Move your pointer to the same Hot Corner to close. Mission Control can also be closed by pressing the **esc** key or the **F3** key.

To turn off a Hot Corner, open the **Mission Control** preference pane and click the **Hot Corners...** button in the lower left corner. Select the – from the drop-down menu for each corner that you want to turn off.

To learn how to avoid accidentally triggering the Mission Control Hot Corner, see Avoid Accidentally Triggering a Hot Corner on page 42.

Hot corners can also be configured from the **Desktop & Screen Saver** preference pane.

Replace the Mission Control Background

Do you hate the boring default **Mission Control** background? The folks at Apple seem to have a love affair with gray linen. Not me. In this tweak I'll show you how to replace the boring Mission Control background.

First, find an image that matches the native resolution of your display. If you need instructions on how to do this, check out Configure Desktop Wallpaper From a Folder on page 32. You will need a **PNG** file. If the image is in another format such as **JPEG**, you can convert it using **Preview**. From the **Preview** application, choose **File > Export...** and select PNG for the **Format**. Name the file **defaultdesktop.png** and save it to a convenient location.

Next, open a **Finder** window. Enter ⇧⌘G (shift+command+G) to open the **Go to folder** dialog box. Enter the following into the field and click **Go**.

`/System/Library/CoreServices/`

Find the **Dock** application in this folder, secondary click on it, and select **Show Package Contents**. Open the **Contents** folder, then open the **Resources** folder. Find the file named **defaultdesktop.png**, which is the default Mission Control background. Rename it to something else because you may want to restore it later. I suggest renaming it to **old defaultdesktop.png** so you can easily find it later. OS X will ask for your password to complete the change. Drag the new **defaultdesktop.png** image you created in the last step into the **Resources** folder. OS X will prompt you to enter your password again. Log out and log back in for the change to take effect.

To restore the default Mission Control background, open **Finder** and enter ⇧⌘G (shift+command+G) to open the **Go to folder:** dialog box. Enter the following into the field and click **Go**.

```
/System/Library/CoreServices/
```

Find the **Dock** application in this folder, secondary click on it, and select **Show Package Contents**. Open the **Contents** folder, then open the **Resources** folder. Find the file named **defaultdesktop.png**, which is the current Mission Control background. Drag it to the trash. OS X will ask for your password to complete the change. If you took my suggestion, all you have to do is to rename the file called **old defaultdesktop.png** to **defaultdesktop.png**. OS X will prompt you to enter your password again. Log out and log back in for the change to take effect.

Navigate Between Desktop Spaces

Let's exit **Mission Control** so I can show you how to navigate between desktops and application windows without using Mission Control. Navigating between spaces outside of **Mission Control** is similar to navigating between them inside of **Mission Control**.

Swipe left or right with either three or four fingers on the trackpad. If you are using a Magic Mouse, swiping left or right with either one or two fingers will navigate between your desktops. You can also hold down the ^ (control) key and press the left or right arrow to move left or right through your desktop spaces. By default, switching to an application automatically switches your desktop to the space in which the app resides.

Move a Window To Another Space

There are several methods to move a window to another space. You could use **Mission Control** as described earlier, but there always multiple ways to do things in OS X. Another method is to drag the window over to the left or right edge of the desktop until the pointer reaches the edge of the screen and can no longer move any further. After a short delay, OS X will move the window to the neighboring desktop space.

Remove the Workspace Edge Delay

If you moved a window between desktop spaces by dragging it to the left or right edge of the screen, you noticed a slight delay before OS X moved the window to the neighboring space. You can completely remove this delay by entering the following commands in **Terminal**.

```
defaults write com.apple.dock workspaces-edge-delay -float 0

killall Dock
```

Now you can move a window to the neighboring desktop space without the delay. However, I've found that without a delay, a window will fly across the desktop spaces before I have a chance to drop it on the desired space. So the delay we just eliminated is actually somewhat useful, albeit longer than necessary. The following commands will configure a ¼ second delay, which is just long enough to prevent a window from flying out of control across multiple spaces.

```
defaults write com.apple.dock workspaces-edge-delay -float 0.25
```

```
killall Dock
```

Feel free to play with the decimal number after **float** to adjust the delay to your personal taste.

To revert to the default OS X behavior, enter the following commands.

```
defaults delete com.apple.dock workspaces-edge-delay
```

```
killall Dock
```

Turn Off Automatic Space Rearrangement

After working with spaces for a while you may notice something odd. Your desktop spaces seem to automatically rearrange themselves. No, your Mac is not haunted by gremlins and you're not losing your mind. By default, OS X rearranges desktop spaces based on their most recent use. Therefore, Desktop 4 can work its way up to become Desktop 2 if the applications on Desktop 4 are used more often than the applications on Desktops 2 and 3. If you find this behavior confusing or disturbing, OS X allows you to disable it.

To disable automatic desktop space rearrangement, open the **Mission Control** preference pane by launching the System Preferences application and selecting the **Mission Control** icon or from the Apple menu by selecting > **System Preferences... > Mission Control**. Next, uncheck the check box next to **Automatically rearrange Spaces based on most recent use**.

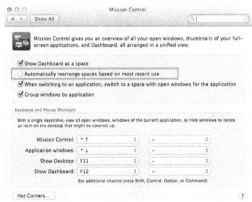

Pin an Application to a Desktop

If you really value organization, OS X allows you to pin an application to a specific desktop space to ensure that the app will always open in the desktop space to which you assigned it. By pinning applications to desktops, you can ensure certain applications appear on particular desktops. Another option is to create themed desktop spaces. For example, you can have one desktop for all of your social media applications, another for your productivity apps, another for browsers, etc. How you organize your applications onto your desktops is up to you.

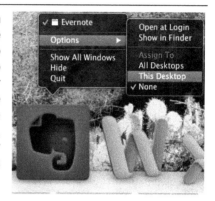

To pin an application to a specific desktop, first navigate to the desktop to which you want to pin the application. If you need to create a new desktop space, first launch **Mission Control** and click the **Add Desktop Button**. Find the application in the **Dock**. If the application is not in the Dock, launch the application using **Launchpad** to make it appear in the Dock. **Secondary click** on the app icon in the Dock to reveal the **Options** submenu as shown at the right. By default, a checkmark will be next to **None**, which allows the application to be run in any desktop space. To assign an app to the current desktop, select **This Desktop**.

Pinning an application to a desktop does not prevent you from moving that application to another desktop using **Mission Control** later. Also, the app does not have to be added to the Dock. Once an application has been assigned to a desktop, it will always appear on the assigned desktop regardless of how it was launched.

Pin an Application to Every Desktop

OS X also offers an option to pin an application in every desktop. This is a handy feature if you have an app you use frequently such as Safari and desire quick access to it. Find the application in the **Dock**. If the app is not in the Dock, launch it using **Launchpad** to make it appear in the Dock. **Secondary click** on the app icon in the Dock to reveal the **Options** submenu as shown at the right. To assign an app to every desktop, select **All Desktops**.

Create Keyboard Shortcuts for Spaces

Another method to move quickly between desktop spaces is to set up keyboard shortcuts. Keyboard shortcuts allow you to jump between desktops without swiping. Keyboard shortcuts are by far the quickest way to jump between desktop spaces because you can move from Desktop 1 to Desktop 4 with a single command.

To set up keyboard shortcuts, open the **Keyboard** preference pane by launching the System Preferences application and selecting the **Keyboard** icon or from the Apple menu by selecting ** > System Preferences... > Keyboard**. Next, select the **Keyboard Shortcuts** pane if not already selected. Click on **Mission Control** in the left-hand pane.

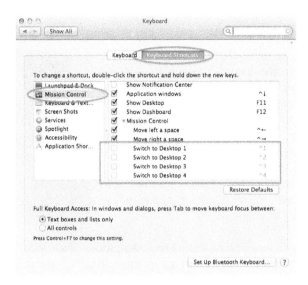

You may have to scroll to the bottom of the right-hand pane to see all of the **Switch to Desktop** shortcuts. Check the check boxes next to each of your desktops to enable the shortcuts. Once enabled, simply type the number of the desktop space you want to go while holding down the **^** (control) key. OS X will immediately jump to that space. Note that if you add more desktop spaces, you will have to return to the Keyboard preference pane to configure shortcuts for the new spaces.

Quick Look

When application windows are grouped in **Mission Control**, it is sometimes difficult to differentiate between windows because they are grouped one on top of the other. This is especially true if you have a lot of windows open on the same desktop and are using a computer with a small screen like the 11-inch MacBook Air. The solution is **Quick Look**.

To see the contents of any window in **Mission Control**, hover over it with your pointer and press the spacebar to zoom. The window underneath your pointer will be highlighted in a blue border. To toggle the zoom, hit the spacebar again to turn off **Quick Look** and the window will shrink back to its normal size.

An alternative method to activate Quick Look is to scroll up with two fingers on the trackpad. First, hover your pointer over the window you are interested in seeing. The window will be highlighted with a blue border. Next, scroll up using two fingers to activate Quick Look. Scroll down with two fingers to turn off.

Change the Quick Look Size

If the default Quick Look size is not big enough for you, this tweak will allow you to increase the size of the window. To make the Quick Look window expand to full size in **Mission Control**, open **Terminal** and enter the following commands.

```
defaults write com.apple.dock expose-cluster-scale -float 1

killall Dock
```

If that size is too big, you can change the numeric value after **float**. For example, using 0.5 makes the window expand larger than the default but not as large as the previous set of commands. Enter the following commands and Terminal and see if the size works for you. Try changing the numeric value after **float** to find the size that is right for you.

```
defaults write com.apple.dock expose-cluster-scale -float 0.5

killall Dock
```

To revert to the default, enter the following commands in **Terminal**.

```
defaults delete com.apple.dock expose-cluster-scale

killall Dock
```

Ungroup App Windows in Mission Control

OS X will group windows from the same application for a cleaner display in **Mission Control**. In the picture below, the two Preview windows are stacked on top of each other, making it difficult to distinguish between their contents without having to use Quick Look. OS X offers an option to ungroup windows of the same application. This feature makes it easier to quickly discern the contents of multiple application windows without resorting to Quick Look.

In the picture below, the two windows from the Preview application are shown separately, making it easier to distinguish between their contents without having to use Quick Look. This feature requires turning off the option to group windows by application in Mission Control.

To ungroup application windows in **Mission Control**, open the **Mission Control** preference pane by launching the System Preferences application and selecting the **Mission Control** icon or from the Apple menu by selecting > **System Preferences... > Mission Control**. Next, uncheck the check box next to **Group windows by application**

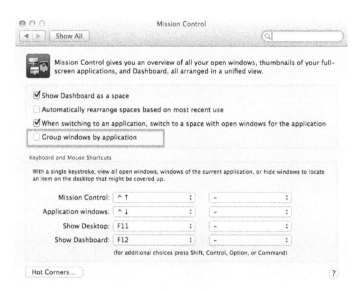

Change the Keyboard Shortcut to Mission Control

The default keyboard shortcut to launch **Mission Control** is ^**up** (control+up arrow). If you want to create your own keyboard shortcut or mouse shortcut, the lower half of the **Mission Control** preference pane allows you to do so.

To change the keyboard shortcut or to create a mouse shortcut, open the **Mission Control** preference pane by launching the System Preferences application and selecting the **Mission Control** icon or from the Apple menu by selecting > **System Preferences... > Mission Control**.

Use the drop-down menu next to **Mission Control** in the lower half of the preference pane to select your desired keyboard shortcut. The second column allows you to create a mouse shortcut. You can use the shift, control, option, or command keys alone or in combination as modifiers for both the keyboard and mouse shortcuts.

The bottom half of the **Mission Control** preference pane also allows you to create or change keyboard and mouse shortcuts for **App Exposé**, to show the desktop, or to show the **Dashboard**.

App Exposé removes desktop clutter to reveal all the windows of the chosen application. To launch **App** Exposé, select an application with multiple open windows and enter ^**down** (control+down arrow). You can than select the desired window by pointing and clicking on it, making it active and placing it on top of all other windows. App Exposé can also be executed with a trackpad gesture of swiping three or four fingers down. Check out the chapter on Gestures to find out how to turn on the gesture for **App Exposé**.

Pressing the **F11** key, clears the desktop of all open windows by pushing them to the right edge of the screen. Note that you may have to hold down the **fn** (function) key while pressing **F11** as this function key is normally used to lower the speaker volume. Press **F11** (or **fn F11**) to return the desktop clutter.

Pressing the **F12** key, launches the **Dashboard**. On older keyboards, the **F4** key launches the **Dashboard**, so you may find using **F12** redundant. On new keyboards, the **F4** key is used to open **Launchpad**. Note that you may have to hold down the **fn** (function) key while pressing **F12** as this function key is normally used to raise the speaker volume.

To turn off any of the shortcuts, select the – option from the drop-down menu.

5

Menu Bar

OS X Mavericks offers some customizations for the **Menu Bar** to include changing its color and reordering and deleting the menu extras in the **Status Menu**. Remember, there are two halves to the Menu Bar. The left half displays the **Apple** and **Application** menus and the right half displays the **Status Menu**.

The OS X default Status Menu is shown below. Note that if you upgraded from a previous version of OS X, your status menu may look different.

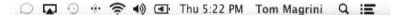

The **Status Menu** displays the status and provides quick access to various OS X features via small icons called **Menu Extras**.

Next to the Menu Extras are icons for **Spotlight** and **Notification Center**. We will cover Spotlight and the Notification Center in another chapter.

Make the Menu Bar Solid Gray

By default, the Menu Bar is translucent. allowing the colors of the desktop wallpaper to show through. OS X allows you to change your Menu Bar to solid gray, which will not change color as the desktop wallpaper changes.

To make the the Menu Bar solid gray, open the **Desktop & Screen Saver** preference pane by launching the System Preferences application and selecting the **Desktop & Screen Saver** icon or from the Apple menu by selecting **> System Preferences... > Desktop & Screen Saver**. Next, uncheck the check box next to **Translucent Menu Bar.**

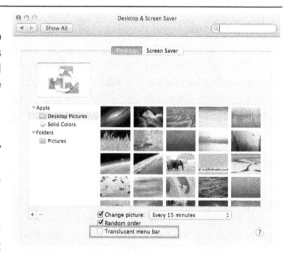

Make the Menu Bar Black in Full Screen Apps

If you don't like a translucent or solid gray Menu Bar, OS X Mavericks provides one more option, but only for full-screen apps. This tweak will turn the Menu Bar solid black for full-screen applications. Lettering and icons will appear white on the black Menu Bar.

To turn the Menu Bar black in full-screen apps, open **Terminal** and enter the following commands. You will need to log out and log back in for the change to take effect.

```
defaults write -g NSFullScreenDarkMenu -bool TRUE
```

To revert to the default Menu Bar, enter the following commands.

```
defaults delete -g NSFullScreenDarkMenu
```

Like before, you will have to log out and log back in again for the changes to take effect.

Remove the Menu Bar from Other Displays

One of the new features in OS X Mavericks is the **Menu Bar** is available at the top of every display. This provides a more independent treatment of each display rather than other displays being merely extensions of the main desktop as in previous versions of OS X. Since the **Menu Bar** is available on all displays, You no longer have to move your pointer back to the main display to access **Menu Bar** features.

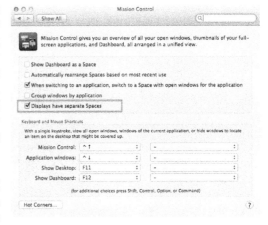

If you prefer the older style of previous OS X versions or if some of your applications are not compatible with how Mavericks handles the **Menu Bar**, you can configure the **Menu Bar** to appear on only your main display.

Open the **Mission Control** preference pane by launching the System Preferences application and selecting the **Mission Control** icon or from the Apple menu by selecting > **System Preferences... > Mission Control**. Uncheck the check box next to **Displays have separate Spaces**. You will need to logout and log back in for the change to take effect.

Reorder Menu Extras

The **Menu Extras** in the **Status Menu** are displayed in the order in which they started. If you launch a program, such as Evernote, its **Menu Extra** will appear at the far left of the **Status Menu**. Evernote's Menu Extra allows you to create a note and save it to Evernote directly from the **Status Menu**. Not all programs have a **Menu Extra**.

If you don't like the order of the **Menu Extras**, OS X allows you to move them by holding down the ⌘ (command) key while clicking and dragging them to a new location on the

Status Bar. The selected Menu Extra will turn gray while you are holding it. Slide it left or right to your desired location. Other Menu Extras will politely move out of the way to make room. Note that you can only reorder the Menu Extras within the Status Bar, the right half of the Menu Bar. You cannot relocate a Menu Extra to the left side as it is reserved for the **Apple** and **Application menus**.

Take care not to drag a Menu Extra off the Menu Bar as you can accidentally remove it from the Status Menu.

You can move most, but not all Menu Extras. You cannot move the Menu Extra for **Spotlight** or **Notification Center**.

Remove a Menu Extra

If you have no need for a particular **Menu Extra**, Mavericks allows you to permanently remove it from the **Status Bar**. To remove a Menu Extra, hold down the ⌘ (command) key while clicking and dragging the Menu Extra off the Menu Bar. Release and poof, the Menu Extra disappears in a puff of smoke!

Add a Menu Extra

If you want to add a **Menu Extra** or put one back that you accidentally removed, first open **Finder**. Next press ⇧⌘**G** (shift+command+G) to bring up the **Go to folder** dialog box. Enter **/System/Library/CoreServices/Menu Extras** into the dialog box and click **Go**. The contents of the Menu Extras folder will be displayed in Finder.

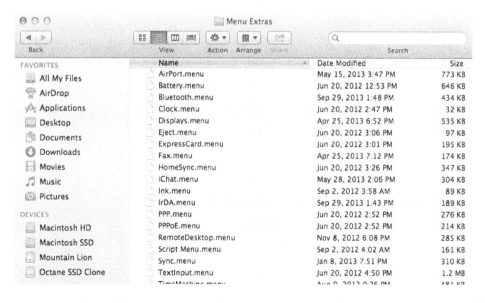

There are more Menu Extras shown in this folder than are displayed in the default OS X Status Bar. Find the Menu Extra you wish to add and double-click on it. The Menu Extra will appear at the far left of the Status Bar. Hold down the ⌘ (command) key while clicking and dragging the Menu Extra to your desired location on the Status Bar.

OS X Menu Extras

Menu Extras are used to show the status of various OS X features and to customize them. In the next few sections, I'll cover the default OS X Menu Extras. OS X Mavericks offers about 24 Menu Extras, most of which are not shown in the default Status Bar.

User Menu Extra

The **User Menu Extra** appears to the left of **Spotlight** if you have multiple user accounts and have configured the **fast user switching** feature. Fast user switching allows you to switch users from the drop-down menu in the User Menu Extra. It also provides quick access to two other features – the log in window and the **Users & Groups** preference pane.

Selecting **Login Window...** will lock your Mac without logging you out. Selecting **Users & Groups Preferences...** will take you to the **Users & Groups** preference pane where you can add or remove users, change your password and profile picture, enable parental controls, and choose login items.

Fast user switching is configured from the **Users & Groups** preference pane. Click on **Login Options** in the left pane and then check the check box next to **Show fast user switching menu as**. The drop-down menu lets you show the **Full Name**, **Short Name**, or **Icon**.

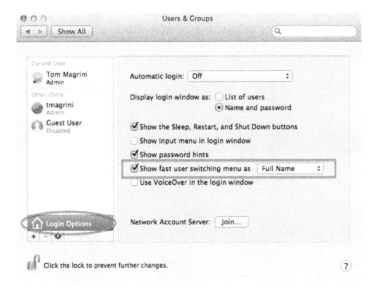

Clock Menu Extra

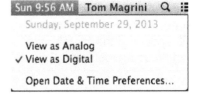

The **Clock Menu Extra** displays the current date and time. The options available from its drop-down menu allow you to view the clock as analog or digital and to access the **Date & Time** preference pane. Its drop-down menu also displays the day of the week and date.

Selecting **Open Date and Time Preferences...** takes you directly to the **Clock** pane of the **Date & Time** preference pane.

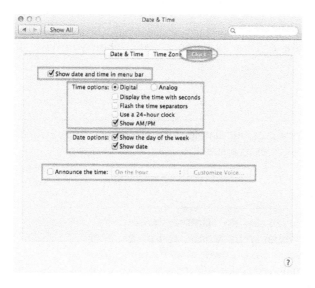

The first option available on the **Clock** pane is to **Show date and time in the Menu Bar**. Unchecking this box does essentially the same thing as dragging the **Clock Menu Extra** off the Menu Bar – it tells OS X to not display the date and time on the Menu Bar.

If you choose to display the date and time on the Menu Bar, you have various time and date options available to you in the next two sections. The time can be shown in either analog or digital format. If you select digital format, you have three additional options. The time can be displayed with or without seconds, the colons that separate the time can flash, and you have the option of displaying a 12-hour or 24-hour clock. If you select the 12-hour clock, you have an additional option of showing AM and PM. Check or uncheck the options to display the time in the format you desire.

As for the date, you can choose to display or not display it in the Menu Bar. You also have the option of displaying the day of the week. Check or uncheck the date options until the date and time display the way you want them. All changes to the date and time options are effective immediately.

The **Clock** preferences also allow you to configure OS X to announce the time on the quarter, half, or hour. To have OS X announce the time, check the check box next to **Announce the time**. Choose how often you want the time announced and then click **Customize Voice...** to access the voice drop-down to select the voice you wish to use to announce the time.

The **Voice** drop-down menu allows you to choose from a number of pre-installed voices or to download additional voices. Choose one of the voices from the **Voice** drop-down menu or click **Customize...** to see other voices available.

If you select **Customize...**, you'll be presented with another drop-down menu. Check the check box next to the desired voices and click **OK**. To remove voice, uncheck the check box.

You can close the **Date & Time** preference pane when you have finished making your selections.

Volume Menu Extra

The **Volume Menu Extra** is rather simple. All it allows you to do is to change the volume of your speakers. Use the slider to adjust the volume up or down.

Battery Menu Extra

The information displayed by the **Battery Menu Extra** depends on whether your MacBook Pro or MacBook Air is plugged into AC power or is running on battery. When plugged into AC power, the **Battery Menu Extra** will tell you whether the battery is charged or how long it will take to fully charge the battery. When running on battery power, the 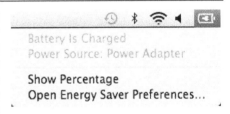 **Battery Menu Extra** will tell you how much time remains before your battery runs out of power.

There is a single option on the **Battery Menu Extra** drop-down menu to **Show Percentage**. By default, OS X shows only a representation of a battery in the status bar. Checking this option displays a percentage to the left of the battery icon.

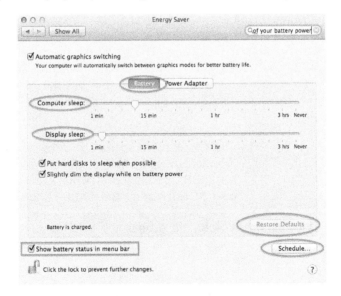

The final choice in the **Battery Menu Extra** drop-down menu, opens the **Energy Saver** preference pane in System Preferences. The **Energy Saver** preference pane allows you to set options to control your Mac's energy usage. If you're using a MacBook Pro or MacBook Air, these options will help you extend the life of your battery.

By default, the top option, **Automatic graphics switching**, is checked. With **Automatic graphics switching** you trade graphics performance to gain better battery life. If you prefer better graphics performance, uncheck this option. You will need to log out and then log back in for the change to take effect.

The next two sliders allow you to set the amount of time your computer is inactive before the computer or display goes to sleep. There are two tabs – **Battery** and **Power Adapter** – with the battery tab only visible if you are using a MacBook Pro or MacBook Air. OS X puts the display to sleep after two minutes of inactivity and the computer goes to sleep after ten minutes when on battery power. When running on AC power, the display will go to sleep after ten minutes of inactivity and the computer will go to sleep after fifteen minutes. Personally I find these settings a little too aggressive. I suggest you adjust them to your personal preference. If you change any of these settings, OS X will warn you that your computer may use more energy. Simply click **OK** to continue.

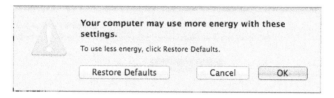

Your Mac's hard disk drive drains a lot of power from your battery, checking the option to **Put hard drives to sleep when possible** will spin down your hard drives to conserve battery power. If you are using a Solid State Drive (SSD), this option is not important as an SSD uses less power than a hard disk drive.

The next option depends if you have selected the **Battery** or the **Power Adapter** tab. On the **Battery** tab the next option is to **Slightly dim the display while on battery power**. Checking this option will automatically reduce the display's brightness before it goes to sleep, helping to further conserve battery power. When the **Power Adapter** tab is selected, this option changes to **Wake for network access**. This option will wake your computer to allow others to access your Mac's shared resources (i.e., printers or iTunes playlists).

If you want to return to the OS X defaults, click the **Restore Defaults** button at the lower right of the **Energy Saver** preference pane.

At the lower left of the **Energy Saver** preference pane is a check box to **Show battery status in Menu Bar**. The check box is checked by default. Uncheck it if you do not want to show the battery status in your **Menu Bar**.

The final option in the **Energy Saver** preference pane is to set a schedule to start up, wake or put your Mac to sleep. Clicking on the **Schedule...** button presents a drop-down dialog box that allows you to set a schedule for when you want your Mac to start up, wake, or go to sleep.

The first check box allows you to start up or wake your Mac at a particular time every day, on weekdays, on weekends, or on particular days of the week. The second check box allows you to sleep, restart, or shutdown your Mac at a particular time every day, on weekdays, on weekends, or on particular days of the week. Click the **OK** button when finished configuring.

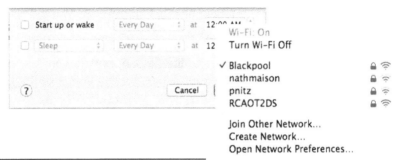

AirPort Menu Extra

The **AirPort Menu Extra** allows you to turn Wi-Fi on and off, connect to a Wi-Fi network, join or create other networks, or open the **Network** preference pane. The drop-down menu is divided into three sections.

The first section displays the status of your Wi-Fi and allows you to turn Wi-Fi off and on.

The second section lists the wireless networks that your Mac is able to see. Wi-Fi networks that are secure and require a password to join will be shown with a padlock. Public Wi-Fi networks which are open and allow anyone to join will not have a padlock.

The third and final section will allow you to join other Wi-Fi networks that are not listed in the list of available Wi-Fi networks. You may wish to use this option, **Join Other Network...** when trying to connect to a network which is hidden (i.e., not broadcasting its network name). Selecting this option brings up another dialog box where you can enter the network name and choose the type of security. Available security options are: WEP, WPA Personal, WPA2 Personal, WEP Enterprise, WPA Enterprise, and WPA2 Enterprise. Once you select the security type, the dialog box challenges you for the network password. OS X will remember this Wi-Fi network, allowing you to connect again without entering the network password. You can click the **Show Networks** button to display the available Wi-Fi networks to which you can connect. Click **Join** when finished entering the network name, security, and password.

Selecting the option **Create Network...** allows you to create what's known as an ad hoc wireless network. An ad hoc wireless network is a temporary Wi-Fi network you may wish to create to transfer files between two computers. Obviously one of the computers is not a Mac, otherwise you would probably have used the AirDrop feature instead.

To create an ad hoc Wi-Fi network enter the network name, channel, the type of security, and the password you would like to use. Note that OS X only supports 40-bit WEP and 128-bit WEP security, neither of which is very secure. However given the temporary nature of ad hoc Wi-Fi networks, either of these options is probably sufficient. If you do not want security you can choose **None** for the security option. Otherwise, if you choose 40-bit WEP, you'll be asked to enter a password of exactly five ASCII characters or 10 hexadecimal digits. For 128-bit WEP, OS X will ask you to enter a password of exactly 13 ASCII characters or 26 hexadecimal digits.

The final option in the **AirPort Menu Extra** drop-down menu is to **Open Network Preferences...** which launches the **Network** preference pane. The **Network** preference pane allows you to turn Wi-Fi off and on and connect to a Wi-Fi network. It also provides a check box at the bottom of the pane to show the **AirPort Menu Extra** in the **Status Bar**. An **Advanced** button allows you to configure various Wi-Fi, TCP/IP, DNS, and other network configurations.

If you're having trouble connecting to a Wi-Fi network the **Assist me...** button towards the bottom of the **Network** preference pane will allow you to run **Network Setup Assistant** or run **Network Diagnostics**. The **Network Setup Assistant** will run you through an automated script to help you connect your Mac to the Internet. **Network Diagnostics** will help you resolve any connectivity issues to get you back onto the Internet whether you connect through an Ethernet or Wi-Fi network.

Hold Down the Option Key with the AirPort Menu Extra

Holding down the ⌥ (option) key while clicking on the **AirPort Menu Extra** provides additional status information. Note the change to the second section of the Airport drop-down menu. In addition to showing the Wi-Fi network to which your Mac is connected, it now provides additional wireless status information that can be used to troubleshoot any connectivity issues.

At the very bottom of the drop-down menu is an option to **Open Wireless Diagnostics...** which is an application that will detect common Wi-Fi problems.

Bluetooth Menu Extra

Bluetooth is a short range wireless technology that allows you to connect mobile phones, headsets, printers, digital cameras, tablets, keyboards, a mouse, and a trackpad to your Mac.

The **Bluetooth Menu Extra** allows you to turn Bluetooth on and off, pair your Mac with another Bluetooth device, send or browse files on a device paired over Bluetooth, and open the **Bluetooth** preference pane. The drop-down menu is divided into four sections.

Bluetooth: On
Discoverable: Off
Turn Bluetooth Off

Send File...
Browse Device...

Devices
Apple Wireless Trackpad ▸
Tom's keyboard ▸

Set Up Bluetooth Device...
Open Bluetooth Preferences...

The first section displays the status of your Bluetooth and allows you to turn Bluetooth off and on.

The second section allows you to send files or browse files on paired Bluetooth devices which support file storage. Launching the OS X **Bluetooth File Exchange** application to send or browse files.

The third section lists all of the Bluetooth devices to which your Mac has been paired. If the name of the device is bolded, it indicates that the device is currently connected. Highlighting any of the connected devices will bring up a secondary menu allowing you to disconnect the device, see its current battery level, or open the appropriate preference pane in the **System Preferences** application.

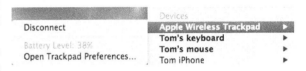

In the final section, selecting **Set Up Bluetooth Device** launches the **Bluetooth Setup Assistant**, which allows you to pair new Bluetooth devices to your Mac. **Open Bluetooth Preferences...** launches the **Bluetooth** preference pane, which lets you turn Bluetooth off and on, pair Bluetooth devices, and connect and disconnect paired devices. It also provides a check box at the bottom of the pane to show the **Bluetooth Menu Extra** in the **Status Bar**.

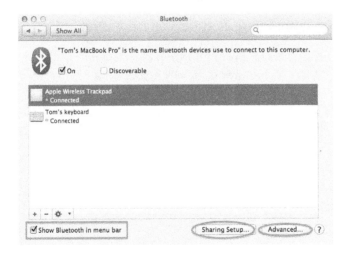

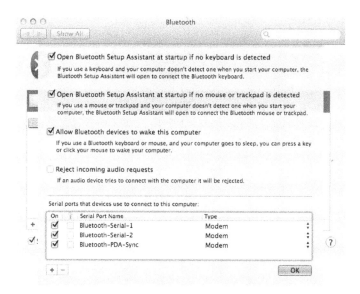

Holding down the ⌥ (option) key while highlighting any device will display the current signal strength of the device.

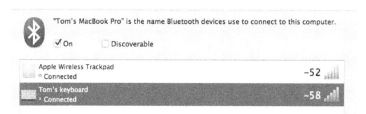

Clicking the **Advanced...** button at the lower right of the **Bluetooth** preference pane displays a drop-down menu with options to run the **Bluetooth Setup Assistant** if a keyboard, mouse, or trackpad is not detected at start up. You can also configure Bluetooth devices to wake your Mac from sleep and reject incoming audio requests.

Hold Down the Option Key with the Bluetooth Menu Extra

Holding down the ⌥ (option) key while clicking on the **Bluetooth Menu Extra** provides additional status information. Note the two new sections added to the drop-down menu. The first section displays the Bluetooth version and MAC address of your Mac's Bluetooth network card. The second section provides an option to **Create Diagnostic Report on the Desktop...** which is handy when if you are working with Apple to troubleshoot a Bluetooth issue.

Highlighting any of the paired devices will display a secondary menu allowing you to disconnect the device, remove it, see its signal strength, MAC address, battery level, or open the appropriate preference pane in the **System Preferences** application.

Time Machine Menu Extra

Time Machine is the OS X built-in backup application which will automatically backup your entire Mac, including all system files, applications, accounts, preferences, email messages, music, photos, movies, and documents to an external drive or **AirPort Time Capsule**. Not only does **Time Machine** back up everything on your Mac, it also remembers how your Mac looked on any given day in the past. **Time Machine** keeps hourly backups for the past 24 hours, daily backups for the past month, and weekly backups, provided your external hard drive or **Time Capsule** has sufficient space.

The **Time Machine Menu Extra** contains three sections. The top section displays the last time Time Machine backed up your Mac and to where it was backed up.

The second section allows you to **Back Up Now**, which will tell Time Machine to immediately start a backup of your Mac. This section also allows you to **Enter Time Machine** to restore any files you may have lost.

The final option to **Open Time Machine Preferences...** will launch the **Time Machine** preference pane where you can turn **Time Machine** off and on, see the day and time of the last back up, and configure your back up destinations. At the bottom of the Time Machine preference pane is a check box next to **Show Time Machine in Menu Bar**. Unchecking this box will remove the Time Machine Menu Extra from the Status Bar.

An **Options...** button at the bottom right of the preference pane displays a drop-down dialog that allows you to exclude devices from being backed up by Time Machine along with two configuration options.

The check box next to **Back up while on battery power** is unchecked by default. Typically it is not a good idea to backup while on battery power as your MacBook Pro or MacBook Air could run out of power before a Time Machine

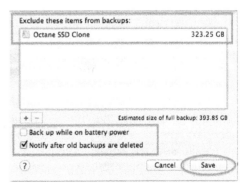

backup is successfully completed. By default, OS X will notify you after old backups are deleted. Uncheck this box, if you do not want to be notified when OS X deleted an old backup. Click **Save** when finished.

AirPlay Mirroring Menu Extra

If you own an Apple TV, the **AirPlay Mirroring Menu Extra** will allow you to send video from your Mac to your Apple TV using an OS X feature called **AirPlay**. **AirPlay** is limited to Macs manufactured beginning in 2011. If your Mac does not support AirPlay, you will not see the AirPlay Mirroring Menu Extra in the status bar.

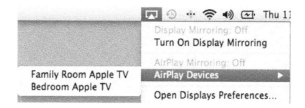

The **AirPlay Mirroring Menu Extra** is split into two sections. The top section displays the current AirPlay status, allows you to connect an AirPlay display, displays the current mirroring status, and turns mirroring on or off. If you select **Connect To AirPlay Display**, you'll be presented with a list of available AirPlay displays.

The option at the bottom **Open Displays Preferences...** launches the **Displays** preference pane.

iChat Menu Extra

The **iChat Menu Extra** allows you to send a new message and to see and change your current status. You can even configure iChat to show the current song you are listening to on iTunes.

Choosing **New Message...** will launch the **Messages** application, allowing you to create and send a new message.

6

Dock

Whether you are starting your Mac for the first or the thousandth time, the most iconic and recognizable feature of the OS X desktop is the **Dock**. The Dock is one of the most customizable features of OS X. By default, the Dock appears as a three-dimensional strip of application and folder icons floating above a reflective glass surface at the bottom of the desktop. The Dock serves a twofold purpose, combining the functions of an application launcher and a taskbar to switch between running applications. The Dock is an ingenious feature of OS X that provides a convenient and speedy method to launch applications, open documents and folders, or switch between running applications with a single click of your trackpad or mouse.

The default Dock for OS X Mavericks is shown above. If you upgraded your Mac from Mountain Lion or an earlier operating system, your Dock may look different as any customization you may have done will have carried forward into Mavericks.

Since the Dock operates as both an application launcher and switcher, applications that are running are denoted by a tiny indicator light beneath their icon along the front edge of the Dock's reflective glass surface. Note the indicator lights beneath the icons for Finder, Safari, iTunes, and the System Preferences in the picture above.

Apps that are not permanently kept in the Dock will appear at the end of the strip of icons when they are run. In the picture, Pages appears  next to System Preferences and to the left of the **divider**. The indicator light beneath the Pages icon denotes it is running.

The **divider** is the light gray line that separates applications from stacks, minimized windows, documents, and the trash. Applications go to the left of the divider. Everything else goes on the right. Note the icon to the left of the Trash. It is a Safari window that has been minimized to the Dock. How did it get there? Clicking on the yellow minimize window control in the upper left corner of a window will minimize it. Clicking on the icon maximizes it, restoring it to its original size before it was minimized.

Put Apps in Order

The first order of business in customizing the **Dock** is to put the application icons in the order in which you want to see them. This is easily accomplished by moving your mouse pointer to the application icon you wish to move, clicking and holding it, and immediately dragging it horizontally along the Dock to its new location. If you click and hold too long without moving the icon, a menu will appear and you won't be able to move the icon. In this case, click anywhere on the Desktop and try again. While you are moving the icon, it will become transparent and other application icons will politely move out of its way. Once in its desired location, simply release your hold.

Remove Apps from the Dock

Once you have your application icons in the right order, the next step is to remove apps that you don't want to see in the **Dock**. Note that when you remove an application from the Dock, you are not removing it from your Mac. You only remove its alias from the Dock. The application remains safely in the **Applications** folder in case you want to use it later.

There are always multiple ways of doing things in OS X. It is your personal choice which method you prefer. You can click and hold the icon you wish to remove until a contextual menu appears. You can also make this menu appear by using a secondary click, holding the control key down while clicking or by using the two-finger tap gesture. If two-finger tap doesn't work, it means you haven't yet customized the trackpad. See the chapter on gestures. Select **Options > Remove from Dock** and the app disappears in a puff of smoke.

An application that is running behaves differently. You can click and hold the icon or use a secondary click to make a contextual menu appear. Select **Options** and a submenu appears. Note the checkmark next to **Keep in Dock**. Select **Keep in Dock** to remove the checkmark. The menu will disappear along with the checkmark. Since the application is running, its icon will not disappear from the Dock until you quit.

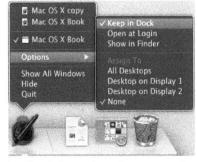

The fastest and easiest way to remove an app icon from the Dock is to drag it up past the middle of the desktop. A small puff of smoke will appear below the icon. Release and poof the app disappears. If the app icon jumps back to the Dock, it means one of two things. Perhaps you didn't move it far enough away from the Dock. Be sure to move it far enough from the Dock until a small puff of smoke appears below the application's icon. The other possibility is the app is running. If the app is running, it won't disappear until you quit it.

Oops! Everyone panics the first time they accidentally remove the wrong application icon from the Dock and see it disappear. Don't worry. This is an easy fix. Simply add the application back to the Dock. We'll cover how to do that next. And remember, removing an application from the Dock only removes its icon. The application is still safely tucked away in the Applications folder.

Add Apps to the Dock

Adding an application to the **Dock** is even easier than removing one. Of course, there are multiple ways to do so. The simplest method is to run the application. Its icon will appear at the end of the strip of apps just to the left of the divider. Drag it to the left to its desired location. The simple act of moving an app icon the the left along the Dock is a signal to OS X that you desire to keep that app in the Dock.

Another method to add a running application's icon to the Dock is to use the secondary click to make the menu appear. Select **Options > Keep in Dock** using your trackpad or mouse to put a checkmark next to **Keep in Dock**.

Another method is to open the Applications folder in Finder, select the application, and drag it to the Dock. Note that you are not moving the app. You are creating an alias on the Dock. Any of these methods will add an app to the Dock.

Control App Behavior

The **Options** menu contains several options to control how an application behaves. Checking **Open at Login** opens the app immediately upon logging in to your Mac. This is handy if you have an app or set of apps you open every time you start your Mac. For example, if you always open Safari, Mail, and iTunes as soon as you login, setting these apps to open at login will save a little time. Use the secondary click to make the **Options** menu appear and select **Open at Login**. A checkmark indicates the application will open when you login or start your Mac. If you no longer want an application to open when you log in, select **Options > Open at Login** to remove the checkmark.

If you want to see the folder where the application is located in Finder, choose **Show in Finder**. This will immediately open the Applications folder with the application highlighted. This option is handy if you need to navigate to the Application folder to uninstall it.

The **Assign To** feature allows you to assign an application to appear on a specific display. Naturally, this option is only relevant if you have multiple displays. As I write this book, I am using two displays and have the option to assign applications to either display. This feature is handy if you prefer certain applications to always appear on the left display and others to appear on the right.

It is quite common to have more than one window open for the same application. As your desktop becomes crowded with open windows from multiple applications, it becomes increasingly difficult to find a specific window. The **Show All Windows** command executes a feature called App Exposé, which temporarily removes the desktop clutter to reveal all the windows of the chosen application. You can than select the desired window by pointing and clicking on it, making it active and placing it on top of all other windows. The App Exposé feature can also be executed with a trackpad gesture of swiping three or four fingers down. Check out the chapter on gestures to find out how to turn on the gesture for App Exposé.

The Other Side of the Divider

The Dock's gray divider separates applications from stacks, minimized windows, documents, and the Trash. The picture shows the default Mavericks Dock. If you upgraded your Mac from Mountain Lion, your Dock may look different as any customization will have carried forward into Mavericks.

 The icon at the end of the Dock that looks like a wire mesh trash can is the **Trash**, a temporary holding area for files you wish to delete. You can move files to the Trash by dragging them onto its icon. Another option is to utilize a secondary click on a file to display a contextual menu with **Move to Trash** as one of the commands.

Once there are items in the Trash, its icon changes to display a full trash can. If you secondary click on the Trash when there are items in it, you have the option to **Empty Trash** or to display its contents in Finder with the **Open** command. The latter feature is handy if you accidentally drag a file into the trash and want to pull it back out. Selecting **Empty Trash** brings up a warning dialog box giving you the option to empty the trash or cancel.

Dragging files to the trash does not delete them. The files you drag into the Trash can always be dragged back out (unless you have emptied the Trash). And you may be surprised to learn that emptying the trash does not delete the trashed files. Similar to other operating systems, OS X merely marks the space on the disk drive occupied by the trashed files as free space that can be written over with new data. If the trashed files have not been written over, a hacker could use a third party application to reclaim the files. This is very disconcerting if the trashed files contain sensitive data such as financial information or other personally identifiable information that could be used to steal your identity. Don't worry. OS X offers a way to permanently delete files.

Permanently Delete Files

 If you want to permanently delete the files in the Trash, you must use the **Secure Empty Trash** feature. Hold down the ⌘ (command) key while secondary clicking on the Trash. The option for **Secure Empty Trash** replaces the **Empty Trash** command. Be sure to keep holding the ⌘ (command) key down until you select **Secure Empty Trash**. If you don't, the command will revert to the **Empty Trash** command. After selecting **Secure Empty Trash**, a

dialog box will warn that the items in the Trash will be permanently deleted and cannot be recovered unless they have been backed up by Time Machine. Click the **Secure Empty Trash** button to permanently delete your trashed files or cancel to go back. The options **Empty Trash** and **Secure Empty Trash** are also available under Finder in the Menu Bar.

Manually selecting between **Empty Trash** and **Secure Empty Trash** can lead to mistakes where files you wanted securely deleted are not. OS X allows you to choose Secure Empty Trash as the default method of emptying the trash. From the **Finder** menu, choose **Preferences...** or enter ⌘, (command+,) to bring up the Finder preference pane. Click **Advanced**. Checking the **Empty Trash securely** check box makes it the default. If you don't want to be warned each time you empty the Trash, turn this off by unchecking the box next to **Show warning before emptying trash**.

Change the Dock's Behavior

Up to this point we have learned how to change the behavior and appearance of icons in the Dock. Now it's time to learn how to customize the behavior and appearance of the Dock itself. Most of the customizations are accomplished using the **Dock** pane in **System Preferences**, however we'll first look at four customizations that can be done directly from the Dock itself.

First, position your pointer on the Dock divider. When the pointer turns into a white arrow, use a secondary click to bring up the Dock menu. Four customization options are available that allow you to hide the Dock when not in use, magnify the icons in the Dock, change the position of the Dock on the screen, and control the animation of windows as they are minimized and maximized.

Although the Dock is a very useful feature of OS X, it takes up a significant amount of real estate at the bottom of the desktop. This can sometimes be problematic when using your pointer at the bottom of a window as the pointer will sometimes interact with the Dock. OS X gives you the option of hiding the Dock when not in use. From the Dock menu, select **Turn Hiding On** to hide the Dock. When not in use, the Dock will conveniently slip

out of sight below the Desktop. To make the Dock reappear, simply position your pointer at the bottom edge of the Desktop. To turn hiding off, secondary click the divider to bring up the Dock menu and select **Turn Hiding Off**. A quick way to toggle hiding on and off is to use ⌥⌘D (option+command+D).

Magnification is a neat feature of OS X and is particularly useful if you prefer a small Dock or your Dock is crowded with a large number of icons. As you add more icons to the Dock, it will become smaller, adjusting its size to fit horizontally across the bottom of the Desktop. If you have lots of icons in your Dock or prefer a small Dock, it may become difficult to distinguish app icons from one another. With magnification on, the icons in the Dock will magnify as you move the pointer over them.

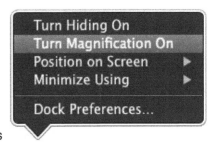

The default position of the Dock is at the bottom of the Desktop. OS X allows you to change the location of the Dock to either the left or right side of the Desktop. Select **Position on Screen** and then choose where you want the Dock, **Left, Bottom,** or **Right**.

The **Minimize Using** option affects the animation of windows as they are minimized or maximized. The default is **Genie Effect**, in which windows minimize or maximize like a genie entering or exiting a magic lamp. A second choice is the **Scale Effect**, where a window scales smaller and smaller until it reaches the Dock as an icon. When maximizing, the window scales larger as it restores itself to its original size.

With the exception of the **Minimize Using** feature, these options can also be accessed from the menu on the Menu Bar.

The final selection, **Dock Preferences** opens the Dock preference pane in **System Preferences**. There are several ways to open the Dock preference pane. It can be opened by launching the System Preferences application and clicking on the **Dock** icon or by selecting the Dock from the Apple menu, **> System Preferences... > Dock**.

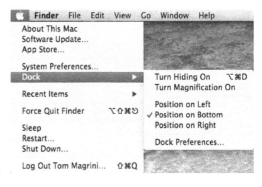

The Dock preference pane offers granular control over the size of the Dock and its magnification level. It also allows you to position the Dock on the screen and change how windows minimize to the Dock. The Dock preference pane is shown with the defaults set. This book is all about customizing your Mac to your personal taste, so let's skip the defaults and get to work customizing the Dock.

At the top of the pane is the **Size** slider, which provides granular control over the size of the Dock horizontally across the bottom of the Desktop or vertically if the Dock is on the left or right. Making the Dock smaller means it will take up less desktop real estate. Sometimes it seems that sliding the size towards large has no effect. This is because OS X scales the Dock to the maximum size horizontally (or vertically if positioned on the left or right) that will fit on the desktop given the number of icons in the Dock.

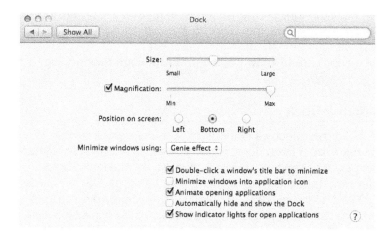

You can also change the size of the Dock directly from the Dock itself. Hover the pointer over the Dock divider until it turns into a double-headed white arrow. Click and hold. Move the white arrow up to make the Dock bigger and down to make it smaller.

The check box next to **Magnification** turns magnification on or off while the slider provides granular control over the amount of magnification of Dock icons. Magnification will make the icons bigger as you move the pointer over them. This is particularly useful if you prefer a small Dock or have a large number of icons.

Position on Screen positions the Dock on the left, bottom, or right side of the desktop. Note that if you choose **Left** or **Right**, the Dock will change from three-dimensions to a more conventional two-dimensional strip. A quicker way to move the Dock around the desktop is to hover your pointer over the divider until it turns to a double-headed white arrow and hold down the Shift key while dragging the Dock to the left, right, or bottom of the desktop. You'll lose any size setting when you change the Dock's desktop position, so you'll have to resize it.

Minimize windows using offers the same two window minimization animations discussed previously - Genie or Scale Effect. Check out the advanced customization section later in this chapter to learn how to configure a third effect, the Suck effect.

At the bottom of the pane, there are five check boxes that provide further control over window minimization and Dock animation. **Double-click a window's title bar to minimize** does exactly what you imagine it would, providing an alternative to clicking on the yellow minimize window control. The option **Minimize windows into application icon** minimizes windows into their application icon on the left side of the Dock, saving a great deal of Dock real estate. To maximize, simply click on the application icon.

Animate opening apps is on by default and causes the application's icon to bounce after you click on it to open the app. Uncheck the box if you do not like this animation.

Checking the next check box, **Automatically hide and show the Dock**, hides the Dock when it is not in use as we discussed previously. Uncheck the box to keep the Dock permanently on the desktop. You can also toggle Dock hiding on and off by entering ⌥⌘D (option+command+D).

OS X puts a tiny indicator light on the Dock underneath the icon of applications that are currently running. If you moved the Dock to the left or right side of the desktop, the indicator light will be on the left or right, respectively, of the icons of the running applications. If you don't care to know which applications are running, uncheck this box.

Clean Up a Cluttered Dock

By default, OS X minimizes windows to the right side of the Dock divider. This can become problematic if you minimize a large number of windows. As you minimize each window, the Dock expands across the Desktop. Once it reaches its maximum size, each successive window minimization causes the Dock to become smaller as OS X crowds more window icons into the right side of the divider. Eventually the overcrowding causes all of the icons in the Dock to become difficult to differentiate, particularly the minimized windows.

OS X has a solution, available in the Dock preference pane. Open the Dock preference pane by launching the System Preferences application and clicking on the **Dock** icon or from the Apple menu, ** > System Preferences... > Dock**. Click the check box next to **Minimize windows into application icon** as shown in the picture below.

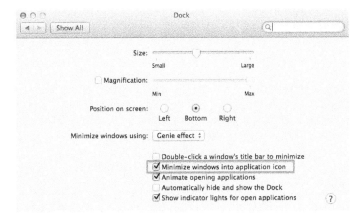

When this option is checked, OS X will minimize windows into their associated application icon instead of minimizing them to the right side of the divider. Minimizing windows will now no longer increase the size of the Dock by adding icons to it. When you want to see all the windows of an application, simply use **App Exposé** on the associated app icon in the Dock.

App Exposé is activated by hovering the pointer over an application icon in the Dock and swiping down with either three or four fingers on the trackpad. Note that **App Exposé** has to be activated in the Trackpad preferences. Refer to Chapter 2 to see how to enable **App Exposé**. If you use a Magic Mouse, see the section called Activate App Exposé with a Scroll Gesture later in this chapter.

Translucent Dock

By default, the Menu Bar of OS X Mavericks is translucent, allowing you to see through it to the desktop background. However, the Dock's glass is opaque. If you prefer the Dock's glass to be translucent to match the menu bar, open **Terminal** and enter the following commands. Hit the **return** key at the end of each line. The last command, **killall Dock**, will cause the Dock to restart.

```
defaults write com.apple.dock hide-mirror -bool TRUE
```

```
killall Dock
```

Enter the following commands to restore the Dock back to its default opaqueness.

```
defaults delete com.apple.dock hide-mirror
```

```
killall Dock
```

Pin the Dock to a Corner

The Dock in OS X Mavericks is centered along the bottom of the desktop. If you prefer, you can pin the Dock to the left or right corner of the desktop. To pin the Dock to the left corner, open **Terminal** and enter the following commands. Hit the **return** key after each line.

```
defaults write com.apple.dock pinning -string start
```

```
killall Dock
```

To pin the Dock to the right corner, enter the following commands in **Terminal**. Hit the **return** key after each line.

```
defaults write com.apple.dock pinning -string end
```

```
killall Dock
```

To return the Dock to its default position at the center of the desktop, enter the following commands in Terminal. Hit the **return** key after each line.

```
defaults delete com.apple.dock pinning
```

```
killall Dock
```

What if you moved your Dock to the left or right side of the Desktop? The first set of commands will pin the Dock to the top of the Desktop while the second set will pin it to the bottom. The last set of commands centers the Dock.

Space Out Apps

All of the application icons are equally spaced next to each other on the Dock. If you'd like to better organize your apps, you can group similar apps together and put a blank space between groups. Launch Terminal and enter the following commands. The first two lines are a single command. **Do not** hit the **return** key until you have entered both lines.

```
defaults write com.apple.dock persistent-apps -array-add '{tile-
data={};tile-type="spacer-tile";}'
```

killall Dock

A blank space will appear at the end of the app icons permanently kept in the Dock. Note the blank space between the icons for System Preferences and Pages in the picture. Drag the blank space to your desired position. Repeat the commands if you want to add more spaces.

Removing the space is rather interesting. Drag it off the Dock until a small puff of smoke appears and release. What makes this interesting is it will appear as if you are dragging nothing because the blank space is invisible! If that is too weird for you, secondary click on the blank space to bring up the **Remove from Dock** option. Select it and poof the space disappears in a puff of smoke!

Space Out the Trash

Another command will add as space in front of the Trash on the right side of the divider. By default, the Trash is the very last icon in the Dock. This tweak will place a space to the left of the Trash to separate it from all of the icons located on the right side of the Dock divider.

Open **Terminal** and enter the following commands. The first two lines are a single command. **Do not** hit the **return** key until you have entered both lines.

```
defaults write com.apple.dock persistent-others -array-add '{tile-
data={};tile-type="spacer-tile";}'
```

killall Dock

A blank space will appear to the left of the Trash. Drag the space to your desired location. Repeat the commands if you want to add more spaces.

Remove the space by dragging it off the Dock up past the middle of your desktop until a small puff of smoke appears and release. Remember the blank space is invisible so it will appear that you are dragging nothing. If you prefer, you can secondary click on the blank space to bring up the **Remove from Dock** option. Select it and poof, the space disappears in a puff of smoke!

Dim Hidden Apps

How do you know which applications are hidden? An indicator light under the icon denotes a running app, but the Dock provides no feedback to tell you which applications are hidden versus which ones are not. The Dock can be customized to make the icon of a hidden application appear dimmed, allowing you to spot the applications you have hidden at a glance. Note the difference between the icons for Pages and Notes and the middle app, Evernote. Evernote is hidden and its icon appears dimmed. Although Evernote's icon is dimmed, you can still interact with it like any other app icon in the Dock. Open Terminal and enter the following commands. Hit the **return** key after each line.

```
defaults write com.apple.dock showhidden -bool TRUE
```

```
killall Dock
```

If you hid applications before entering the commands above, you'll notice no change to the icons. Click on the icons and then hide again. They will now be dimmed.

Use the following commands to change the Dock back to its default behavior of displaying both visible and hidden icons the same way.

```
defaults write com.apple.dock showhidden -bool FALSE
```

```
killall Dock
```

Size the Dock

The Dock will automatically resize itself based on the number of icons docked. As you squeeze more icons into the Dock, the Dock stretches across the bottom of the desktop. The Dock's maximum size is limited by the size of the screen. OS X will not allow you to make the Dock so big that it won't fit on the screen, although the left- and right-most icons will slide off screen when using magnification.

Once the Dock reaches the maximum size allowed by the screen, you can continue to add icons. However, each icon will become smaller in order to allow all icons to fit. If your Dock has become overcrowded with app icons, check out the next chapter where I show you a nifty method to group apps into stacks and use them as application launchers.

OS X gives you the option of resizing the Dock. Move your mouse pointer over the divider. It will turn into a double headed white arrow. Click, hold and move the white arrow up to make the Dock bigger and down to make it smaller. Remember, the maximum size is limited by the size of the screen. While you can make the Dock very small, OS X limits you here too.

You can also utilize **Terminal** commands to more precisely size the Dock. Try out the following commands. They will make your Dock small. Don't worry you can resize it.

```
defaults write com.apple.dock tilesize -int 32
```

```
killall Dock
```

OS X will allow you to replace the 32 in the first command to any integer from 1 to 256. The smaller the number, the smaller the Dock. Try using the integer 1.

```
defaults write com.apple.dock tilesize -int 1
```

```
killall Dock
```

Yes, your Dock is still there. It's that half-inch long blob where your Dock used to be. A Dock this small is really not useable even with magnification. Let's change the Dock to a more reasonable size.

```
defaults write com.apple.dock tilesize -int 64
```

```
killall Dock
```

There, that's better. You can try other integers between 1 and 256. If you were hoping for a gigantic Dock, you're out of luck. Even if you use 256, the size of the Dock is limited to the maximum size that will fit on your screen.

Sometimes getting the Dock sized properly is like adjusting the drivers seat in your car. It's never quite right. If you want to return the Dock to its default size and start over, open Terminal and enter these commands.

```
defaults delete com.apple.dock tilesize
```

```
killall Dock
```

Turn the Dock into a Taskbar

The Dock serves a twofold purpose, combining the functions of an application launcher and a taskbar to switch between running applications. OS X allows you to change the behavior of the Dock so that it operates only as a taskbar, showing only the applications that are currently running. Enter the following commands into **Terminal** to switch the Dock to taskbar only mode.

```
defaults write com.apple.dock static-only -bool TRUE
```

```
killall Dock
```

Once the Dock is operating in taskbar mode, you may want to turn off the indicator lights for the running applications. Since the Dock now shows only running apps, the indicator lights are superfluous. You can turn them off from the **Dock** preference pane, **🍎 > System Preferences... > Dock >** uncheck **Show indicator lights for running applications**.

Running the Dock in taskbar mode is particularly useful if you don't want to use the Dock to launch applications or you have categorized your applications into App Stacks as described in the next chapter. Often users want to put all of the applications they routinely use into the Dock. The problem is the Dock's maximum size is limited and once reached, each application icon becomes smaller and more difficult to differentiate from the others as you add more apps.

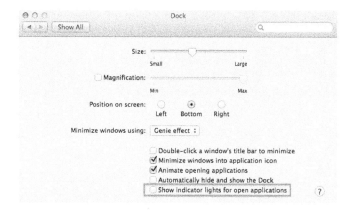

OS X offers several alternative methods to launch applications. **Launchpad** offers a quick and easy method to access and launch any of your applications. Applications can be categorized into folders for easy access and to combat sprawl and clutter. Applications can be organized into App Stacks as described in the next chapter and launched directly from the Dock in taskbar mode. If you are an ex-Windows user, you may want to create aliases on the desktop for your applications. Alternatively, if there is a particular set of applications you use constantly, you can set them to launch when you start or log into your Mac. Another option is to enter ⌘**space** (command+space) to activate Spotlight. Type the first few characters of the app's name and Spotlight will highlight the app under **Top Hit**. Press the **return** key to launch the app.

To change the Dock back to its default behavior, enter the following commands.

```
defaults write com.apple.dock static-only -bool FALSE
```

```
killall Dock
```

Surprise! OS X remembered what your Dock looked like and restored it back to its original state.

Minimize Windows with the Suck Effect

OS X offers two animations when minimizing windows to the Dock, the Genie and Scale effects. The default animation is Genie. OS X offers one more animation, the Suck effect, which is not available from the Dock preference pane. As the name suggests, a minimized window appears as if it is being sucked into the Dock by a powerful vacuum cleaner. Maximizing reverses the effect with the window shooting back to its original position as it pushed by a powerful leaf blower.

To turn on the suck effect, open **Terminal** and enter the following commands. Be sure to hit the **return** key after each line. The change takes place immediately, so minimize a window to see the suck effect.

```
defaults write com.apple.dock mineffect -string suck
```

```
killall Dock
```

To go back to the default animations, enter the following commands in **Terminal**. And then go to ⌘ > **System Preferences... > Dock** and select your choice of effect, genie or scale, from the Dock preference pane. You can also replace **suck** with either **genie** or **scale** in the above command to configure these standard window animations directly in Terminal.

```
defaults delete com.apple.dock mineffect
```

```
killall Dock
```

Dock Magnification

Magnification is a handy feature that allows you to conserve desktop real estate by keeping your Dock small and magnifying icons as you move the pointer over them. The magnification level can be set from the
Dock preference pane. Go to ⌘ > **System Preferences... > Dock**. A slider allows you to control the magnification level from "Min," which is no magnification, to "Max," which is 128 pixels (shown right).

If you want more magnification, you can set magnification levels up to a ridiculously humungous 512 pixels. Open **Terminal** and enter the following commands. The 256 at the end of the first command doubles the OS X maximum magnification level.

```
defaults write com.apple.dock largesize -float 256
```

```
killall Dock
```

Why not go all the way and double the magnification level again?

```
defaults write com.apple.dock largesize -float 512
```

```
killall Dock
```

Now that's ridiculously large! You can enter any integer between 1 and 512 to set the magnification level.

Enter the following commands to revert to the default maximum magnification level.

```
defaults write com.apple.dock largesize -float 128
```

```
killall Dock
```

Toggle Dock Magnification On or Off

Holding down the ⇧⌃ keys (shift+control) while moving your pointer across the Dock will toggle magnification on or off. If you have Dock magnification turned off, holding the ⇧⌃ (shift+control) keys while moving your pointer across the Dock will temporarily turn magnification on. Conversely, if you have Dock magnification turned on, holding the ⇧⌃ (shift+control) keys while moving your pointer across the Dock will temporarily turn magnification off.

Fill Up the Trash Can

By default, the trash icon changes from an empty Trash can to a full one when there are items in the Trash. Empty a full Trash can and the icon reverts back to the empty state.   This is a handy indicator to let you know if there is anything in the Trash. However, if you prefer to always show the Trash as full, enter the following commands.

```
defaults write com.apple.dock trash-full -bool TRUE
```

```
killall Dock
```

To revert back to the trash's normal behavior, enter the following commands.

```
defaults write com.apple.dock trash-full -bool FALSE
```

```
killall Dock
```

Use App Exposé in the Dock

App Exposé is an OS X feature that allows you to see all the windows of an open application regardless of the space the window resides. It differs from Mission Control which allows you to see all windows of every open application within a desktop space. Typically App Exposé is opened by swiping down with either three or four fingers in an application window. The number of fingers is configured in the **Trackpad** preference pane, accessible from > **System Preferences... > Trackpad**. See the chapter on gestures for more information.

If you configured a gesture for App Exposé, that gesture will also work in the Dock. Position your pointer over any application icon and swipe down with with either three or four fingers (depending on how you configured the gesture for App Exposé). Click on the desired window or swipe with three or four fingers in the opposite direction to close App Exposé.

Activate App Exposé with a Two-Finger Scroll Gesture

App Exposé can only be accessed using a trackpad, so you are out of luck if you use a Magic Mouse unless you activate this tweak. This tweak allows you to open App Exposé using a scroll up gesture on an application icon in the Dock. Scroll up with one or two fingers on an Apple Magic Mouse or with two fingers on a trackpad. Scroll in the opposite direction with the same number of fingers to close App Exposé.

Open **Terminal** and enter the following commands to activate this feature.

```
defaults write com.apple.dock scroll-to-open -bool TRUE
```

```
killall Dock
```

Once active, you'll be able to open App Exposé by moving the pointer to an application icon in the Dock and scrolling up. Scroll down to close App Exposé. An additional benefit of this feature is that it also allows you to open and close a stack by scrolling up or down, respectively.

Enter the following commands in **Terminal** to deactivate this feature.

```
defaults delete com.apple.dock scroll-to-open
```

```
killall Dock
```

Stop App Icons from Bouncing

Application icons in the Dock will bounce when one of two events occur: upon launching the app or if the app needs to get your attention. The latter event typically occurs when a dialog box opens with a warning, asks for your input, or wants to tell you a task has been completed. Bouncing can be disabled individually for each event.

To stop app icons from bouncing when you launch an application, head to the Dock preference pane at > **System Preferences... > Dock** and uncheck the box next to **Animate opening applications.**

Some applications will bounce their icon continuously until you respond by clicking on the icon. The incessant bouncing can be irritating if you are busy doing something else and are not at a convenient break point. Stopping icons from bouncing in response to a warning or when the app needs your attention requires configuration using the Terminal. However, the downside to this customization is that you won't know when an application requires your attention. Open **Terminal** and enter the following commands.

```
defaults write com.apple.dock no-bouncing -bool TRUE
```

```
killall Dock
```

To turn bouncing back on for warnings, enter the following commands in **Terminal**.

```
defaults delete com.apple.dock no-bouncing
```

```
killall Dock
```

Single Application Mode

Hiding applications is a handy technique to keep your desktop free of clutter and distractions to help you stay focused. A Dock shortcut allows you to accomplish two commands simultaneously – open an application while hiding all other apps.

Hold down the ⌥⌘ (option+command) keys while clicking on an application icon in the Dock. The app will immediately open and all other open windows from all other running applications will instantly be hidden. You can also use this shortcut even if the application is already open.

If you like this behavior, you can make it permanent by configuring the Dock to operate in single application mode. Enter the following commands in **Terminal** to turn on single application mode.

```
defaults write com.apple.dock single-app -bool TRUE
```

```
killall Dock
```

To turn off single application mode and return the Dock to its default behavior, enter the following commands in **Terminal**.

```
defaults delete com.apple.dock single-app
```

```
killall Dock
```

Change the Hide/Show Animation Speed

If you like keeping your Dock hidden, you'll notice that OS X animates the Dock's disappearance and reappearance to/from underneath the screen. OS X allows you to completely eliminate this animation, making the Dock hide and unhide instantly.

Enter the following commands in Terminal to eliminate the Dock animation.

```
defaults write com.apple.dock autohide-time-modifier -int 0
```

```
killall Dock
```

OS X also allows you to increase the length of the animation. Setting the animation to a larger number slows the animation down. A smaller number speeds it up. The following commands will set the animation to 5 seconds so you can see the Dock animation in slow motion. You can even use decimals like 0.15 and 0.5 to tune the length of the animation to your exact specifications.

```
defaults write com.apple.dock autohide-time-modifier -float 5
```

```
killall Dock
```

To restore the Dock to its default animation, enter the following commands.

```
defaults delete com.apple.dock autohide-time-modifier
```

```
killall Dock
```

Find an App's Location

Another handy Dock shortcut is to hold the ⌘ (command) key while clicking on an app icon. This shortcut opens the application's location in Finder with the application highlighted.

Spring Loaded Dock Icons

Applications icons in the Dock are spring loaded like folders in Finder. If you drag a file, pause, and hover over an application icon, **App Exposé** will launch allowing you to drop the file into one of the app's windows. Hit **space** if you don't want to wait out the spring load delay.

Add a Preference Pane

If you find yourself frequently using a **Preference Pane** from the System Preferences application, you may find it convenient to add it to the Dock. A preference pane can only be added to the right side of the Dock, where Stacks and the Trash are located.

To add a preference pane to the Dock, open **Finder.** Enter ⇧⌘G (shift+command+G) to open the **Go to folder:** dialog box. Enter the following into the field and click **Go**.

```
/System/Library/PreferencePanes/
```

Locate the preference pane you want to add to the Dock and drag it to the right side of the Divider. You now will be able to access the preference pane directly from the Dock without having to first launch the System Preferences application. To remove a preference pane from the Dock, drag it off like any other item you wish to remove until a puff of smoke appears and release.

Lock the Dock

You spent a significant amount of time customizing the Dock to get it to look and perform exactly the way you like it. However, it is very easy to accidentally reorder, remove icons, or resize or reposition the Dock. All it takes is one bad click from your trackpad or mouse to ruin all of your customization work. It is easy to prevent this from happening by locking the Dock. If you are satisfied with the way your Dock looks, OS X allows you to individually lock the Dock's contents as well as its size, position, and magnification settings.

To prevent unintentional changes to the contents of the Dock, open Terminal and enter the following commands. Hit the **return** key after each line.

```
defaults write com.apple.dock contents-immutable -bool TRUE
```

```
killall Dock
```

The following commands will prevent accidental changes to the size of the Dock. After running these commands, you'll notice the **Size** slider in the Dock Preference pane will be grayed out.

```
defaults write com.apple.dock size-immutable -bool TRUE
```

```
killall Dock
```

To lock the Dock's position on the Desktop, enter the following commands.

```
defaults write com.apple.dock position-immutable -bool TRUE
```

```
killall Dock
```

To prevent changes to your Dock's magnification setting, enter the following commands.

```
defaults write com.apple.dock magnify-immutable -bool TRUE
```

```
killall Dock
```

The following commands will prevent changes to the Dock's minimization effect.

```
defaults write com.apple.dock mineffect-immutable -bool TRUE
```

```
killall Dock
```

To lock the Dock's autohide feature, enter the following commands.

```
defaults write com.apple.dock autohide-immutable -bool TRUE
```

```
killall Dock
```

After locking the Dock's size, magnification, position, minimization, and hiding, these five settings will be grayed out on the Dock Preference pane accessible from > **System Preferences... > Dock**.

Now that your Dock is locked, what do you do if you need to make changes later? I'll show you how to unlock the Dock next.

Ensure that the Dock preferences pane is closed before executing any of the lock or unlock commands. Sometimes having the preferences pane open interferes with changes made using the Terminal application.

Unlock the Dock

What happens if you want to make changes to a locked Dock? Well, unlock it, of course! Each of the locks for contents, size, position, magnification, and minimization effect can be unlocked individually.

To unlock the Dock contents to add, move, or remove items from the Dock, enter the following commands in Terminal.

defaults delete com.apple.dock contents-immutable

killall Dock

Entering these commands will allow you to change the size of the Dock.

defaults delete com.apple.dock size-immutable

killall Dock

To unlock the Dock's position on the screen, enter the following commands in Terminal.

defaults delete com.apple.dock position-immutable

killall Dock

To unlock your Dock's magnification setting, enter the following commands.

defaults delete com.apple.dock magnify-immutable

killall Dock

To unlock your Dock's minimization effect setting, enter the following commands.

defaults delete com.apple.dock mineffect-immutable

killall Dock

To unlock the Dock's autohide feature, enter the following commands.

defaults delete com.apple.dock autohide-immutable

killall Dock

Once you have unlocked your Dock, the settings you unlocked will no longer be grayed out in the Dock preferences pane accessible from > **System Preferences... > Dock**.

7

Stacks

Stacks are another iconic and cool feature of OS X, offering quick access to frequently used folders directly from the Dock. Stacks are located to the right of the divider, the light gray line separating applications from the stacks, minimized windows, and the trash. Applications go to the left of the divider. Everything else goes on the right. The picture shows the default Mavericks Dock with a single Downloads stack located to the left of the trash. If you upgraded your Mac from Mountain Lion or an earlier operating system, your Dock may look different as any customization you may have done will have carried forward into Mavericks.

Unless you upgraded from a previous version of OS X, Mavericks gets you started with one stack, linking to the Downloads folder. The Downloads stack is the exact same Downloads folder you see under Favorites in the sidebar of Finder. Anything downloaded using Safari, Mail, Messages, or AirDrop will be saved here.

The icon for the Downloads stack does not look like a folder. It looks like a document. That is because Downloads is configured to display as a stack and it takes on the appearance of the only item in the stack, a PDF document about stacks.

When you click on the Downloads stack, its contents spring from the Dock in a fan. Clicking on any item in a stack opens it. At the very top of the stack is a link to open the Downloads folder in Finder. Of course, you can change this behavior and view the contents as a Fan, a Grid, or a List. An automatic option lets OS X select the most appropriate view depending on the number of items in the stack. Use a secondary click on the Downloads stack to access the menu to configure how the stack is displayed and how its contents are viewed and sorted.

OS X offers four options to view the stack contents. Automatic is the default, automatically switching between fan and grid view depending

on the number of items in the stack. Choosing Fan will always display the contents as a stack fan, however, only the first ten items will display. OS X will tell you how many more items are available in Finder. Clicking the circular icon with the arrow will open the folder in Finder so you can see the remaining items.

As their names imply, grid displays stack contents as a grid and list as a list. Both the grid and list options behave differently than the fan view. Clicking on a folder in a stack fan will open the folder in Finder. Clicking on a folder in a grid or list stack will open the sub-folder directly in the grid or list view, allowing you to navigate through many layers of folders to your intended destination. If you don't want to navigate further in the grid or list, hold the ⌘ (command) key while clicking a folder and it will open in Finder.

In addition to changing how you want the contents to display, the menu allows you to change the stack icon to a folder.

OS X offers five sorting options. A stack can be sorted by **Name**, **Date Added**, **Date Modified**, **Date Created**, or **Kind**. The default is to sort by name. In a fan the closest icon to the Dock is based on the sort type. For example, if a fan is sorted by name, the closest item to the Dock is the first item in alphabetical order. Similarly, when the fan is sorted by date added, the item with the most recent date will be closest to the Dock.

Add Stacks

You can customize the right side of the Dock by adding stacks for folders like Applications or other frequently accessed folders or devices. Adding folders you frequently use as stacks is

much more efficient than navigating to them through Finder. The picture shows stacks for Applications, Documents, Downloads, and a hard disk drive.

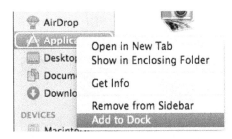

To add a stack, simply locate the folder you wish to add in Finder, click and drag it to the Dock. It's that easy. Another method is to locate the folder in the sidebar and secondary click on it to bring up the menu. Choose **Add to Dock**. Any item in the sidebar can be added to the Dock as a stack with the exception of AirDrop. And OS X allows you to create as many stacks as you want.

To add a disk drive, look under **Devices** in th Finder Sidebar. Secondary click the device and select **Add to Dock**. Note that the icon for a removable storage device will turn into a question mark on top of a disk drive icon when the media is removed from your Mac.

Once your stacks are in the Dock, you can arrange their order. Rearrange stacks by dragging them left or right. Remember, you cannot drag a stack to the left of the divider.

OS X will not allow you to move them to the left side of the Dock divider as that section is reserved for applications.

You can even drag individual documents into the Dock, although technically, a document icon is not a stack. The only options available with a secondary click are to remove the document, open it, open it at login, and to open its location in Finder. Despite these limitations, adding a document to the Dock is particularly useful if you frequently access it.

You can click and drag items in a stack to move them to another folder, stack, onto the Dock, to the desktop, into the trash, to an external disk drive, or any other location.

Remove Stacks

Removing a stack is done the same way as you would remove any Dock icon. Simply click and drag it off the Dock until a small puff of smoke appears below the icon. Release and the stack will disappear in a puff of smoke. Stacks can also be removed by secondary clicking on the stack and selecting **Options > Remove from dock**.

This Happens All the Time

You think you are dragging a file from the Downloads stack, but you accidentally drag the entire Downloads folder off the Dock and poof, it's gone! Don't panic. You can put the Downloads folder back on the Dock with one command.

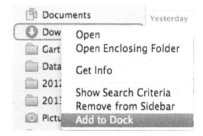

Open Finder and secondary click on Downloads under **Favorites** in the sidebar. Choose **Add to Dock**. I told you not to panic. To avoid accidentally removing or rearranging items in the Dock, lock it. See "Lock the Dock" in the last chapter for instructions on how to lock and unlock the Dock.

Highlight Stack Items

OS X offers a feature that will highlight an item in a stack as you hover over it with the pointer. Highlighting is disabled by default. To enable it, open Terminal and enter the following commands. Don't hit the **return** key until you have completely entered the first two lines.

```
defaults write com.apple.dock mouse-over-
hilite-stack -bool TRUE
```

```
killall Dock
```

When the stack is viewed as a fan, both the item name and the icon is highlighted in blue. If viewed as a grid or list, the item is highlighted with a gray background.

To disable highlighting and go back to the default, enter the following commands. Don't press **return** until you have completely entered the first two lines.

```
defaults delete com.apple.dock
mouse-over-hilite-stack
```

```
killall Dock
```

Temporarily Highlight Stack Items

If you don't want to permanently highlight stack items, OS X allows you to use highlighting on an as needed basis. If you want to temporarily highlight items, click and hold the stack icon. Do not remove your finger from the trackpad or mouse as the stack expands. With your finger still pressing down on the trackpad or mouse, move up the stack listing. Whatever item your pointer is hovering over will be highlighted. Continue to hold the trackpad or mouse until you hover over the desired stack item and then release. The highlighted item will open immediately.

Another option is to click and hold the stack icon. Release immediately after the stack expands. Now type the first few letters of the desired item's name. OS X will highlight items as you type. Once the desired item is highlighted, hit enter. The item will open immediately.

Add a Recent Items Stack

To save you the trouble of looking for a recently opened application, document, or server, OS X keeps a list of Recent Items under the menu. Select > **Recent Items** to display a list of the last ten applications, documents, and servers. Ten is the default and can be changed in the **General** preference pane. Access the pane by clicking **System Preferences > General**. Look for **Recent Items** near the bottom of the pane and select none, 5, 10, 15, 20, 30, or 50 items.

But what if you want to use the Dock instead of the menu to access your recent items? Adding a recent items stack to the Dock is one of the most useful OS X tweaks. Open Terminal and enter the following commands. Do not press the **return** key until you have completely entered the first three lines.

```
defaults write com.apple.dock persistent-others -array-add '{
"tile-data" = { "list-type" = 1; }; "tile-type" = "recents-tile";
}'
```

killall Dock

OS X will place a recent items stack on the Dock to the left of the trash. By default, the recent items stack will list the most recently accessed applications with the contents viewed as a fan. A secondary click on the stack icon will access a menu, allowing you to change the type of recent items are in the stack and how the stack is viewed. The recent items stack can show the recent applications, documents, servers, volumes, or a list of favorite items. Like all stacks, contents can be viewed as a fan, grid, list, or automatic.

OS X allows you to create as many stacks as you want. If you want another recent items stack, run the commands again. By default, each new stack will appear as a recent applications stack. Use the secondary click to show the recent items you want. To remove a recent items stack, simply drag it off the Dock.

If you ever need to clear the recent items displayed in a stack or set of stacks, go to > **Recent Items > Clear Menu**. If you have a large number of recent items, you will have to scroll down to access the **Clear Menu** command at the very bottom. The stacks will look like they disappeared, but they are still there. They simply have no contents.

Create App Stacks

If your Dock is crowded with applications making it difficult to quickly find the application you are looking for, a solution to the overcrowding is to organize your apps into app stacks. You can organize your apps by any method imaginable – by application type like productivity, social media, utilities, or browsers or by how often you use them. This feature is particularly useful if you like a neat and tidy Dock or if you switched the Dock to taskbar mode, where it only shows the running applications.

Can't you just drag the Aplications folder to the Dock to create an Applications Stack? Yes, that is one solution. However, if you are like most Mac users, the applications folder will be crowded with apps, making a single Applications stack as difficult to navigate as a crowded Dock.

Creating App Stacks is a multi-step process.
1. Create a new folder in your Home Directory called "Stacks." Open the folder.
2. Create new folders for each app category or theme in the Stacks folder using ⇧⌘N or **File > New Folder**. Each of these folders will become an app stack.
3. Open a new Finder Window using ⌘N or **File > New Finder Window**. Click on the Applications folder in the sidebar.
4. In the Applications folder, select an application you wish to add to one of your app stack folders. Holding down both the option and command keys ⌥⌘, drag the

application to one of your app stack folders. Holding down the ⌥⌘ keys will create an alias for the application. If you simply dragged the application icon to the app stack folder, OS X will either copy the application or move it. You don't want to copy the app – it wastes disk space – nor do you want to move it. You only need to create aliases to the applications, similar to the alias on the Dock.

5. Repeat step 4 for each application you want to move to your app stack folders.
6. Click and drag each of the app stack folders to the Dock to the right of the divider.

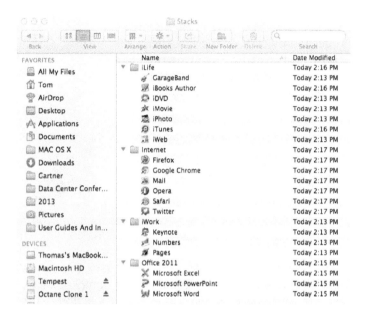

Dragging the folders from the Stacks folder to the Dock creates the four app stacks shown. By default, the contents of an app stack are sorted by name and displayed as a fan. Secondary click on the app stack to set the sort, display, and view options.

To add new applications to an app stack, open the Stacks folder you created in step 1 and repeat steps 1 through 5. You will have to delete the old app stack from the Dock and drag the folder with the new applications to the Dock. This is because new applications added to the stacks folders will show up as a blank, white icon. You will need to recreate the app stack by dragging the folder to the Dock for the icons of the new applications to properly render.

To remove an app stack, simply drag it off the Dock until a small puff of smoke appears under its icon. Release and poof, the stack disappears.

Create Document Stacks

If there are certain folders you frequently access, the quickest and easiest method to open items in these folders is to create a

Document Stack on the Dock. A Document Stack can be created for any folder that exists in your Home directory. The picture shows, in order, a Desktop, Document, Application, and Download stack.

To create a Document Stack, simply locate the desired folder in Finder and drag it to the right side of the Dock. Secondary click on the newly created Document Stack to configure sort, display, and content viewing items.

To remove a Document Stack, simply drag it off the Dock until a puff of smoke appears under the icon and release your hold.

Create a Desktop Stack

If you like a clean and clutter-free desktop like I do, you probably configured the OS X tweak "For a Really Clean Desktop," from the chapter on customizing the Desktop. However, a lot of items are saved to the Desktop by default. If they no longer appear on the Desktop, where do they go? In reality, OS X doesn't save these items to the Desktop. They are saved to the **Desktop** folder in your **Home** directory. You can access this folder in **Finder**, but because so many items get saved to the Desktop folder by default, I suggest you add a Desktop Stack to your Dock for quicker access to these items.

To create a Desktop Stack, open **Finder**. If the Desktop folder is in the Finder sidebar, drag it to the Dock. Remember, stacks go on the right side of the divider. If the Desktop folder is not in the Finder sidebar, you can find it in your Home directory. Drag the folder to the right side of the Dock. You may want to also drag it to the Finder Sidebar to provide another method to quickly access the Desktop folder. Secondary click on your newly created stack to configure sort, display, and content viewing items.

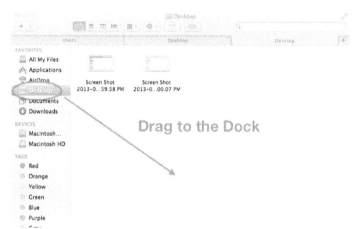

To remove a Desktop Stack, drag it off the Dock until a puff of smoke appears under the icon and release your hold.

Create a Volumes Stack

If you have numerous internal or external hard drives, wouldn't it be cool to see them all in one stack? While OS X does allow you to drag each one individually from the **Device** list in the **Finder** sidebar, you have to use this hack to see them all in a single stack like the one shown in the picture.

If you like a clean, uncluttered desktop as I do, you probably wish OS X wouldn't show all of your disk drives on the Desktop. See the chapter on customizing the Desktop to learn how to turn this off. Once OS X is no longer displaying your hard drives on the Desktop, a **Volumes Stack** makes accessing any of your internal or external hard drives a breeze.

Creating a Volumes Stack is a multi-step process.
1. Open Finder and enter ⇧⌘G (shift+command+G) to open the **Go to the folder:** dialog box.
2. Enter **/Volumes** in the dialog box and hit **return** to open the **Volumes** folder.
3. Click **Column** View in the Finder toolbar. The **Volumes** folder will be highlighted and grayed. This is because **Volumes** is a hidden folder.
4. Click and drag the **Volumes** folder to the right side of the Dock to create the Volumes stack.

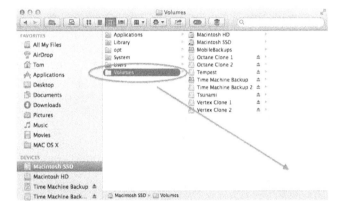

By default, the contents of a Volumes Stack are sorted by name and displayed as a fan. Secondary click on the stack to set the sort, display, and view options.

Here is my Volumes Stack showing my two internal drives. But why are their three devices? I have two partitions on one of my drives. OS X will show each partition as a separate device.

To remove a Volumes Stack, simply drag it off the Dock until a small puff of smoke appears under it. Release and poof, the stack disappears. If you changed the **Finder** preferences so external drives no longer display on the desktop, you may wish to turn this feature back on. Otherwise the only place you will be able to see your external drives is under **Devices** in the **Finder** sidebar. See the chapter on customizing the Desktop to learn how to change the **Finder** preferences to make external drives appear on the Desktop.

A Better List View

There are three different ways to view the contents of a stack: Fan, Grid, or List. The default OS X List view displays files, folders, or apps with very small, barely discernible icons. Scrolling is accomplished by nudging the pointer to the top or bottom of the list. The default stack list is shown below at the left.

OS X offers another stack list view shown at the right. The alternative list features larger icons, a title, and a scroll bar when the number of items in the stack requires the ability to scroll. Scroll as you would in any document. There is no need to nudge the top or bottom of the list.

To change to the alternative list view, enter the following commands in **Terminal**.

```
defaults write com.apple.dock use-new-list-stack -bool TRUE
```

```
killall Dock
```

The size of the icons in this list view can be changed by displaying the stack and then holding the ⌘ (command) key while tapping the plus or minus key to make them larger or smaller, respectively.

To revert back to the OS X default list view, enter the following commands.

```
defaults delete com.apple.dock use-new-list-stack
```

```
killall Dock
```

Activate Stacks with a Scroll Gesture

Typically a stack is opened using a single click or click and hold (when using temporary highlighting). Another method available is to use a scroll up gesture using a single finger on a Apple Magic Mouse or two fingers on a trackpad.

To enable this feature, open **Terminal** and enter the following commands.

```
defaults write com.apple.dock scroll-to-open -bool TRUE
```

```
killall Dock
```

Once active, you'll be able to open a stack by moving the pointer to the stack and scrolling up. Scroll down to close the stack. An additional benefit of this feature is that it also activates App Exposé when you use the scroll gesture on an application icon in the Dock. Give it a try on an application with multiple windows open. All open windows of the application will be shown in App Exposé.

Enter the following commands in Terminal to disable this feature.

```
defaults delete com.apple.dock scroll-to-open
```

```
killall Dock
```

Slow Motion Stack Animation

Next time you open a stack, hold down the ⇧ (shift) key while clicking on the stack. The stack will open in slow motion. This is a pretty cool effect, especially if you are opening an applications stack with lots of colorful icons. Holding the ⇧ (shift) key while closing the stack works in slow motion too.

Quickly Open a Stack in Finder

If you ever need to open a stack in Finder, a shortcut is to hold down the ⌥⌘ (option+command) keys. The folder linked to the stack will immediately open. This is the same as clicking on the **Open in Finder** control at the top of a fan or the bottom of a grid and list stack. This shortcut works for any stack except a recent items stack.

Locate a Stack

Another handy Dock shortcut is to hold the ⌘ (command) key while clicking on a stack. This shortcut opens the stack's location in Finder with the folder highlighted.

Spring Loaded Stacks

Try dragging a file onto a Stack, pause while hovering over the Stack and suddenly a Finder window will open allowing you to move the file into the Stack. If you hold down the ⌥ (option) key while dragging and hovering, you will copy the file instead of moving it. Holding down the ⌥⌘ (option+command) keys dragging and hovering will allow you to create an alias for the file.

8

Spotlight

Spotlight is the OS X system-wide search feature that allows you to find almost anything on your Mac quickly and easily. Spotlight creates an index of your Mac so you can quickly find applications, system preferences, documents, folders, mail, messages, contacts, events, reminders, images, webpages, music, movies, and fonts. Spotlight can even find specific words in documents and in Safari's history. Spotlight can also look up a word in the dictionary, search the web or Wikipedia, or serve as a simple calculator. Spotlight is accessed by clicking on its icon in the Menu Bar to reveal a drop-down text search field. The default keyboard shortcut for Spotlight is ⌘**space** (command+space).

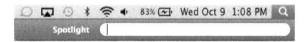

As you type into the search field, Spotlight will display results, refining them as you type. Results will be displayed in categories, with the **Top Hit**, the result OS X determined to be the most likely, highlighted at the top of the list. If you press **return**, OS X will launch the Top Hit.

By default, OS X Mavericks will display results in categories: Applications, System Preferences, Documents, Folders, Presentations, Spreadsheets, PDF Documents, Mail & Messages, Contacts, Events & Reminders, Images, Webpages, Music, Movies, Fonts, Developer, Dictionary, and Web Searches. Spotlight will skip categories lacking a result.

At the very top of the results list is an option to **Show All in Finder**. Selecting this option opens a Finder window with the results organized into categories. This is a handy feature as many searches often return more results than Spotlight can display.

At the bottom of the results list is a link to **Spotlight Preferences...**, which opens the Spotlight preference pane.

Any item in the Spotlight search results can be previewed by highlighting it. Hover your pointer over an item to reveal the Quick Look preview. Click to open any item in the Spotlight results. If an item is already highlighted because you were previewing it, pressing the **return** key will open it.

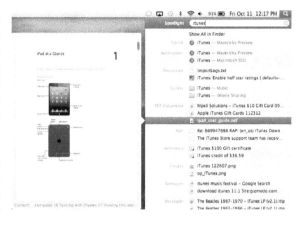

To see the location of an item in the file system, hold down the ⌥⌘ (option+command) keys after the preview appears. The file path will be shown at the bottom of the preview.

Perform a Boolean Search

If you enter two or more words into **Spotlight**, the search is performed using a Boolean **AND**. This means that Spotlight will only display results containing all of the search terms. Spotlight can also perform a search using a Boolean **OR** of two or more search terms. Using an **OR** will display results that contain at least one of the search terms. To perform a search using a Boolean **OR**, place the word **OR** or the | character between each of the words. The | key is found just above the **return** key.

To further narrow your search results, it is often handy to include a Boolean **NOT**. By placing a **NOT** or a – before a word, Spotlight will eliminate results containing that word.

Placing quotes around two or more words will search for that exact phrase.

`"OS X Mountain Lion"`	Will return search results containing the exact phrase "OS X Mountain Lion"
`Mountain Lion` `Mountain AND Lion`	Spotlight will only return results containing both words. Results may be about OS X Mountain Lion or the animal.
`Mountain | Lion | "OS X"` `Mountain OR Lion OR "OS X"`	Will return results containing one, two, or all three of the words in the search list. Results will contain items about mountains, lions, mountain lions, OS X Mountain Lion, in fact any OS X version
`Mountain | Lion "OS X"` `Mountain OR Lion AND "OS X"`	Will return results containing OS X Lion, OS X Mountain Lion, and items about a mountain

`Mountain Lion -"OS X"`
`Mountain Lion NOT "OS X"`
`Mountain AND Lion NOT "OS X"`
	Will return results about mountain lions (the animal). The – before OS X would eliminate items about OS X, OS X Mountain Lion, and OS X Lion

Remove Spotlight Search Categories

By default, **Spotlight** will search 16 different categories of items on your Mac. OS X allows you to remove categories from the results in the **Spotlight** preference pane.

To remove categories, open the Spotlight preference pane by launching the System Preferences application and selecting the **Spotlight** preference pane or from the Apple menu by selecting > **System Preferences... > Spotlight**. Next, click **Search Results** at the top of the pane if it is not already selected.

By default, all of the items are checked. If you want to remove a particular category, uncheck the check box next to it. Changes take effect immediately. The more categories you uncheck, you'll have fewer items to sort through.

Removing a category only removes it from the search results. It does not change the Spotlight index. Therefore, if you turn the category back on, Spotlight will not have to index your Mac again.

Remove the Calculator Category

Spotlight includes a simple calculator function. Entering 2+2 will display the result 2+2 = 4 under the **Calculator** category in the search results. Since OS X already has a much more powerful and versatile calculator, you may find little use for this feature.

You may have noticed that the **Calculator** category was missing from the list of categories in the Spotlight preference pane. If you want to remove the Calculator category, open **Terminal**, enter the following command, and press **return**.

```
defaults write com.apple.spotlight CalculationEnabled FALSE
```

You must restart your Mac for the change to take effect. Once your Mac restarts, the Calculator category will no longer appear in the results list.

To revert back to the default, enter the following command in **Terminal**, press the **return** key, and restart your Mac.

```
defaults write com.apple.spotlight CalculationEnabled TRUE
```

Remove the Look Up Category

Spotlight includes a **Look Up** category, allowing you to look up a word in the dictionary. Since OS X already includes a separate application called **Dictionary**, you may not have a need for this feature.

You may have noticed that the **Look Up** category was missing from the list of categories in the Spotlight preference pane. If you want to remove the Look Up category, open **Terminal**, enter the following command, and press **return**.

```
defaults write com.apple.spotlight DictionaryLookupEnabled FALSE
```

You must restart your Mac for the change to take effect. Once your Mac restarts, the Look Up category will no longer appear in the Spotlight search results list.

To revert back to the default, enter the following command in **Terminal**, press the **return** key, and restart your Mac.

```
defaults write com.apple.spotlight DictionaryLookupEnabled TRUE
```

Reorder the Search Categories

Spotlight lists results in the category order shown in the Spotlight preference pane. The categories appear immediately below the **Top Hit**. Any category without a result is skipped. OS X allows you to change the order in which the categories are displayed.

To change the category order, open the Spotlight preference pane by launching the System Preferences application and selecting the **Spotlight** preference pane or from the Apple menu by selecting > **System Preferences... > Spotlight**. Click **Search Results** at the top of the pane if it is not already selected.

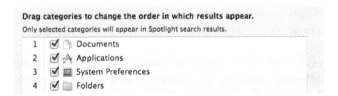

The list can be reordered by dragging categories up or down the list. For example, if you want to search for **Documents** before **Applications** and **System Preferences**, drag Documents to the top of the list ahead of Applications as shown above.

Change the Spotlight Keyboard Shortcut

The default keyboard shortcut for **Spotlight** is ⌘space (command+space). OS X allows you to configure any of the keys between **F1 and F12** as an alternate shortcut.

To change the keyboard shortcut for Spotlight, open the Spotlight preference pane by launching the System Preferences application and selecting the **Spotlight** icon or from the Apple menu by selecting **> System Preferences... > Spotlight**. The Spotlight keyboard shortcut is available under both the **Search Results** and **Privacy** tabs.

Using the Spotlight keyboard shortcut is a quick way to display the menu bar when an application is in full-screen mode

Exclude Volumes from Spotlight

Spotlight searches everything on your Mac by default. However, OS X allows you to exclude specific volumes or folders from being searched.

To exclude a volume or folder, open the Spotlight preference pane by launching the System Preferences application and selecting the **Spotlight** icon or from the Apple menu by selecting **> System Preferences... > Spotlight**. Click **Privacy** at the top of the pane if it is not already highlighted.

Click the **Add Button**, denoted by the **+** at the bottom left, to open a **Finder** window allowing you to browse to the volume or folder you want to exclude. Click the **Choose** button. OS X will ask, "Are you sure you want to prevent Spotlight from searching" followed by the volume or folder name. Click **OK** to continue.

The volume or folder will be added to the exclusion list. To remove a folder previously excluded, highlight it in the list of excluded folders and click the **–** at the bottom left.

Improve Spotlight Search Results

Spotlight allows you to narrow your search to specific types of files using the search modifier **kind**. For example, in the picture at the right shows results of a Spotlight search for music by the English folk rock band Mumford & Sons. By entering **kind:music mumford** into the Spotlight search field, the results were limited to only audio files by Mumford & Sons.

To search for music files, enter the following search modifier followed by the search term(s).

`kind:music`

If I was searching for an image called "squashed," I would enter **kind:image squashed** in the Spotlight search field as

shown at the right. Using a search modifier zeroed in on the specific image file. Had I simply typed "squashed" into the search field, Spotlight would have returned documents, PDFs, webpages, developer files, a definition, and web and Wikipedia search links – all of which I'd have to sort through to find the file.

To search for image files, enter the following search modifier followed by the search term(s).

`kind:image`

The following list of search modifiers can be used to improve your searches. Enter the search term after the modifier. Entering a Spotlight search modifier alone without a search term afterwards will return all files of that type.

`kind:alias`	The alias search modifier will return results that are aliases to files or folders.
`kind:app`	The app search modifier is used to locate applications. For example, kind:app Microsoft will return Microsoft applications.
`kind:audio`	The audio search modifier will return results which are audio files.
`kind:avi`	The avi modifier is used to specifically find AVI files.
`kind:bookmark`	The bookmark search modifier will return results from your Safari bookmarks.
`kind:chat`	The chat search modifier will return results from your iChat files.
`kind:contact`	The contact search modifier will search your Contacts.
`kind:developer`	The developer search modifier will return results from the developer category.
`kind:document`	Document will return results that document

	files including text and image files.
`kind:event`	The event search modifier will return results from Calendar events.
`kind:folder`	This search modifier will return results that are folders.
`kind:font`	The font search modifier is used to search for fonts.
`kind:gif`	The gif search modifier will return results that are images in GIF format.
`kind:history`	The history search modifier will return results from your Safari history.
`kind:image`	The image search modifier returns results that are image files.
`kind:jpeg`	The jpeg search modifier will return results that are images in JPEG format.
`kind:mail`	The mail search modifier is used to search Mail files.
`kind:movie`	The movie search modifier will return results that are movies regardless of format.
`kind:music`	The music search modifier returns results that are music files regardless of format.
`kind:pdf`	The pdf search modifier is used to locate PDF files.
`kind:preferences`	When searching for system preferences use the preferences search modifier.
`kind:presentation`	The presentation search modifier returns files that are presentations whether they were created in PowerPoint or Keynote.
`kind:quicktime`	The quicktime search modifier is use to locate QuickTime movies.
`kind:reminder`	The reminder search modifier returns results from the Reminder application.
`kind:spreadsheet`	The spreadsheet search modifier returns files that are spreadsheets whether they were created in Excel or Numbers.
`kind:tiff`	The tiff search modifier returns images in TIFF format
`kind:webpage`	The webpage search modifier will return results from your Safari history.

Search for Files from Specific Applications

Spotlight has the capability to search for files produced by specific applications. For example, to search for this book, written in Microsoft Word, I would enter **kind:word Mac OS X** into the Spotlight search field.

The following list shows search modifiers that you can use to look for specific files produced by Apple's iWork suite and the Microsoft Office productivity suite.

```
kind:pages        kind:word
kind:numbers      kind:excel
kind:keynote      kind:powerpoint
```

Search Using Tag Color

If you use Finder tags, **Spotlight** allows you to search for files based on the color of their tag using the search modifier **tag**. For example, to find files with a red tag, you would enter **tag:red** into the Spotlight search field. If you're looking for files tagged with a red tag you can enter:

```
tag:red
```

The search would find files that have been tagged with the color red. Valid tag colors in OS X Mavericks are red, orange, yellow, green, blue, purple, or gray.

Once you have begun to routinely tag files, you most likely will rename tags to something more descriptive than their color. OS X allows you to search for tags based on their color or their name. Let's say you renamed the green tag to "vacation." Either of the following searches would return all of your files tagged with the green tag "vacation."

```
tag:green
```

```
tag:vacation
```

For more information on using tags, see the chapter on Finder.

Search by Document Author

Spotlight allows you to use the search modifier **author** to search for documents written by a specific author. For example, to search for documents written by myself, I would enter the following into the Spotlight search field.

```
author:Magrini
```

Search by Date

Spotlight has the capability to search for files based on the date they were created or modified using the search modifier **date**. The date can be a specific date, a range of dates, today, or yesterday. For example, entering **date:7/4/13** in the Spotlight search field will return files created or modified on July 4, 2013.

Spotlight also allows you to search for date ranges. The following search would return all files created or modified during the month of July 2013.

```
date:7/1/13-7/31/13
```

You can also use greater than and greater than or equal to in order to find files created or modified on or after a certain date. The following search would return all files created or modified after September 1, 2013. The second search returns all files created or modified on and after September 1, 2013.

`date:>9/1/13`

`date:>=9/1/13`

You can also search for files created or modified before a specific date. In this example, Spotlight returns all files created or modified before September 1, 2013.

`date:<9/1/13`

This search returns all files created or modified on and prior to September 1, 2013.

`date:<=9/1/13`

Spotlight also allows you to search for files created or modified yesterday or today.

`date:yesterday`

`date:today`

Spotlight understands yesterday and today. How about tomorrow? Yes, Spotlight does understand what tomorrow means. However, results are limited to Calendar events and Reminders since your Mac can't predict what files you will create or modify in the future.

`date:tomorrow`

In addition to the **date** search modifier, Spotlight understands **created** and **modified**.

`created:<=10/1/13`

`modified:7/1/13`

Use Multiple Search Modifiers

Any of the search modifiers can be used together to narrow your search. For example, the following Spotlight search would find all Microsoft Word documents I created or modified during the month of September 2013.

`kind:word date:9/1/13-9/30/13 author:Magrini`

This search looks at Safari's history and returns any webpages about Mavericks that I visited after August 1, 2013.

`kind:history Mavericks created:>8/1/13`

Handy Keyboard Shortcuts

Spotlight features a number of useful keyboard shortcuts. Use any of the following keyboard shortcuts when Spotlight displays its search results.

⌘B	Opens Safari and searches the Internet for the term(s) listed in the Spotlight search field.
⌘D	Opens the **Dictionary** application and looks up the term(s) in the Spotlight search field.
⌘K	Opens the **Dictionary** application and looks up the term(s) in Wikipedia.
⌘L	Shows the definition of the search term(s) in a Spotlight preview window.
⌘O	Opens the currently highlighted search result.
⌘R	Opens the containing folder of the currently highlighted result.
⌘T	Launches the Top Hit.
⌘down	Jumps down and highlights the first result in the next category of search results.
⌘up	Jumps up and highlights the first result in the next category of search results.

Copy a Spotlight Result to Finder

Any of the files in the **Spotlight** search results can be dragged into any open **Finder** window to create a copy of the file.

Create an Alias of a Spotlight Result

You can create an alias of any of the files in the **Spotlight** search results by holding down the ⌥⌘ (option+command) keys while dragging the item to its destination.

Open the Containing Folder

Holding down the ⌘ (command) key while clicking an item in the **Spotlight** search results will open a Finder window of the folder which contains the item. You can also use **⌘R** (command+R) or **⌘return** (command+return) to open the containing folder in Finder.

Save a Spotlight Search

OS X allows you to save **Spotlight** searches for later reuse. To save a Spotlight search, click **Show All in Finder** result the top of the Spotlight search results list. This will open a Finder window displaying all of the results from the Spotlight search. Click the **Save** button at the upper right of the Finder window.

A drop-down sheet will appear asking you to specify a name for the search and location to save it. By default, OS X saves searches to the **Saved Searches** folder in your **Home** directory. Clicking the arrow next to **Save As** opens the Saved Searches folder, allowing you to see other searches you have

saved. A check box, which is checked by default, allows you to add the saved search to the **Sidebar** where it will be available in every Finder window. Click the **Save** button to save your search or **Cancel**.

If you left the **Add To Sidebar** check box checked, your search will appear in the **Sidebar** of every Finder window as shown to the left. What you have just created is a **Smart Folder**, a saved instance of a Spotlight search that will dynamically update its content based on your search criteria. Simply click on the Smart Folder under **Favorites** in the Sidebar of any Finder window to run the search again. Content meeting your saved search criteria is added dynamically to the Smart Folder. We'll cover Smart Folders in more detail in the chapter on Finder.

Use Spotlight as an App Launcher

Spotlight can be used as an application launcher. This is a handy feature if you're trying to open an application that is not in the Dock or if you're running your Dock in taskbar mode where it only displays running applications.

Start Spotlight by clicking on its icon in the Menu Bar or by entering ⌘**space**. Begin typing the name of the application into the Spotlight search field. Spotlight will zero in on the application after entering a few letters of its name. Normally the application will appear as the **Top Hit**. You can launch the application by pressing **return**, Using the ⌘**T**

(command+T) keyboard shortcut to launch the **Top Hit**, or clicking on the app within the search results.

Often you can use an application's initials to quickly find and launch it. For example, **Photo Booth** can be launched by entering **pb**. QuickTime can be launched using **qt**. Similarly, you can use **ip** for **iPhoto**, **it** for **iTunes**, **wo** for **Word**, **ex** for **Excel**, **pa** for **Pages**, **nu** for **Numbers**, **ke** for **Keynote**, **ev** for **Evernote** and so forth.

Change the Spotlight Keyboard Shortcut

The **Spotlight** preference pane only lets you choose ⌘**space** or one of the **F** keys as its keyboard shortcut. However, the **Keyboard** preference pane allows you to choose any combination of keys as the keyboard shortcut for Spotlight.

To assign your own keyboard shortcut for Spotlight, open the **Keyboard** preference pane by launching the System Preferences application and selecting the **Keyboard** preference pane or from the Apple menu by selecting **> System Preferences... > Keyboard**. Click on the **Shortcuts** tab.

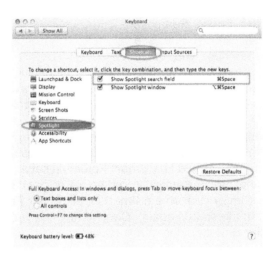

Next, select **Spotlight** from the left-hand pane. **Show Spotlight Search Field** is the first choice in the list of shortcuts in the right-hand pane. By default, ⌘**space** is the shortcut. Click on **Show Spotlight Search Field** to highlight it and click on ⌘**space**. You will now be able to enter your own custom shortcut in the field provided. Be sure to select a shortcut that is not used by another function. If you select a shortcut already in use, a yellow triangle will appear. The yellow triangle will also appear in the left pane to denote a conflict with one of the previously assigned shortcuts.

To revert back to the OS X default shortcut of ⌘**space**, click the **Restore Defaults** button at the lower right of the preference pane. Note that clicking this button restores all keyboard shortcuts to their OS X defaults.

Create Spotlight Comments

Adding **Spotlight Comments** to your files is a convenient way to organize related content without having to create folders in Finder. The Spotlight Comments feature allows you to enter descriptive metadata into a file's **Get Info** window. This metadata will facilitate searching for a file or group of files.

For example, if you are working on a large project, you may create or collect a number of different files from several applications. While all are related to your project, they may not be saved in the same location in Finder. Of course, you could create a folder in Finder and save or move your files to that folder. Another option is to use Spotlight Comments and never care where your files are located.

To add Spotlight Comments to a file, first locate the file in Finder. Next, highlight it, secondary click, and select **Get Info** or press ⌘ i (command+i). This will open the Get Info window.

In OS X Mavericks, the fifth section is labeled **Comments**. Expand it by clicking on the little triangular shaped caret to the left of **Comments**. Enter your metadata in the field provided. You can enter multiple words. If you want to add multiple comments, separate them with commas as shown below.

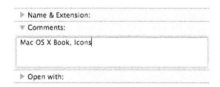

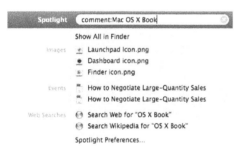

To perform a Spotlight search using your Spotlight Comments, use the search modifier **comment:** followed by one of your comments.

comment:Mac OS X Book

In the picture to the left, Spotlight found three image files I tagged with Mac OS X Book.

To search for files tagged with multiple comments, type **comment:** into the Spotlight search field before each comment.

comment:Mac OS X Book comment:Icons

This Spotlight search returned a single file, which I tagged with both the Mac OS X Book and Icons comment.

Spotlight Comments are a great way to quickly find files while still keeping them organized in their respective folders.

Rebuild the Spotlight Index

Sometimes you will swear that **Spotlight** is not finding a file you know is on your Mac or on an external drive. You are not crazy. Sometimes the Spotlight index becomes corrupted, causing inaccurate searches. When this happens, it is time to rebuild the Spotlight index.

To rebuild the Spotlight index, open **Terminal** and enter the following commands. The first command erases the existing Spotlight index. While the second command turns Spotlight back on, forcing it to reindex the drive. Enter your password into **Terminal** when prompted.

```
sudo mdutil -E /
```

```
sudo mdutil -i on /
```

If you click on Spotlight in the Menu Bar, you can verify Spotlight is rebuilding its index. The rebuilding process takes some time and is dependent upon the size and speed of the drive and the number of files it contains. Once the rebuilding process is complete, Spotlight will provide accurate search results.

Spotlight helps you quickly find things on your computer.

Spotlight will be available as soon as the contents of your computer have been indexed.

Indexing Tom's MacBook Pro

Estimating indexing time

9

Notification Center

Notification Center is a one-stop shop that consolidates all your notifications from FaceTime, Mail, Messages, Reminders, Calender, Safari, iTunes, Maps, Game Center, and many third party applications such as Evernote, Facebook, LinkedIn, and Twitter. OS X allows you to choose which applications will notify you as well as the style of each notification.

Notifications can be delivered to the desktop in the form of a banner or alert, depending on the style chosen. A notification may disappear after a set period of time, allowing you to see the notification yet continue to work. Other notifications may require action on your part to respond or dismiss the notification. All previous notifications are stored and are available in the **Notification Center**, a hidden panel on the right edge of the OS X desktop.

To unhide Notification Center, start with your fingers on the right edge of your trackpad and swipe left with two fingers. Swiping in the opposite direction hides Notification Center. Alternately, you can click on the Notification Center Menu Extra in the Menu Bar. Click the Menu Extra again to close Notification Center.

If you click on any of the notifications, you will launch the application that created the notification. For example, clicking on one of the Mail notifications will take you to the OS X Mail application where you can read and respond to the selected email. Doing so will mark the notification as read and the notification will be removed from Notification Center. Clicking the **X** at the top right of any application dismisses all notifications associated with that application.

Any application utilizing Apple's push notification service or local notifications can send notifications to Notification Center. OS X allows you to customize which applications are allowed to send notifications to the desktop and Notification Center via the **Notifications** preference pane in the **System Preferences** application.

Choose Which Apps Will Notify

All of the applications listed in the **Notifications** preference pane will display alerts in the upper right-hand corner of your desktop. These alerts are also saved to **Notification Center**. The default number of applications configured in Notification Center could easily inundate you with annoying and superfluous alerts. OS X allows you to turn off notifications from any of the applications listed in the preference pane.

To turn off notifications, open the **Notifications** preference pane by launching the **System Preferences** application and selecting the **Notifications** preference pane or from the Apple menu by selecting **** > **System Preferences...** > **Notifications**.

The **Notifications** preference pane is split into left- and right-hand panes. The left-hand pane lists the applications that are **In Notification Center**. Applications in this category will send notifications to your desktop and save them to Notification Center. By default, all applications are a part of the **In Notification Center** category.

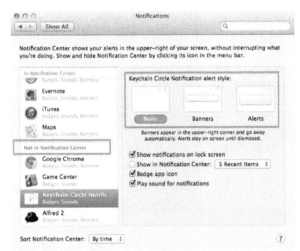

Move your pointer to the left-hand pane and scroll down. You will find a category called **Not In Notification Center** at the bottom of the pane. Any application in this category will not save notifications in Notification Center, however, they may still send notifications to your desktop.

To remove an application from **Notification Center**, simply drag it from **In Notification Center** into the **Not In Notification Center** category at the bottom of the left-hand pane.

Once in the **Not In Notification Center** category, an application will no longer save its alerts to Notification Center. However, the application will continue to send notifications to your desktop. This, of course, is a completely valid configuration. Another valid configuration is for an application to not send notifications to the desktop and only save them in Notification Center. If you want to stop an application from sending notifications to your desktop, you must click on **None** in the **Notification Alert Style** at the top of the right-hand pane. When **None** is selected as the notification style, the application will stop sending notifications to your desktop.

Choose the Notification Style

The OS X **Notification Center** can be configured to send either banners or alerts to your desktop. There is a difference between a banner and an alert. A **banner** is a notification that will appear on your desktop and disappear after set amount of time. An **alert** is a notification that will stay on your desktop until you respond or dismiss it. Alert styles and options such as history, badging, and sound are configured on a per application basis.

To choose a notification style, open the **Notifications** preference pane by launching the **System Preferences** application and selecting the **Notifications** preference pane or from the Apple menu by selecting > **System Preferences... > Notifications**.

Click on an application in the left-hand pane of the Notifications preference pane. Once an application has been selected, the right-hand pane will change to show the alert style currently configured, which is highlighted in blue.

Choose **None**, **Banners**, or **Alerts** to change the alert style that will appear on your desktop. Choosing **None** will stop notifications from appearing on your desktop.

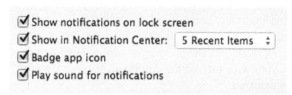

Once you have chosen your alert style, you need to configure the various options shown below the alert style in the right-hand pane. In OS X Mavericks, there will be either four or five options depending on the application selected. The options are: **Show notifications on lock screen**, **Show message preview**, **Show in Notification Center**, **Badge app icon**, and **Play sound for notifications**. The check boxes for all of the options are checked by default.

The **Show notifications on lock screen** option is obvious. By default, OS X will show alerts when your Mac is locked. This creates a potential security and privacy issue as anyone can read your notifications even when your Mac is locked. If you want to turn this feature off, uncheck the check box.

The **Show message preview** option is only applicable to apps such as **Mail** and **Messages**. By default, OS X will show a preview of your messages only **when unlocked**. The **always** option will show message previews regardless of whether your Mac is locked or unlocked. Again, this presents

a potential security and privacy issue. Uncheck the check box to turn message preview off.

By default, the **Show in Notification Center** option is checked and the 5 most recent notifications will be available in Notification Center. OS X allows you to choose the number of recent items saved. You have the option of saving 1, 5, 10, or 20 items.

The **Badge app icon** option will show the number of notifications on a badge on the app's icon in the **Dock**. The app must be in the Dock. If you don't want the application icon to get badged, uncheck the check box.

By default, every alert plays a sound when it appears. While this seems pretty cool, it can become annoying after a while. If you would rather the app not make a sound, uncheck the check box next to **Play sound for notifications**.

Change the App Order in Notification Center Panel

OS X allows you to manually reorder the apps in **Notification Center** so the apps and their associated alerts always appear in the order you desire.

To change the order in which alerts are displayed in Notification Center, open the **Notifications** preference pane by launching the **System Preferences** application and selecting the **Notifications** preference pane or from the Apple menu by selecting > **System Preferences... > Notifications**.

You can rearrange the order of the apps in the left-hand pane by dragging them up or down in the **In Notification Center** list. Make sure you have **Sort Notification Center**, located at the bottom left of the Notifications preference pane, configured to sort **Manually**. Once finished, close the Notifications preference pane. The alerts saved to Notification Center will be displayed in your desired order. Any application without an alert will be skipped.

Sort Notifications by Time

OS X can automatically sort the notifications in **Notification Center** by the time the alerts are received.

To sort the apps in Notification Center based on time, open the **Notifications** preference pane by launching the **System Preferences** application and selecting the **Notifications** preference pane or from the Apple menu by selecting > **System Preferences... > Notifications**.

Verify that **Sort Notification Center**, located at the bottom left of the Notifications preference pane, is configured to sort **By time**. When sorted by time, the apps with the most recent alerts will float to the top of Notification Center.

Turn Off Share Buttons

The share button in Notification Center is on by default. This feature puts share buttons for Messages, Facebook, Twitter, and LinkedIn in Notification Center.

To turn this feature off, open the **Notifications** preference pane by launching the **System Preferences** application and  selecting the **Notifications** preference pane or from the Apple menu by selecting > **System Preferences... > Notifications**.

Select **Share Button** from the left-hand pane and uncheck **Show share button in Notification Center**. You will no longer have the ability to send or post messages directly from Notification Center.

Set Up Twitter, Facebook, & LinkedIn

Notification Center can be set up so you can receive alerts from and post messages to Twitter, Facebook, and LinkedIn.

To add your Twitter, Facebook, and LinkedIn accounts, open the **Mail** application. OS X Maverick seems to require you have at least one email account set up before you add your social media accounts. The easiest email account to set up is your iCloud account. Once you have an email account set up, select **Mail > Accounts...**

from the **Mail** menu in the Menu Bar. An account dialog box will appear that will allow you to add your Twitter, Facebook, and LinkedIn accounts.

You can also add your social media accounts in the **Internet Accounts** preference pane in the **System Preferences** application. Launch the **System Preferences** application and select **Internet Accounts** or from the Apple menu select > **System Preferences... > Internet Accounts**.

To add a social media account, click on the account type you wish to add. Enter your username and password in the fields in the  drop-down dialog box. Once configured, you'll receive alerts from and be able to post to your social media accounts directly from Notification Center by clicking the appropriate **Share Button**.

Send Messages from Notification Center

OS X Mavericks adds the ability to send a message in the **Messages** application directly from Notification Center.

To send a Message, open Notification Center. Click the **Messages Share Button**. A field will appear allowing you to enter the destination and your Message. Click **Send**.

Tweet from Notification Center

Once you have set up your Twitter account, you can tweet directly from the Notification Center. To tweet, open Notification Center. Click on the **Twitter Share Button**. A field will appear allowing you to enter your tweet and optionally, your location. Click **Send**.

Post to Facebook from Notification Center

Once you have set up your Facebook account, you can post directly from the Notification Center. To post to Facebook, open Notification Center. Click on the **Facebook Share Button**. A field will appear allowing you to choose the type of post (Public, Friends, Only Me, etc.). Enter your post and optionally, your location. Click **Send**.

Post to LinkedIn from Notification Center

Once you have set up your LinkedIn account, you can post directly from the Notification Center. To post to LinkedIn, open Notification Center. Click on the **LinkedIn Share Button**. A field will appear allowing you to choose how you want to share your post. Enter your post and click **Send**.

Swipe to Dismiss a Notification

OS X allows you to dismiss any notification that appears on your desktop by swiping on the notification dialog from left to right with two fingers

on your trackpad. If you are using a Magic Mouse, swipe left to right with one finger. The notification will fade away as it moves towards the right edge of the screen. If the notification includes a **Snooze** button, this gesture is equivalent to Snooze.

Respond to Messages

OS X Mavericks added the capability to respond to **Messages** directly from the Alert without the need to open the Messages application.

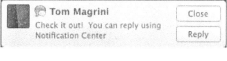

If you configured Messages to send notifications to your desktop in the Notifications preference pane, you will be alerted whenever someone sends you a Message. The alert will give you the option to **Close** or **Reply**. If you click the **Reply** button, a field will appear for you to type a response. Press the **return** key to send your reply.

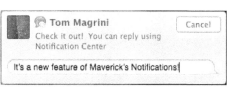

Turn Do Not Disturb On

Apple introduced a handy new feature for Notification Center in OS X Mavericks – **Do Not Disturb**. The Do Not Disturb feature turns Notification Center off for the remainder of the day.

To turn the **Do Not Disturb** feature on, first open Notification Center. Next, swipe in a downward motion with two fingers with your pointer located anywhere within Notification Center to reveal the Do Not Disturb switch at the very top.

Click the switch to the **ON** position to turn Do Not Disturb on. OS X Mavericks will automatically turn Do Not Disturb off tomorrow. Any notifications received while Do Not Disturb is on are still visible in the Notification Center. To turn Do Not Disturb off, switch the Do Not Disturb switch to **OFF**.

Temporarily Disable Notification Center

You can temporarily turn alerts off by holding the ⌥ (option) key down while clicking the **Notification Center** Menu Extra in the **Menu Bar**. In OS X Mavericks, this turns on the **Do Not Disturb** feature. Alerts will resume the next day. The icon for Notification Center will turn gray to indicate alerts are temporarily disabled.

Schedule Do Not Disturb

Not only can you turn the **Do Not Disturb** feature on in Notification Center, it can also be scheduled to turn on and off automatically at a particular time each day.

To schedule Do Not Disturb, open the **Notification** preference pane by launching the System Preferences application and selecting the **Notification** icon or from the Apple menu by selecting > **System Preferences... > Notification**. Click on **Do Not Disturb** in the left pane if not selected already.

To schedule Do Not Disturb check the check box next to **From** and then select the times during which you want Do Not Disturb on. You also can turn on Do Not Disturb when you are mirroring your display to TVs and projectors. This is quite handy if you're giving a presentation to a group of people and do not want notifications to interrupt your presentation, especially if the notifications could potentially be embarrassing and not appropriate to the audience.

By default, your Mac will not accept FaceTime calls when Do Not Disturb is turned on. If you would like to accept FaceTime calls, check the appropriate check box. You also can choose to accept FaceTime calls from **Everyone** or just from your list of **Favorites**.

Safari Push Notifications

Safari 7.0 adds push notifications for websites supporting Apple's push notification service. This allows websites to send notifications to OS X Mavericks even when Safari is not running. Websites can use push notification to send you breaking news, sports, or other information.

Before a website can send you push notifications, you must choose to opt in. If a website supports push notifications, you'll see a drop-down notification asking you if you would like to receive notifications from this website. Click **Allow** to opt in or **Don't Allow** to opt out. Don't worry, you can always change your mind later.

Once you opt-in, you'll see notifications appear on your desktop. Notifications will also be saved in Notification Center.

If you no longer find notifications from a particular website useful, you can opt out from receiving further notifications. Similarly, if you opted out and you can opt back in.

To change your Safari notification choice, open the **Safari** preferences from the **Safari** menu by selecting **Safari > Preferences...** or by entering **⌘,** (command+comma). Once the Safari preferences launch, select **Notifications**. The websites that have asked for permission to send you push notifications will be listed. Next to each website are two radio buttons for **Allow** and **Deny.** The radio button showing the current status will be selected.

If you want to delete a website from the list, highlight it and click the **Remove** button. You also have the option of removing all websites from the push notification list by clicking the **Remove All** button. This effectively turns off Safari push notifications until you opt in to another website.

Clicking **Notification Preferences...** in the lower right corner of the Safari preferences opens the **Notification Center** preference pane. Scroll down the **In Notification Center** list in the left-hand pane and select the Safari Alerts. You then can configure the alert style, whether you want notifications to appear when your Mac is locked and the number of recent items in Notification Center.

Assign a Hot Corner to Notification Center

The OS X **Hot Corners** feature allows you to assign a specific action to each of the four corners of your desktop. A **Hot Corner** is activated by moving your pointer to one of the corners to execute the associated command. It is often quicker to use a **Hot Corner** than to use a keyboard shortcut or to click on an icon.

To assign a **Hot Corner** to **Notification Center**, first open the **Mission Control** preference pane by launching the **System Preferences** application and selecting the **Mission Control** preference pane or from the Apple menu by selecting **⌘ > System Preferences... > Mission Control**.

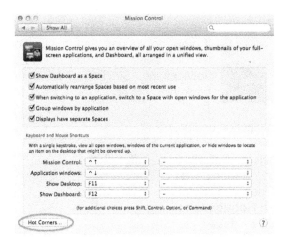

Next, click the **Hot Corners...** button at the lower left of the pane to reveal the drop-down dialog box shown at the right. Since the Notification Center Menu Extra is located at the top right of the desktop, it makes sense to assign the top right-hand Hot Corner to Notification Center. Click **OK** when finished, then close the Mission Control preference pane.

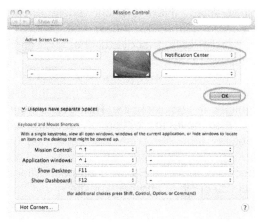

Now you can open Notification Center by moving your pointer to the upper right-hand corner of the desktop. Move your pointer to the same Hot Corner to close Notification Center.

To turn off Hot Corners, open the **Mission Control** preference pane and click the **Hot Corners...** button in the lower left corner. Select the – from the drop-down menu for each corner that you want to turn off.

To learn how to avoid accidentally triggering the Notification Center Hot Corner, see Avoid Accidentally Triggering a Hot Corner on page 42.

Create a Keyboard Shortcut to Notification Center

OS X allows you to assign keyboard shortcuts to execute any number of actions. If you would like to create a keyboard shortcut to open Notification Center, open the **Keyboard** preference pane by launching the System Preferences application and selecting the **Keyboard** preference pane or from the Apple menu by selecting **⚫ > System Preferences... > Keyboard**. Click on the **Shortcuts** tab.

Next, select **Mission Control** from the left-hand pane. **Show Notification Center** is the second choice in the list of shortcuts in the right-hand pane. By default, the check box is not checked. Check the check box and select a shortcut key combination in the field provided. Be sure to select a shortcut that is not used by another function. If you select a shortcut that is already assigned to another function, a yellow triangle will appear to the right of the shortcut. The yellow triangle will also appear in the left pane to denote a conflict with one of the assigned shortcuts. I've found the key combination of ⌥⌘tab

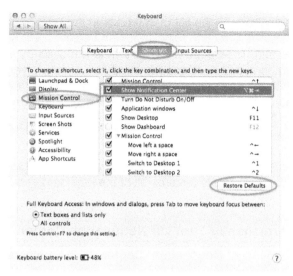

(option+command+tab) works well for me since it isn't assigned to another function.

To remove the shortcut, simply uncheck the check box next to **Show Notification Center** or click the **Restore Defaults** button at the lower right of the preference pane. Restore Defaults restores all of the keyboard shortcuts to their OS X defaults.

Create a Keyboard Shortcut for Do Not Disturb

In addition to creating a keyboard shortcut to open Notification Center, OS X allows you to assigned a keyboard shortcut for the **Do Not Disturb** feature. Open the **Keyboard** preference pane by launching the System Preferences application and selecting the **Keyboard** preference pane or from the Apple menu by selecting > **System Preferences... > Keyboard**. Click on the **Shortcuts** tab.

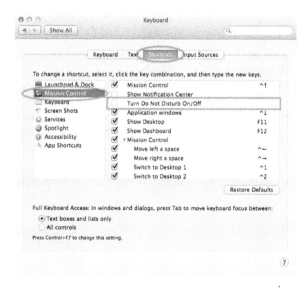

Next, select **Mission Control** from the left-hand pane. **Turn Do Not Disturb On/Off** is the third choice in the list of shortcuts in the right-hand pane. By default, the check box is not checked. Check the check box and select a shortcut key combination in the field provided. Be sure to select a shortcut that is not used by another function. If you select a shortcut that is already assigned to another function, a yellow triangle will appear to the right of the shortcut. The yellow triangle will also appear in the left pane to denote a conflict with one of the assigned shortcuts. Once configured, the keyboard shortcut will act as a toggle to turn Do Not Disturb on and off.

To remove the shortcut, simply uncheck the check box next to **Turn Do Not Disturb On/Off** or click the **Restore Defaults** button at the lower right of the preference pane. Restore Defaults restores all of the keyboard shortcuts to their OS X defaults.

Permanently Turn Off Notification Center

If you find **Notification Center** to be bothersome, OS X allows you to turn it off permanently.

To turn off Notification Center permanently, open **Terminal** and enter the following commands. The first two lines are a single command. Be sure to enter the entire two lines before hitting the **return** key. Note that there is a space between **–w** and **/System**.

```
launchctl unload -w
/System/Library/LaunchAgents/com.apple.notificationcenterui.plist
```

```
killall NotificationCenter
```

Take a look at your Notification Center Menu Extra in the Menu Bar. It's gone!

To revert to the OS X default and turn Notification Center back on, enter the following commands in **Terminal**. Be sure to enter the entire two lines before hitting the **return** key. Note that there is a space between **–w** and **/System**.

```
launchctl load -w
/System/Library/LaunchAgents/com.apple.notificationcenterui.plist
```

```
killall NotificationCenter
```

You should now see the Notification Center Menu Extra back in its usual place in the Menu Bar.

10

Dashboard

 The **Dashboard** is an OS X application capable of running mini-applications called **widgets**. By default, the Dashboard runs as a space. Swiping right with four fingers reveals the Dashboard space located in its default location to the left of Desktop 1, the main OS X desktop. The Dashboard can also be accessed using the **F12** key or by clicking on the Dashboard icon in the Dock or Launchpad. Note that you will have to hold the **fn** (function key) while pressing **F12** if you own own a MacBook Pro or MacBook Air. On older Macs, the **F4** key may open the Dashboard.

Widgets can be rearranged, added, and deleted. OS X includes over a dozen widgets including a calculator, calendar, contacts, clock, and weather widgets. Additional widgets can be downloaded from Apple at the following url:
http://www.apple.com/downloads/dashboard/.

Turn Off the Dashboard Space

Dashboard can run in a separate space, which is the OS X default, or the widgets can be run from any Desktop space, appearing in the foreground of your desktop. Configuring the Dashboard to run in the foreground provides more convenient access to the widgets.

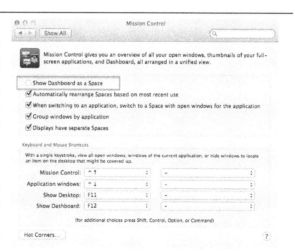

To turn off the Dashboard space, open the **Mission Control** preference pane by launching the **System Preferences** application and selecting the **Mission Control** preference pane or from the Apple menu by selecting > **System Preferences... > Mission Control**. Uncheck the check box next to **Show Dashboard as a Space**.

Launching the Dashboard dims your desktop and the widgets appear in the foreground. Press the **F12** key or click the Dashboard icon in the Dock to close the Dashboard.

Move the Dashboard

The **Dashboard** is accessed like any other space in **Mission Control** by clicking on it to make it active. If OS X is configured to show the **Dashboard** as a separate space, it will appear at the far left of the desktops in Mission Control by default. In OS X Mountain Lion, the Dashboard is always located to the far left of the Desktops and cannot be moved. OS X Mavericks does not have that restriction. The Dashboard can be moved by dragging it amongst the Desktops at the top of Mission Control

Assign a Hot Corner to the Dashboard

The OS X **Hot Corners** feature allows you to assign a specific action to each of the four corners of your desktop. A **Hot Corner** is activated by moving your pointer to one of the corners to execute the associated command. It is often quicker to use a **Hot Corner** than to use a keyboard shortcut or to click on an icon.

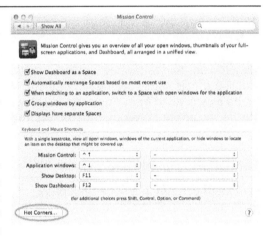

To assign a **Hot Corner** to the **Dashboard**, first open the **Mission Control** preference pane by launching the **System Preferences** application and selecting the **Mission Control** preference pane or from the Apple menu by selecting **☺ > System Preferences... > Mission Control**.

Next, click the **Hot Corners...** button at the lower left of the pane to reveal the drop-down dialog box shown at the left. Choose which corner you want to use to launch the Dashboard. Click **OK** when finished, then close the Mission Control preference pane.

Now you can open the Dashboard by moving your pointer to the Hot Corner you configured. Move your pointer to the same Hot Corner to close the Dashboard.

To turn off Hot Corners, open the **Mission Control** preference pane and click the **Hot Corners...** button in the lower left corner. Select the – from the drop-down menu for each corner that you want to turn off.

To learn how to avoid accidentally triggering the Dashboard Hot Corner, see Avoid Accidentally Triggering a Hot Corner on page 42.

Add New Widgets

By default, OS X Mavericks comes with a rather Spartan **Dashboard** containing only four widgets: calculator, calendar, clock, and weather.

OS X allows you to add widgets by clicking on the large, circled + sign located at the lower corner of the Dashboard. This will open what appears to be a Launchpad for widgets, listing all available widgets on your Mac. Apple's website has a page dedicated to Dashboard widgets at the following url: http://www.apple.com/downloads/dashboard/. This page contains thousands of widgets, organized in categories.

 If you have configured the Dashboard to not run as a separate space, adding widgets is done the same way. You'll find the large circled + sign in the lower left corner of your Desktop.

Remove a Widget from the Dashboard

Dashboard widgets are deleted much the same way as they are added. To delete a widget, click on the large circled – sign at the lower left of the Dashboard, if run as a separate space, or at the lower left of the desktop. An **X** will appear at the upper left corner of each widget. Click the **X** to remove the widgets. Widgets are only removed from the Dashboard. They are not deleted and can be added back at any time.

Rearrange Widgets

Dashboard widgets can be rearranged by clicking and dragging them to a new location on the Dashboard. Click along the upper edge of the widget to drag it.

Open Duplicate Widgets

If you haven't tried to open multiple copies of the same widget, you may never know this feature existed. I happened to stumble upon it accidentally. OS X doesn't limit you to one instance of a Dashboard widget. The most obvious use is to open multiple weather or clock widgets so you can see the weather or time in different locations. Or you could have multiple sticky notes.

To open duplicate widgets, repeatedly add the same widget as many times as needed.

Put a Widget on your Desktop

The **Dashboard** is handy if you have a lot of widgets. It provides a convenient space to collect all the widgets and run them simultaneously. The Dashboard can be configured two ways: as a separate space or in the foreground of your desktop. When the Dashboard runs in the desktop foreground, OS X dims your desktop and the widgets appear in the foreground.

What if you want a particular widget to appear on your desktop? OS X has a command for that! This is one of my favorite tweaks as I like to have the weather widget on my desktop.

First, open the **Mission Control** preference pane and uncheck the check box next to **Show Dashboard as a Space**.

Next, launch the **Terminal** application and enter the following command.

```
defaults write com.apple.dashboard devmode TRUE
```

Log out and log back in for this tweak to take effect.

To move a Dashboard widget to your desktop, make sure you are on **Desktop 1**, the main OS X desktop. Clear the desktop of windows by closing or minimizing them. Launch the Dashboard by hitting the **F12** key or clicking on its icon in the Dock. Your desktop will dim and the Dashboard will appear in the foreground. Click and hold the top edge of the widget you want on your desktop and then close the Dashboard by pressing the **F12** key. The Dashboard will disappear and your chosen widget will be dropped onto the desktop. Drag it to its final location.

Sometimes a widget refuses to appear after you have dropped it on to the desktop. Don't worry! Open **Terminal**, if it isn't open already. Enter the following command and the misbehaving, hidden widget will magically reappear.

```
killall Dock
```

To ensure success, make sure you are on Desktop 1. Widgets will not move to other desktops. Make sure you have unchecked **Show Dashboard as a Space** in the Mission Control preference pane. Also, make sure you have closed or minimized all windows on Desktop 1 before trying to drop a widget on to the desktop.

To remove a widget from your desktop, first open the **Mission Control** preference pane and check the check box next to **Show Dashboard as a Space**. Next, click on the large circled – sign at the lower left of the Dashboard. An **X** will appear at the upper left corner of each widget. If a widget is located on the desktop, only a circled **X** will appear where the widget is located. "Hidden" widgets from failed attempts to move a widget to the desktop will also only show a circled **X**. Click the **X** to remove the widgets.

If you no longer want the option to move Dashboard widgets to the desktop and want to revert to the OS X default, open **Terminal** and enter the following command. Log out and log back in for the tweak to take effect.

```
defaults delete com.apple.dashboard devmode
```

Move the Dashboard to Another Display

One of the major changes in OS X Mavericks is that the **Dashboard** acts like any other space. And like any other space in Mavericks, the Dashboard can be moved to another display if you have a multiple display system.

141

To move the Dashboard to another display, open **Mission Control** by hitting the **F3** key or by swiping four fingers up on the trackpad. Drag the **Dashboard** space to the left or right edge of the screen to move it to your second (or third) display.

Remove the Dashboard

If you find the **Dashboard** to be less than useful because it's getting a little long in the tooth. Browsing Apple's Dashboard widget page is like taking a trip in Mr. Peabody's Wayback machine to a time before iPhones and iPads. Apple's widget browser is out-of-date and just plain ugly. There I said it. Many of the widgets haven't been updated in years and few are being actively developed or maintained. Mavericks does little to help. The only noticeable improvement to the Dashboard is the slightly improved background. Many Mac users feel that Dashboard has outlived its usefulness.

The solution to this problem is to simply remove the Dashboard so you never have to worry about widgets again.

To remove the Dashboard, open **Terminal** and enter these commands. Press the **return** key after entering each line.

```
defaults write com.apple.dashboard mcx-disabled -bool TRUE
```

```
killall Dock
```

If you change your mind and want the Dashboard back and enter the following commands.

```
defaults write com.apple.dashboard mcx-disabled -bool FALSE
```

```
killall Dock
```

11

Launchpad

Launchpad is a feature that blurs the line between iOS and OS X. Similar to iOS, Launchpad allows you to see every application installed on your Mac on one or more pages. From Launchpad, you can search, launch, organize, and delete apps.

To open Launchpad, click on its icon in the Dock, press the **F4** key (on newer Macs), use the ⌥⌘L (command+option+L) shortcut, or pinch your thumb and three fingers together using the trackpad. For information on configuring gestures, refer to Chapter 2. When you open Launchpad, your desktop background will blur and any windows will disappear to reveal a grid of applications icons similar to the home screen on an iPad or iPhone. The Dock, if hidden, will reappear.

Launchpad offers a search field at the top center allowing you to easily find applications, particularly ones that may be hidden in a folder. Small dots at the bottom center represent pages. You can swipe left or right to with one finger on a Magic Mouse or two fingers on a trackpad or hold down the ⌘ (command) key while pressing the left or right arrow keys to navigate between pages. You also can click on one of the dots to jump directly to that page. All four arrow keys can be used to move up, down, left, or right within the grid to highlight an application. Pressing the **return** key launches the highlighted application, as does clicking on an icon.

Folders can be created the same way they are in iOS, by dragging one icon on top of another. Once a folder is created, it can be renamed and other applications can be dragged into it. Folders are opened by clicking on them or by holding down the ⌘ (command) key while typing the down arrow. Holding ⌘ while typing the up arrow closes an open folder.

You can close Launchpad by clicking on the desktop wallpaper, hitting the **F4** key again, or using the Show Desktop gesture by spreading your thumb and three fingers apart.

Add Finder to Launchpad

Try launching **Launchpad**. Now type **Finder** in the search field. You should get **No Results**, which is displayed at the center of Launchpad. Noticeably absent from Launchpad is one of the most critical apps in OS X, Finder.

To add Finder to Launchpad, first open a **Finder** window using the icon in the **Dock**. Enter ⇧⌘G (shift+command+G) to open the **Go to folder:** dialog box. Enter the following into the field and click **Go**.

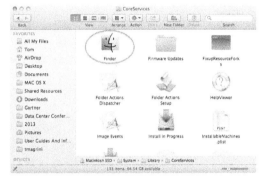

`/System/Library/CoreServices/`

Locate **Finder** in this folder and drag and drop it onto the **Launchpad** icon in the Dock. Now, check out Launchpad and there's Finder.

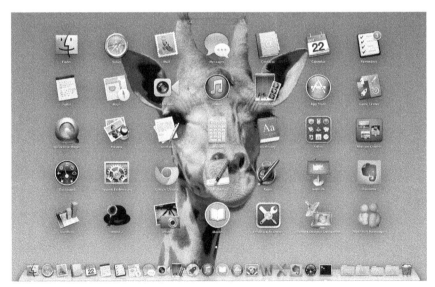

Change the Number of Apps per Page

By default, OS X lays out a 7 column by 5 row grid in Launchpad, allowing 35 app icons per page. If you want more application icons to appear on each Launchpad page, you do so by making the grid larger (i.e., more columns and/or more rows).

For example, if you want Launchpad to display 48 application icons per page, you would need to resize the grid to 8 columns by 6 rows. To resize Launchpad, open **Terminal** and enter the following commands.

```
defaults write com.apple.dock springboard-columns -int 8
```

```
defaults write com.apple.dock springboard-rows -int 6
```

```
killall Dock
```

Increasing the size of the grid decreases the size of each icon, making them smaller than the OS X default setting. With Launchpad displaying more icons per page, it takes less pages to display all of your applications.

I suggest you experiment, trying different combinations of column and row sizes. Simply replace the number after **-int** with an integer. I've tried grids as large as 12x12, but I found the application icons too small to be usable. I've found that an 8 column by 8 row grid is the largest grid size where the app icons are still usable.

Conversely, you can make the Launchpad grid smaller (i.e., fewer columns and/or rows) so that fewer application icons are displayed on each page.

For example, if you want Launchpad to display 20 application icons per page, you would need to resize the grid to 5 columns by 4 rows. To resize Launchpad, open **Terminal** and enter the following commands.

```
defaults write com.apple.dock springboard-columns -int 5
```

```
defaults write com.apple.dock springboard-rows -int 4
```

```
killall Dock
```

Decreasing the size of the grid increases the size of each icon, making them larger than the OS X default setting. With Launchpad displaying less icons per page, it takes more pages to display all of your applications.

To revert back to the OS X default of 7 columns by 5 rows, enter the following commands.

```
defaults delete com.apple.dock springboard-columns
```

```
defaults delete com.apple.dock springboard-rows
```

```
killall Dock
```

You probably noticed that as you changed the Launchpad grid size, your application icons spread out across multiple pages. Creating an 8-column by 8-row grid supporting 64 icons, doesn't mean Launchpad will automatically rearrange the icons for you. Unfortunately, you'll have to rearrange them manually. I suggest you determine what grid size works best before rearranging any of the application icons.

Change the Amount of Background Blur

When you open **Launchpad**, any windows immediately disappear and OS X blurs your desktop wallpaper. OS X allows you to change the amount of blurring. The picture below shows the default level of background blur.

If you do not like the background blurring, see the next section to learn how to disable it.

To change the amount of background blurring, open **Terminal** and enter the following commands.

```
defaults write com.apple.dock springboard-blur-radius -int 255
```

```
killall Dock
```

The number after **-int** denotes the amount of blur with 255 being the maximum. Valid values are integers between 0 and 255 with 0 denoting no blur and 255 being the maximum amount of blur. I suggest you experiment with a number of values until you tune the blur to your liking. The picture below shows the same background as the picture above with background blurring tweaked to the maximum (255).

To revert back to the OS X default amount of blur, open **Terminal** and enter the following commands.

```
defaults delete com.apple.dock springboard-blur-radius
```

```
killall Dock
```

Change the Background Visual Effect

When you open **Launchpad**, any windows immediately disappear and OS X blurs your desktop wallpaper. If you don't like the blurring effect, you can configure OS X to leave your background image alone.

To change the background visual effect, open **Terminal** and enter the following commands.

```
defaults write com.apple.dock springboard-background-filter -int 0
```

```
killall Dock
```

Now when you open Launchpad, your desktop wallpaper will no longer be blurred.

To revert back to the OS X default of a blurred background, enter the following commands in **Terminal**.

```
defaults write com.apple.dock springboard-background-filter -int 1
```

```
killall Dock
```

Notice the number after **-int**. There are four possible values, each with its own visual effect.

0	No visual effect.
1	Blurs the desktop wallpaper. This is the OS X default.
2	Turns the desktop wallpaper black and white.
3	Turns the desktop wallpaper black and white and blurs it.

Remove the Launchpad Delay

When opening **Launchpad**, you'll notice an ever-so-slight delay before it appears. The same slight delay in the animation also occurs when you exit Launchpad. If you would like Launchpad to appear and disappear immediately, enter the following commands in **Terminal**. The first command removes the delay when opening Launchpad, while the second removes the delay when exiting.

```
defaults write com.apple.dock springboard-show-duration -int 0
```

```
defaults write com.apple.dock springboard-hide-duration -int 0
```

```
killall Dock
```

To revert back to the OS X default Launchpad animation, enter the following commands in **Terminal**.

```
defaults delete com.apple.dock springboard-show-duration
```

```
defaults delete com.apple.dock springboard-hide-duration
```

```
killall Dock
```

Remove the Page Scrolling Delay

OS X introduces a delay when scrolling between pages in **Launchpad**. If you prefer pages appear immediately without the delay, enter the following commands in **Terminal**.

```
defaults write com.apple.dock springboard-page-duration -int 0
```

```
killall Dock
```

To restore the default scroll animation between Launchpad pages, enter the following commands.

```
defaults delete com.apple.dock springboard-page-duration
```

```
killall Dock
```

Assign a Hot Corner to Launchpad

The OS X **Hot Corners** feature allows you to assign a specific action to each of the four corners of your desktop. A **Hot Corner** is activated by moving your pointer to one of the corners to execute the associated command. It is often quicker to use a **Hot Corner** than to use a keyboard shortcut or to click on an icon.

To assign a **Hot Corner** to **Launchpad**, first open the **Mission Control** preference pane by launching the **System Preferences** application and selecting the **Mission Control** preference pane or from the Apple menu by selecting > **System Preferences...** > **Mission Control**.

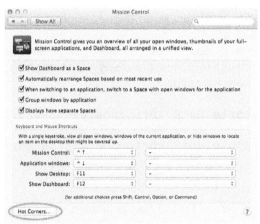

Next, click the **Hot Corners...** button at the lower left of the pane to reveal the drop-down dialog box shown at the right. Choose which corner you want to use to open Launchpad. Click **OK** when finished. Then close the Mission Control preference pane.

To turn off Hot Corners, open the **Mission Control** preference pane and click the **Hot Corners...** button in the lower left corner. Select the – from the drop-down menu for each corner that you want to turn off.

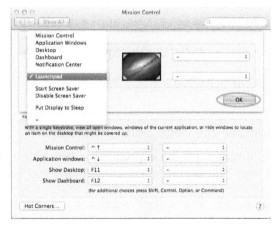

To learn how to avoid accidentally triggering the Launchpad Hot Corner, see Avoid Accidentally Triggering a Hot Corner on page 42.

Change the Launchpad Keyboard Shortcut

The default OS X keyboard shortcut for Launchpad is ⌥⌘L (option+command+L). If you would like to change this keyboard shortcut, open the **Keyboard** preference pane by launching the System Preferences application and selecting the **Keyboard** preference pane or from the Apple menu by selecting > **System Preferences...** > **Keyboard**. Click on the **Shortcuts** tab.

Next, select **Launchpad & Dock** from the left-hand pane. **Show Launchpad** is the second choice in the list of shortcuts in the right-hand pane. By default, the check box is checked and ⌥⌘L (option+command+L) is assigned as the keyboard shortcut. To change the shortcut, click on the ⌥⌘L which will change into a field where you can enter a new shortcut. Enter a shortcut key combination in that field.

Be sure to select a shortcut that is not used by another function. If you select a shortcut that is already assigned to another function, a yellow triangle will appear to the right of the shortcut. The yellow triangle will also appear in the left pane to denote a conflict with one of the assigned shortcuts.

To remove the shortcut, simply uncheck the check box next to **Show Launchpad** or click the **Restore Defaults** button at the lower right of the preference pane. Restore Defaults restores the keyboard shortcuts to their OS X defaults.

Need to Start From Scratch?

If you need to revert back to the OS X **Launchpad** defaults for any reason, enter the following commands in **Terminal**. This will reset Launchpad to its out-of-the-box settings. Any tweaks, including folders you may have created, will be reset back to the defaults.

```
defaults write com.apple.dock ResetLaunchPad -bool TRUE

killall Dock
```

12

Finder

 Finder is the OS X file manager application, which provides a user interface to manage files, disk drives, and network drives and to launch applications. A Finder window is the window that opens when you launch Finder from the Dock or double-click a folder or disk icon. We will focus on customization of the Finder window in this chapter to make Finder more useful.

A Finder window has three major components. At the very top of the Finder window is the **Toolbar**, which contains various tools to manipulate the Finder window and its contents. The **Sidebar** is located at the left and is divided into four sections. In the Sidebar, **Favorites** lists shortcuts to favorite or frequently used items such as All My Files, Desktop, Documents, Movies, Music, Pictures, AirDrop, and the Applications folder. Underneath the Favorites list is the **Devices** list (i.e., a list of internal and external hard drives). Below Devices is **Shared**, a list of shared computers and network shares to which your Mac is connected. The final section is the list of **Tags**, which are useful method of organizing your files. Finally, the **Right Pane** displays the contents of the selected folder.

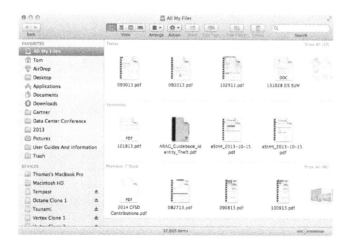

Clicking on the Finder icon in the Dock launches a Finder window showing the **All My Files view**, which displays files organized chronologically with the most recent at the top of the window. You can return to this view by clicking **All My Files** under **Favorites** in the Sidebar.

OS X Mavericks added several features to Finder with the most significant being support for full-screen mode and Tabs. Full-screen mode is awesome when you are scrolling through a folder full of files displayed as icons. As for Tabs, they have been used in browsers for years. Finder tabs is a much needed improvement that will increase your productivity as you no longer have to deal with dozens of Finder windows. To open a new tab enter ⌘T (command+T). Files can be dragged between tabs and a tab can be dragged to the desktop to create a new Finder window. Each tab can have its own view and icon size.

Modify the Sidebar

The **Favorites** list in the sidebar provides quick access to folders that you access frequently. Folders can be added to the Favorites list by first locating the folder in Finder and then dragging it onto the Sidebar. The order of the items listed under favorites can be re-arranged by dragging them until the list is ordered the way you want to see it. Any item in the Favorites list can be removed by dragging it off the Sidebar until a puff of smoke appears underneath its title.

Secondary clicking on an item in the **Favorites** list opens a submenu allowing you to open the folder in a new tab, see the enclosing folder, get info about the folder, remove it from the Sidebar, or add it to the Dock.

 A secondary click on items in the list of **Devices** provides somewhat different options allowing you to open the device in a new tab, show its enclosing folder, eject it, get info on the device, encrypt it, rename it, remove it, or add it to the Dock.

Similarly, the list of **Tags** offers options to open a new tab containing all files with the selected tag, rename a tag, remove a tag from the Sidebar, delete a tag from the system, or change its color.

Hiding Sidebar Lists

Hovering your mouse over any of the Sidebar categories (Favorites, Devices, or Tags) reveals a **Hide/Show** toggle switch to the right of the category name. Clicking **Hide** collapses the category while clicking **Show** expands it.

Choose Which Items Appear in Sidebar

Using the **Finder Preferences**, you can configure which items are displayed in the Sidebar.

Select **Preferences...** from the **Finder** menu in the Menu Bar. You can also access the preferences by entering ⌘, (command+comma). Once the preference pane appears, make sure **Sidebar** is selected from the set of four icons at the top of the pane. Using the check boxes, check and uncheck items until you have configured the Sidebar to your liking.

The items checked will appear in Sidebar, while the unchecked items will be hidden.

Add the Trash to the Sidebar

Missing from the **Finder** Sidebar is one of the most often used folders in OS X, the **Trash**. It only takes a couple of steps to add the Trash to the Sidebar.

First, open a Finder window. Enter ⇧⌘G (shift+command+G) to open the **Go to folder:** dialog box. Enter the following into the field and click **Go**.

~/Trash

Next, switch the view to **Column**. The Trash folder will be highlighted, but it will be grayed to indicate that it is a hidden folder. Simply drag it into the Sidebar. I recommend putting it at the bottom as shown, but its location is your choice.

You now can use the Trash folder in the sidebar to drop files into the Trash. However, the Sidebar Trash folder doesn't quite operate like the Trash in the Dock. Besides the fact that the icon is wrong (it's a folder instead of the Trash icon), you cannot empty the Trash by secondary clicking on the Sidebar Trash icon. The only method to empty the Trash is to Secondary Click on the Trash icon in the Dock. Despite its limitations, the Sidebar Trash folder remains a convenient method to drag files into the Trash directly within a Finder window.

To delete the Trash folder from the Sidebar, drag it away from the Sidebar until a puff of smoke appears underneath. Release and the Trash icon disappears.

Rename Sidebar Items

Any folder that you added to the Finder **Sidebar** can be renamed by secondary clicking on it to display a contextual menu. From that menu, you can open the folder in a new tab, show its enclosing folder, get info, rename it, remove it from the Sidebar, or add the item to the Dock. Renaming an item in the Sidebar not only renames the Sidebar shortcut, but it also renames the original folder.

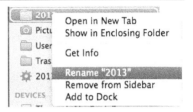

Change the Sidebar Icon Size

By default, OS X sets the size of the icons in the Sidebar to medium. If you have a lot of items in the Sidebar, you may want to set the icons to a smaller size to avoid having to scroll. Conversely, you may simply like Sidebar to display larger icons.

To change the icon size in Sidebar, open the **General** preference pane by launching the System Preferences application and selecting the **General** icon or from the Apple menu by selecting > **System Preferences... > General**. Use the drop-down menu next to **Sidebar icons size** to choose either **Small**, **Medium**, or **Large** for the icon size. The three Sidebar icon sizes are shown below.

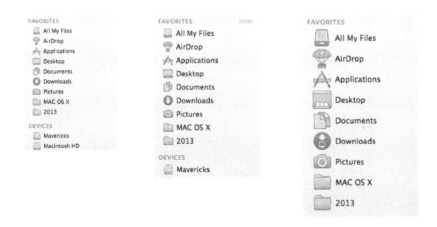

Hide the Sidebar

OS X offers a number of features to change the look of your Finder windows. The various "bars" can be toggled on or off as needed. You can choose to show or hide the Path Bar, Status Bar, Tab Bar, and Sidebar.

To hide the Sidebar, choose **View > Hide Sidebar** or enter ⌥⌘S (option+command+S). The Sidebar can be toggled back on by selecting **View > Show Sidebar** or by entering ⌥⌘S. Another method is to hover in your pointer over the dividing line between the Sidebar in the right-hand pane until the resizing pointer appears. The resizing pointer can be used to change the width of the Sidebar. It can also be used to hide the Sidebar by moving the resizing pointer all the way to the left until the Sidebar disappears.

Customize the Toolbar

The Finder **Toolbar**, located at the top of the Finder window, provides a number of tools to manipulate the contents of folders displayed in the Finder window's right-hand pane. The picture below shows the default Finder Toolbar in OS X Mavericks.

From left to right, the Toolbar provides forward and back buttons to navigate through folders similar to navigating forward and back in the Safari browser.

The next set of four icons change how the contents of a folder are viewed – by **Icon** view, by **List** view, by **Column** view, or by **Cover Flow**.

The **Arrange** button offers a drop-down where you can sort files in the Finder window by name, kind, application, date last opened, date added, date modified, date created, size, or tag. The final option is to provide no sorting.

The **Action** button provides a contextual drop-down menu that changes based on the item that is selected.

The **Edit Tags** button allows you to add, change, and remove tags.

Next is a Spotlight search field that we will cover in detail later in this chapter. Finally, located in the upper right-hand corner is the button allowing you to take Finder to full screen mode.

Finder Tabs, a new feature of OS X Mavericks, are located underneath the toolbar. You can open a new tab by clicking the **+** to the far right of the tabs.

OS X allows you to customize the Finder **Toolbar**, adding, removing, and rearranging tools as you see fit. Secondary click in any open area of the Toolbar to reveal a contextual menu. This menu allows you to choose how the tools appear. Tools can

✓ Icon and Text
Icon Only
Text Only
Hide Toolbar

Customize Toolbar...

be displayed using both their Icon and Text, Icon Only, or Text Only. An option to completely hide the toolbar is also available. The final option, **Customize Toolbar...** allows you to add, rearrange, and remove tools using the drop-down tools palette with the entire selection of tools available.

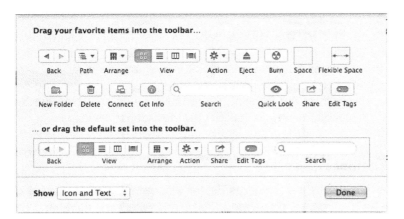

The **Path** tool displays the full path to the location shown in the right-hand pane of Finder. You can also see the path by holding down the ⌘ key while clicking on the title shown at the top of the toolbar.

The **Eject** tool will eject optical media from the optical drive and will unmount any drive whose contents are displayed in Finder's right-hand pane.

The **Burn** tool is used to burn files and folders to optical media such as a CD or DVD.

The **Space** and **Flexible Space** tools are used to space out the tools in the toolbar by adding a blank space between tools or sets of tools.

The **New Folder** tool does as its name implies. It creates a new folder in the current folder displayed in the right-hand pane.

The **Delete** tool sends the selected file(s) and folder(s) to the Trash.

The **Connect** tool is used to connect to network servers and shared drives. Clicking it launches the **Connect to Server** dialog box which allows you to connect to a server and save it to your favorites.

The **Quick Look** tool opens a preview of the selected file without launching the application in which it was created. Quick Look allows you to preview a file before deciding to open it. The Quick Look window provides a **Open with** button, allowing you to launch the underlying application that created the file.

The **Get Info** tool opens the Get Info window with displays information about the selected file such as its tags, kind, size, location, date created, date modified, its file extension,

Spotlight comments, the default application which opens the file, and a preview. The Get Info tool can be used on multiple files.

The **Share** button allows you to share a selected item using Email, Messages, AirDrop, Twitter, Facebook, or Flickr.

To add a tool to the Toolbar, select and drag it to your desired location. Existing tools located on the Toolbar can be rearranged by dragging them. A tool is removed by dragging it off the Toolbar and onto the drop-down tools palette.

The **Show** option at the lower left allows you to choose how the tools appear - Icon in text, icon only, or text only. Click the **Done** button when finished customizing the Finder toolbar.

Here is my Finder toolbar customized with the tools I frequently use.

Tools located on the Toolbar can be moved without having to use the drop-down tools palette. To move a tool, hold the ⌘ key down while dragging the tool to its new location. You can also use the ⌘ key to remove a tool. Hold down ⌘ while dragging the tool off the Toolbar. The tool will disappear in a puff of smoke.

To revert back to the default set of tools, drag the default set onto the Finder Toolbar to replace the existing toolset.

Tag Files & Folders

Tags are another feature that Apple touts as being new in Mavericks. Tags are not really new as OS X has previously supported a file tagging system called **Labels**, which uses the same colored labels that Apple now calls Tags. However, Tags are a much improved version of the Label feature. The main differences between the Tags feature in Mavericks and previous versions of OS X is that you can apply more than one Tag to a file or folder and can create custom tags.

Tagging files is a major shift in the way you work with the OS X file system. Files no longer need to be saved in a specific folder in order to create a relationship between them. Tags remove the need to have deeply nested folders within the file system in order to create relationships between different files. It doesn't matter where files are saved because Tags can be used to relate them to each other. The OS X search capabilities in both Finder and Spotlight allow you to immediately locate files based on their Tags regardless of where they reside in the file system.

Tagging files with a color and name is a convenient way to organize related files, such as files from a project, without having to create a special folder or modify the locations of the files. In Mavericks, you can customize the name to something like "Kitchen Remodel" or "Physics Project" instead of being limited to categorizing only by color.

To tag a file that is open, move the pointer to the right of the filename in the title bar, click on the drop-down arrow, and click on the Tags field. You can choose a tag from the list or create a new one.

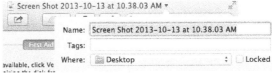

Note that this method does not work on all applications, most notably Microsoft Office, which does not offer a drop-down menu next to the filename.

There are several methods to tag an item in Finder. The first is to select the item, click the **Edit Tags** button in the toolbar, and select the appropriate tag. That method is shown in the picture at the left. Another method, shown at the right, is to select the file, secondary click on it, and add a Tag. Files can be tagged with one or more tags as needed. A third method is to select the file or files you want to Tag and select a Tag from the bottom of the Finder **File** menu. The fourth method is to select the files in Finder and click on the appropriate Tag in the Sidebar. The fifth method is to choose a Tag when saving a file for the first time.

To change or remove a tag from an open file, click on the arrow next to the file name in the title bar to reveal the drop-down menu. Remove or modify any existing tags.

To change or remove a tag from an item in Finder, select the file and click the **Edit Tags** button in the Toolbar. Remove or modify any existing tags. An alternate method is to secondary click on an item and remove or change any existing tags from the contextual menu that appears.

Customize Tags

Tags can be renamed in **Finder Preferences**. Select **Preferences...** from the **Finder** menu in the Menu Bar. You can also access preferences by entering ⌘, (command+comma). Once the Finder preferences appear, make sure **Tags** is selected from the set of four icons at the top of the pane.

To rename a tag, click on its name and rename it. The tag will appear under **Tags** in the Sidebar if its check box is checked. In the example to the right, all of the Tags except the Gray tag will be listed in the Sidebar.

The bottom section of the Tags preference pane is used to configure which tags appear in Finder menus. To remove a Tag, drag it off the preference pane. To add a Tag, drag it from the list at the top into the **Favorite Tags** box at the bottom.

An even quicker way to create a new tag is to click the Edit Tags button in the Finder toolbar. At the top of the drop-down menu is an option to enter the name of a new Tag.

Begin typing in the field, and you will be given the option to create a new Tag. Press **return** when finished.

Manage Tags

Tag management consists of associating and changing the Tag color and organizing tags in the **Sidebar**. By default, newly created custom Tags will not have an associated color, which can make tagged files sometimes difficult to find. OS X offers an **All Tags...** search option, which is located at the very bottom of the Tag list in the Finder Sidebar. This features displays all Tags including any custom tags.

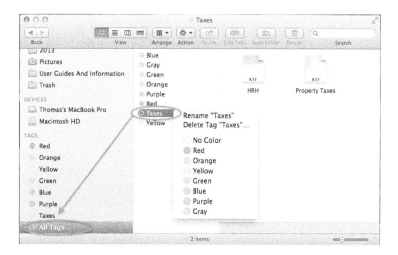

The **All Tags...** search displays all tags available including both the seven default color tags included in Mavericks as well as any custom tags you created. Clicking on the Tag in the first column displays any files associated with the selected Tag. Secondary clicking on a Tag reveals a contextual menu from which the Tag can be renamed, deleted, or a color associated. A Tag can be added to the Sidebar Tag list by dragging it into the Sidebar. The tag list can be rearranged by dragging the Tags into the order you wish to see them. A Tag can be removed from the Tag list in the Sidebar by dragging it off the Sidebar.

Tag management can also be accomplished using the Tags section of the Finder preferences, which is accessible by selecting **Preferences...** from the **Finder** menu or by entering ⌘, (command+comma).

The pane is split into two sections. The top section lists the tags that are shown in the Tag list in the Finder Sidebar. Use the check box to the right of the Tag to add or remove it from the Sidebar. If you remove a Tag, it is still available to associate to files and folders, however it will not be displayed in the Sidebar Tag list. The **Favorite Tags** located in the bottom section lists the Tags available in for use in Finder menus. To add a Tag, drag it from the list at the top into the Favorite Tags. To remove one, drag it off the pane.

Secondary clicking on any Tag in the preference pane reveals a contextual menu allowing you to rename, delete, or assign a color to a Tag.

Search for Tags

All files associated with a Tag can be easily and quickly retrieved using the Sidebar in Finder. However, there is no easy way to find files and folders tagged with multiple Tags in the Sidebar. The only method is to perform a tag search using Spotlight.

If you have a file tagged with tag called "Taxes" and another tag called "2013," the Tag list in the Finder Sidebar will display all files and folders tagged with either Tag, but cannot display items assigned both Tags. Either tag will retrieve the files you are looking for, but, you will have to sift through the items to find the one(s) tagged with both Tags.

To find items tagged with multiple Tags, do a Spotlight search. Using our example above to find items tagged with both "Taxes" and "2013," enter the following into the Spotlight search field in the upper right of the Menu Bar. Note that "Taxes" is not case sensitive.

```
tag:taxes tag:2013
```

You can directly select the file from the list of search results in Spotlight or choose **Show All in Finder**. A Finder window containing all files meeting your search criteria will open after you select **Show All in Finder** from the list of Spotlight search results.

If you want to save the search for future use, click the **Save** button, located in the upper right below the Tabs. When you click the **Save** button, a drop-down will appear allowing you to rename the search, save it, and display it in the Sidebar. I recommend saving frequently used searches to the Sidebar so you can access them quickly and easily.

Create a Smart Folder

By saving a search you are essentially creating a **Smart Folder**. A Smart Folder is a saved search that is continuously updated as items match the search criteria. Smart Folders always remain current even as you add and delete items matching the search criteria. All items are conveniently displayed in a Smart Folder as if they were located in a single folder, regardless of where they actually reside. While the items only appear to be located in one folder, they remain safely tucked away in the folders in which you saved them.

OS X offers two ways to create a Smart Folder. The first is to select **File > New Smart Folder** from an open Finder Window or use the shortcut ⌥⌘N (option+command+N). The second method is to execute a search by selecting **File > Find**, by using the ⌘F shortcut, or by typing search criteria into the **Search** field of a Finder window.

Regardless of the method chosen to create a Smart Folder, you will first enter search criteria into the Finder **Search** field. Although you can enter any search criteria, I'll use the example from the last section and enter the following into the search field.

`tag:taxes tag:2013`

To add additional search criteria or to refine existing criteria, click the **+** button next to **Save**. Doing so reveals the search drop-down shown below. You can choose where to search with **This Mac** being the default. You also have the option of only searching within the current folder. That option is directly to the right of **This Mac**. In the picture below the current folder is **Desktop**. Clicking on **Desktop** would limit the search to only the Desktop folder. A third option is to search the **Shared** folder.

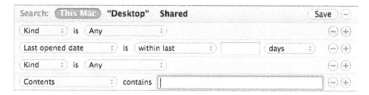

Add search criteria by clicking the **+** button. Any search line can be removed by clicking the **−** button. Clicking the **up/down** carets on any search attribute reveals a list of over 100 attributes against which you can search.

Once you have perfected the search criteria, click the **Save** button to reveal a drop-down allowing you to name your Smart Folder, save it to a folder, and add it to **Sidebar**. By default, all Smart Folders are saved to the **Saved Searches** folder, however, you can choose where to save your Smart Folder. By default, the check box next to **Add to Sidebar** is checked. Uncheck it if you do not want to save your Smart Folder to the Sidebar, otherwise your new Smart Folder will appear in the Sidebar at the bottom of the list of Favorites.

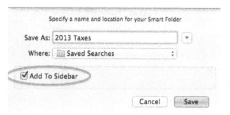

Create a Custom Shortcut to Assign Tags

Even though there are five methods to assign a tag, oddly OS X does not have a keyboard shortcut for this function. If you feel you need a sixth method, the solution is to create a custom application shortcut via the Keyboard preference pane.

To create your own keyboard shortcut to assign a tag in Finder, open the **Keyboard** preference pane by launching the System Preferences application and selecting the **Keyboard** preference pane or from the Apple menu by selecting **> System Preferences... > Keyboard**. Click on the **Shortcuts** tab.

Next, select **App Shortcuts** from the left hand pane. Click on the **+** to add a new custom keyboard shortcut. The drop-down will appear from the top of the preference pane.

Select Finder for the **Application**. Enter Tags... with exactly 3 periods after Tags into the **Menu Title** field. Next, enter your keyboard shortcut into the **Keyboard Shortcut** field. I recommend ⇧⌘T (shift+command+T) as it is easy to remember and is assigned to a rarely used command to show/hide the Tab Bar. Click **Add** when finished.

To assign a Tag to a file or folder in Finder using your keyboard shortcut, simply highlight the file or folder and enter ⇧⌘T or your chosen keyboard shortcut. The Tag menu shown to the right will appear below the file allowing you to choose an existing tag or create a new one.

Close and Open a File or Folder

Holding down the ⌥ key while clicking on a file or folder in Finder will open the item while simultaneously closing the Finder window. You can also accomplish the same thing by entering ⌥⌘O (option+command+O).

Manage Finder Tabs

Finder Tabs are a welcome feature to OS X Mavericks. By default, new Finder windows are opened in a new tab instead of an entirely new window as in previous versions of OS X. Opening new windows in a tab eliminates the clutter that eventually results when opening several folders.

To change the OS X Mavericks default to behave like previous versions of OS X, open the **Finder** preferences by selecting **Finder > Preferences...** or by entering **⌘,** (command+comma). Next, select **General** if not selected already. Uncheck the check box next to **Open folders in tabs instead of new windows**.

If you would like to open a folder in a tab, but have configured OS X to open folders in a new window, you can hold down the **⌘** (command) key while clicking on the folder to open it in a new Finder tab.

If you have multiple Finder windows open, you can merge them all into a single window with each window becoming a tab. To merge all windows, click on any Finder window then select **Window > Merge All Windows**.

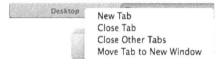

Any of the Tabs in a finder window can be moved to a separate, new window. Secondary click on the tab you want to move to a new window and select **Move Tab to New Window.**

The contextual menu revealed when secondary clicking on any tab also allows you to create a **New Tab**, **Close Tab**, or **Close Other Tabs.**

Hide the Tab Bar

The **Tab Bar** appears just below the Finder toolbar and displays all of the open tabs in Finder with the name of the folder on the tab. Like OS X folders, tabs are spring-loaded meaning the tab will expand if you drag a file or folder and hover over it until the spring load delay timer expires. Hit the **space** bar if you want to open the tab immediately. Similarly, files and folders can be dragged onto a tab to move, copy, or make an alias.

The Tab Bar can only be hidden when Finder is displaying a single tab. Once multiple tabs are opened, OS X will no longer allow you to hide the Tab Bar. To hide the Tab Bar, select **View > Hide Tab Bar** or enter **⇧⌘T** (shift+command+T). The Tab Bar will automatically unhide when a second tab is opened.

Change the Icon Size, Spacing, Arrangement, & Sort

The default icon size in OS X is 64 x 64 pixels. While this is good for most applications, you may find it too small when trying to view pictures or movies in a Finder window. OS X allows you to change the default icon size to make it smaller or larger.

To change the default icon size, click any open space in a Finder window to reveal a contextual menu. Choose **Show View Options**. Or you can select **Show View Options** from under Finder's **View** menu or enter ⌘J (command+J). The panel shown to the right will appear with the name of the folder located in the title bar at the top of the window. If the box next to **Always open in icon view** is checked, all sub-folders will open in icon view.

The next section allows you to change the arrangement of the icons and how they are sorted. Use the drop downs to choose your desired arrangement and sorting methods.

In the next section, you can change the icon size using the slider. Icons can be made as small as 16 x 16 pixels or as large as 512 x 512 pixels. The largest size is handy when sorting through a folder containing pictures or movies.

The next section allows you to change the text size for the label shown at the bottom of files and folders. The default text size is 12 points. Supported text sizes are 10, 11, 12, 13, 14, 15, and 16 points. By default, the label position is at the bottom of an item. OS X allows you to choose to display the label at the bottom or to the right of an item.

The next section contains two check boxes. The first, **Show item info**, will display the size of picture files and the length of movie files when checked. This option is unchecked by default. The second check box, **Show icon preview**, is checked by default and will provide a preview of the contents of a file. If you uncheck it, OS X will display only default icons rather than rendering previews of the content.

The next section allows you to change the background upon which icons are displayed. The default is white and you have the choice of choosing a color or a picture.

Clicking on the **Use as Defaults** button located at the bottom of the window makes your selections the default for the folder and all of its sub-folders.

Show the User Library Folder

Another new feature in Mavericks is that OS X now allows you to toggle a switch in order to make the **Library** folder in the **Home** directory visible. In previous versions of OS X, you would either have to enter a command into **Terminal** or hold down the ⌥ (option) key while selecting the Finder **Go** menu. Holding the ⌥ keydown would make a hidden option to open the Library folder appear. This option can still be used in OS X Mavericks when needed.

To make the **Library** folder in your **Home** directory visible, open **Finder** and navigate to you **Home** directory. Your Home directory is represented by an icon that looks like a house. You can also navigate quickly to your Home directory by entering ⇧⌘G (shift+command+G) and entering the following into the the the **Go to folder** dialog box. Replace *username* with your username.

/Users/*username*

Next click any open space in the Finder window showing your Home directory. Choose **Show View Options**. Or select **Show View Options** from under Finder's **View** menu or enter ⌘J. The panel shown to the right will appear. Check the check box next to **Show Library Folder** to make the user Library visible.

Change the Spring Load Delay

Try dragging a file or folder onto another folder, pausing for a moment. Suddenly the folder will spring open to reveal its contents. This is an OS X feature called spring loaded folders. Once a spring loaded folder opens, you can repeat to drill down through the directory structure until you reach your desired destination folder. The delay, the amount of time you must pause on a folder before is springs open can be tweaked or turned off all together.

To adjust the spring load delay, open the Finder preferences by selecting **Finder > Preferences...** or by entering ⌘, (command+comma). Next, select the **General** tab if not selected already. Adjust the spring load delay using the slider located at the bottom of the pane.

If you are in a hurry and don't want to wait for the spring load delay timer to expire, hit the spacebar to bypass the spring load delay and open the folder immediately.

Select the Folder Displayed in New Windows and Tabs

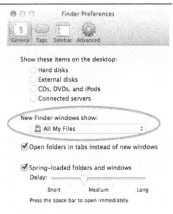

OS X displays the **All My Files** view when new **Finder** windows and tabs are opened. If you prefer new windows and tabs display another folder, such as your **Home** directory, you can set this attribute in the Finder preferences.

To set the directory location for new Finder windows and tabs, open the Finder preferences by selecting **Finder > Preferences...** or by entering ⌘, (command+comma). Next, select the **General** tab if not selected already. Use the drop-down menu under **New Finder windows show** to select your desired location. This attribute will set the location for both new Finder tabs as well as new windows.

Close All Finder Windows

Sometimes you'll end up with a lot of open Finder windows. Wouldn't it be great if there was an easy and quick way to close all of them? OS X has a solution. Hold down the ⌥ (option) key while clicking the red **Close** button in the upper left-hand corner of any Finder window. All Finder windows will close. You also can enter ⌥⌘W (option+command+W) to close all Finder windows. By the way, this trick works for any application.

Show the Path Bar

There are a number of ways to view the path taken to arrive at the folder currently displayed in Finder. You could press and hold the **Back** button in the upper left of the toolbar to display the path taken to reach the folder currently shown.

Another method is the hold the ⌘ (command) key down while clicking on the name of the folder in the title bar. This will reveal the path taken to reach the folder displayed in Finder.

Yet another method is to display the Finder **Path Bar** at the bottom of every Finder window. To turn on the Finder Path Bar, select **View > Show Path Bar** or enter ⌥⌘P (option+command+P). When the Path Bar is toggled on, every Finder window will display a Path Bar at the bottom.

To turn the Finder Path Bar off, select **View > Hide Path Bar** or enter ⌥⌘P.

Shorten the Path Bar

OS X lists the path from the root of the disk drive to the current directory, which, depending on the depth of your directory structure can result in ridiculously long paths. If most of your file browsing is done in your **Home** directory, it would be better if the path was shortened to reflect your location as it relates to your Home directory.

To shorten the path shown in the **Path Bar**, open **Terminal** and enter the following command. The change takes effect immediately.

```
defaults write com.apple.finder PathBarRootAtHome -bool TRUE

killall Finder
```

The following two pictures compare the Path Bar before and after executing the above commands. Notice the second path is quite a bit shorter.

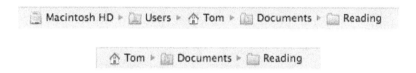

To revert to the OS X default, enter the following commands.

```
defaults delete com.apple.finder PathBarRootAtHome

killall Finder
```

Path Bar Tips & Tricks

You can drag files onto any folder listed in the **Path Bar** to move them. If you want to copy the file instead, hold down the ⌥ (option) key while dragging. To create an alias in that location in the Path Bar, hold down ⌥⌘ (option+command) while dragging. You can even drag between different Finder windows. Drag and hover your pointer over the Path Bar of the inactive Finder window and it will become active after a few moments.

You can see the contents of any folder in the **Path Bar** by double-clicking on it. Its contents will replace the items displayed in the current Finder window. If you hold down the ⌘ (command) key while double-clicking, the folder will open in a new tab. Holding down the ⌥ (option) key while double-clicking opens the folder in a new Finder window while simultaneously closing the source window or tab.

A folder can be moved by dragging it off the Path Bar and into any other folder, window, tab, onto the Desktop, or into the **Sidebar**. Holding down the down the ⌥ (option) key while dragging will make a copy of the folder while holding down ⌥⌘ (option+command) will create an alias in the new location. A folder can even be dragged within the Path Bar to move it to its new location.

If you change your mind while dragging, press the **esc** key to cancel the operation. If you change your mind after completing the move, copy, or alias creation, select **Edit > Undo** or type ⌘**Z** (command+Z) to undo.

Sometimes a path is so long that it cannot fit in the Path Bar. In that case, OS X will truncate the folder names. Pointing to a truncated folder name with expand it so you can read it.

Show the Path in the Title Bar

If you prefer to not use the Path Bar, OS X allows you to configure Finder's Title Bar to display the path. By default the Title Bar simply shows the name of the folder currently displayed. If you would like to show the path instead, open Terminal and enter the following commands. The change takes effect immediately.

```
defaults write com.apple.finder _FXShowPosixPathInTitle -bool TRUE

killall Finder
```

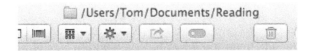

To revert back to the OS X default, enter the following commands.

```
defaults delete com.apple.finder _FXShowPosixPathInTitle

killall Finder
```

Show the Status Bar

The Finder **Status Bar** shows the number of items contained within a folder and the amount of free space left on the drive in which the folder is located.

To turn the Finder Status Bar on, select **View > Show Status Bar** or enter ⌘**/** (command+/). When the Status Bar is toggled on, every Finder window will display the Status Bar at the bottom of the window.

A handy feature of the Finder Status Bar is that it provides a slider you can use to change the size of the icons displayed in the Finder window. Slide the slider left or right to make the icons smaller or larger, respectively.

To hide the Finder Status Bar, select **View > Hide Status Bar** or enter ⌘**/** (command+/).

Show File Extensions

For those of you switching from a Microsoft Windows PC to a Mac and are worried because you miss the comfort of seeing those 3- and 4-letter file extensions after every filename, OS X allows you to turn on file extensions. By default, OS X turns them off.

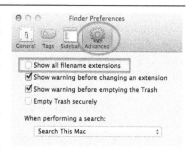

To show file extensions, open the Finder preferences by selecting **Finder > Preferences...** or by entering ⌘**,** (command+comma). Next, select the **Advanced** tab if not selected already. Check the check box next to **Show all filename extensions**.

Note that OS X will also warn you if you change a filename extension. To turn off this warning, uncheck the check box next to **Show warning before changing an extension**. However, changing a file extension could make a file unusable.

Quickly Duplicate a File

OS X offers a number of methods to duplicate a file. You can select a file in Finder, secondary click to reveal the contextual menu and choose **Duplicate**. Or you could select **File > Duplicate**. A quicker method is the hold down the ⌥ (option) key and drag the file to a blank space in Finder and release.

Cut & Paste Files

There are a few things that freak out Microsoft Windows users who are moving to a Mac. First, there is no right mouse button (there isn't a left either). Second, the **delete** key on a Mac keyboard acts like the backspace key on a PC. So how do you delete? Hold down the **fn** key while pressing **delete**. Third, OS X doesn't display file extensions by default, proving that learning the difference between all of those 3- and 4-letter file extensions was a terrible waste of your time. Fourth, windows do not have scroll bars. You'll see what to do about that next. Finally, the **Cut** command and ⌘**X** doesn't work in Finder. OMG! How do you cut and paste a file?

No need to panic. Since OS X is based on the UNIX operating system, there is no concept of cut and paste. Cut and paste is equivalent to a move in OS X. To accomplish a cut and paste, you would move a file by dragging and dropping it in its new location. But if you really, really can't live without cut and paste, there is a workaround.

Select the file in Finder, then copy it by selecting **Edit > Copy** or by entering ⌘C. Navigate to the file's new location and hold down the ⌥ key while selecting the **Edit** menu. When the ⌥ key is held down, **Paste Item** will become **Move Item Here**. You can also enter ⌥⌘**V** (option+command+V) to move the file. This effectively is the same thing as a cut and paste in the PC world. Moving a file is so much easier.

Change the Scroll Bars

By default, scroll bars only appear when you are actually scrolling in OS X. This is very different from Microsoft Windows where scroll bars are a permanent fixture on the right edge of every window. If you are a former Windows PC user and really miss your scroll bars, OS X can be configured so those ugly scroll bars are permanently fixed to the right and bottom edges of every OS X window.

To change the behavior of the scroll bars, open the **General** preference pane by launching the System Preferences application and selecting the **General** icon or from the Apple menu by selecting **> System Preferences... > General**. Next, click **Mouse & Trackpad** in the left-hand pane.

When set to **Automatically based on mouse or trackpad**, scrollbars will not appear unless the document requires scrollbars and you have placed either one finger on the mouse or two fingers on a trackpad in preparation to scroll.

If you like your scroll bars hidden until you are actually scrolling, choose **When scrolling**. Once you're done scrolling, the scrollbars will hide themselves. If you are suffering from scroll bar separation anxiety, select **Always.**

Microsoft made sure that former PC users would not suffer from scrollbar separation anxiety by ensuring its Microsoft Office Suite for Mac by including ugly scroll bars permanently affixed to the right edge of every Office document

You have two options for clicking within a scroll bar – to **Jump to the next page**, which is the default behavior, or to **Jump to the spot that's clicked**. When **Jump to the next page** is selected, clicking within the scroll bar will page up or page down a single page at a time.

When **Jump to the spot that's clicked** is selected, clicking within the scroll bar will take you to that spot in the document. For example, clicking the very bottom of the scroll bar will take you to the end of a document. Clicking ¼ of the way down the scroll bar, will allow you to jump about a quarter way through the document. This can be a handy feature when you need to navigate quickly through a long document.

Remove Scrolling Inertia

OS X mimics the scrolling experience of iOS devices where a flick of your fingers causes the window to scroll rapidly. This feature is called **Scrolling Inertia** and is on by default. Flicking your fingers across a trackpad or Magic Mouse will cause the window to scroll rapidly. Compared to normal scrolling, it appears the window was scrolling about 100 mph. If you don't like Scrolling Inertia, OS X allows you to turn it off.

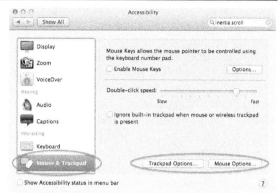

To turn off Scrolling Inertia, open the **Accessibility** preference pane by launching the System Preferences application and selecting the **Accessibility** icon or from the Apple menu by selecting **> System Preferences... > Accessibility**. Next, select **Mouse & Trackpad** in the left-hand pane. To turn off Scrolling Inertia on a trackpad, click **Trackpad Options...** To turn off Scrolling Inertia on a mouse click **Mouse Options...**

Both the trackpad and mouse options will reveal a drop-down configuration dialog box. **Do not uncheck** the box next to **Scrolling** as it will turn off scrolling for the device chosen. Instead, use the drop-down menu next to **Scrolling** to select **without inertia**. Click the **Done** button when finished.

Scrolling Inertia can also be turned off using the following Terminal command. Both methods provide the same result. Log out and back in for the change to take effect.

```
defaults write -g AppleMomentumScrollSupported -bool FALSE
```

To revert back to the OS X default and turn Scrolling Inertia on, enter the following command in **Terminal**. Log out and back in for the change to take effect.

```
defaults delete -g AppleMomentumScrollSupported
```

Change the Scrolling Speed

OS X allows you to change the speed at which you scroll through documents. If you find the default setting too slow or too fast you can tweak it until you get the scroll speed just right.

To change the scrolling speed, open the **Accessibility** preference pane by launching the System Preferences application and selecting the **Accessibility** icon or from the Apple menu by selecting > **System Preferences... > Accessibility**. Next, select **Mouse & Trackpad** in the left-hand pane. Click **Trackpad Options...** or **Mouse Options...** to configure the scrolling speed on each device.

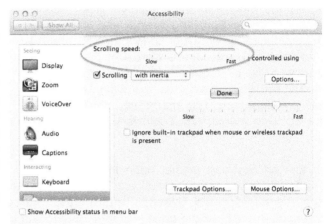

Both the trackpad and mouse options will reveal a drop-down configuration dialog box. Use the slider at the top of the dialog box to adjust the scrolling speed. Click the **Done** button when finished.

Smoother Scrolling

Dragging a file to the top or bottom of a Finder window in **Column** or **List** view can create a rather herky-jerky scrolling experience as the window often scrolls a little bit then stops and restarts. There also seems to be a short delay before Finder begins scrolling.

This OS X tweak provides much smoother and responsive scrolling and eliminates the delay. Open **Terminal** and enter the following commands. The change will take effect immediately.

```
defaults write com.apple.finder NSDraggingAutoscrollDelay -int 0

killall Finder
```

To revert back to the default OS X scrolling, enter the following commands in **Terminal**. The change takes effect immediately

```
defaults delete com.apple.finder NSDraggingAutoscrollDelay

killall Finder
```

Change the Search Scope

When using the search function in **Finder**, OS X searches your entire Mac by default. OS X allows you to change the default search scope to limit it to the currently displayed folder or a previous search scope.

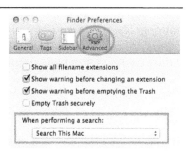

To change the search scope, open the Finder preferences by selecting **Finder > Preferences...** or by entering ⌘, (command+comma). Next, select the **Advanced** tab, if not selected already. Use the drop-down menu under **When performing a search** to select your desired default scope.

Remove the Empty Trash Warning

Every time you empty the **Trash**, OS X asks you if you are sure you want to permanently erase the items in the Trash. If you find this warning unnecessary or annoying, OS X allows you to turn it off.

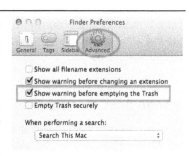

To tell OS X to stop confirming that you want to empty the Trash, open the Finder preferences by selecting **Finder > Preferences...** or by entering ⌘, (command+comma). Next, select the **Advanced** tab if not selected already. Next, uncheck the check box next to **Show warning before emptying the Trash**.

Quiet the Trash

OS X makes a noise that sounds like the crinkling of paper when emptying the **Trash**. This can be annoying if you're working in a quiet office environment or are listening to music. The sound of the trash emptying can disturb your concentration or the concentration of others.

To quiet the Trash when emptying, open Terminal and enter the following commands. The change takes effect immediately.

```
defaults write com.apple.finder FinderSounds -bool FALSE

killall Finder
```

Enter the following commands in Terminal to revert to the OS X default. The change takes effect immediately.

```
defaults delete com.apple.finder FinderSounds

killall Finder
```

Calculate Folder Sizes

When you're viewing items in **List View** in **Finder**, you will notice that only files have an entry under the **Size** column. By default, OS X does not calculate the size of folders. Therefore, you will see a pair of dashes in the size column for all folders.

If you would like to see the amount of disk space your folders are taking up, you need to tell OS X to **Calculate all sizes**.

To turn on this feature, select **View > Show View Options** from the Finder View menu or enter **⌘J** to display View Options preference pane. Check the check box next to **Calculate all sizes**.

This attribute is set on a per-folder basis. So if you would like to make this the default for all folders click the **Use as Defaults** button at the bottom of the preference pane. However, be careful to ensure that the other attributes on the preference pane are set to properly display folders as you would like to see them.

Change the Columns Displayed in List View

OS X displays the following three columns in the **Finder List View**: **Date Modified**, **Size**, and **Kind**. The Finder List View also supports other attributes such as Date Created, Date Last Opened, Date Added, Version, Comments, and Tags.

To change the columns shown in the Finder List View, select **View > Show View Options** from the Finder View menu or enter **⌘J** to display the View Options preference pane. Check the check boxes next to the items you wish to display in **List View**.

Multiple Item Inspector

The Get Info feature provides lots of information about a file. If you select multiple files and choose **File > Get Info** or enter **⌘I**, OS X will open a Get Info pane for each file selected. That might not be what you intended if you wanted to see the combined size of a group of files.

To launch the **Multiple Item Inspector** window, hold down the ⌥ (option) key while selecting **File > Show Inspector** or enter ⌥⌘I (option+command+i). Additional files can be added to an open Multiple Item Inspector window by holding down the ⌘ (command) key while clicking on them. The Multiple Item Inspector will dynamically update as new files are added.

Change the Title Bar Font & Size

Finder utilizes the Lucida Grande font in its **Title Bar** like other OS X applications. If you would like to change the font used in the Title Bar of Finder windows to your favorite font, enter the following commands in **Terminal**.

```
defaults write com.apple.finder NSTitleBarFont -string Times
```

```
killall Finder
```

I specified the **Times** font. Feel free to replace **Times** with your favorite. If your favorite font consists of multiple words, remove the spaces in the name. For example, you would enter **Times New Roman** as **TimesNewRoman**.

You can also change the size of the Title Bar font. To change the font size, enter the following commands in **Terminal**.

```
defaults write com.apple.finder NSTitleBarFontSize 14
```

```
killall Finder
```

To revert back to the OS X defaults, enter the following commands in **Terminal**.

```
defaults delete com.apple.finder NSTitleBarFont
```

```
defaults delete com.apple.finder NSTitleBarFontSize
```

```
killall Finder
```

Change the Default Font

Finder utilizes the Lucida Grande font like all other OS X applications. If you would like to do a little bit of personalization, this tweak will change the font used in both the Title Bar and in the file and folder name labels. This hack works on all Finder views except **Icon View**.

To change the default font for Finder, enter the following commands in **Terminal**.

```
defaults write com.apple.finder NSSystemFont -string Times
```

```
killall Finder
```

I specified the **Times** font. Feel free to replace **Times** with your favorite. If your favorite font consists of multiple words, remove the spaces in the name. For example, you would enter **Times New Roman** as **TimesNewRoman**.

To revert back to the OS X default font, enter the following commands in **Terminal**.

```
defaults delete com.apple.finder NSSystemFont
```

```
killall Finder
```

Increase the Window Resize Area

Any application window can be resized by hovering your pointer over any of its borders until the pointer changes to a double headed arrow resizing cursor. The area in which the pointer changes to the resizing cursor is quite thin and it is sometimes difficult to get the pointer in exactly the right spot to make the resizing cursor appear.

This hack will increase the size of the area in which the pointer will change into the resizing cursor. Open **Terminal** and enter the following command. You will need to logout and log back in again for the change to take effect.

```
defaults write -g AppleEdgeResizeExteriorSize 15
```

Feel free to try different numbers at the end of the command to make the area larger or smaller as you see fit.

To revert back to the OS X default, enter the following command in **Terminal**. You will have to logout and log back in for the change to take effect.

```
defaults delete -g AppleEdgeResizeExteriorSize
```

Quick Look

Quick Look is an OS X feature allowing you to preview any file by highlighting it and pressing **space** or with a three finger tap on the trackpad. Once you're previewing a file, you can double-click on the window to launch the file in the application in which was created. The **Share** button located at the top right of the preview window allows you to share the file via **Messages**, **Mail**, or **AirDrop**. You can even use Quick Look to preview items located in a Stack in the Dock or in a Spotlight search results list. Did you receive an attachment or URL that e-mail? You can preview it using Quick Look. Use the **space** bar or a three finger tap on the trackpad to close a Quick Look preview. You can even delete a file from a Quick Look preview. Hold down the ⌘ (command) key while pressing the **delete** key to delete a file while previewing it.

Select Text in Quick Look

The one thing that **Quick Look** doesn't seem to allow you to do is to select text in order to copy it to another document. To do so requires launching the file in the application that created it, selecting the text, copying it, and closing the file. This hack will allow you to directly select text in a **Quick Look** preview window. This is a great timesaver because you no longer have to open a file in order to select text.

To enable text selection in **Quick Look**, enter the following commands in **Terminal**. The change takes effect immediately.

```
defaults write com.apple.finder QLEnableTextSelection -bool TRUE

killall Finder
```

Highlight text by dragging across it with your pointer and copy it by selecting **Edit > Copy** or entering ⌘**C** (command+C). You can also select all text in the document by selecting **Edit > Select All** or entering ⌘**A** (command+A).

Note that with this tweak turned on, you will have to click and drag in the Title Bar instead of the default of clicking and dragging anywhere in the preview to move a file in Quick Look.

To revert back to the OS X default, into the following commands in **Terminal**. The change takes effect immediately.

```
defaults delete com.apple.finder QLEnableTextSelection

killall Finder
```

Take Quick Look to Full-Screen with a Gesture

This is a nice little tweak that will let you switch **Quick Look** preview to full-screen mode by swiping up with two fingers on a trackpad or Magic Mouse. To enable this tweak, enter the following commands in **Terminal**. Note that the first two lines are a single command. Do not press the **return** key until you have entered both lines. The change takes effect immediately.

```
defaults write com.apple.finder QLPreviewFakeMagnifyWithScrollwheel
-bool TRUE

killall Finder
```

To revert back to the OS X default, open **Terminal** and enter the following commands. Note that the first two lines are a single command. Do not press the **return** key until you have entered both lines. This change takes effect immediately.

```
defaults delete com.apple.finder
QLPreviewFakeMagnifyWithScrollwheel

killall Finder
```

Clip Text

OS X offers a handy text clipping feature that allows you to highlight text in almost any application and drag it onto the desktop or to a folder. OS X immediately creates a Rich Text Format (RTF) file using the first few words of the text as the filename. To view your clipped text, use **Quick Look** or double-click on the file to open it.

If you want to insert your text clipping into a document, simply drag the file onto the document window and position where you want the text inserted before releasing. The text clipping remains available for other uses until you delete the file.

Eliminate .DS Store Files

If you share a network drive between your Mac and PC, you may notice small **.DS Store** files littered across the directory structure when using your PC. You don't see them when using your Mac because they are hidden files which contain data about the directory. However, they are not essential and you can configure OS X to stop saving .DS Store files to network drives.

To stop OS X from writing .DS Store files to network drives, open **Terminal** and enter the following command. Press the **return** key after entering the entire command. Log out and log back in for the change to take effect.

```
defaults write com.apple.desktopservices DSDontWriteNetworkStores –
bool TRUE
```

To revert back to the OS X default, enter the following command in **Terminal**.

```
defaults delete com.apple.desktopservices DSDontWriteNetworkStores
```

Log out and log back in for the change to take effect.

Move Your Home Directory

OS X creates your home directory on the start up drive under a folder called **Users**. If you have a large number of large files such as movies or if your start up drive is a lower capacity solid-state drive (SSD), it may be advantageous for you to move your **Home** directory to another drive in your system. If anything were to happen to your primary drive and you have to erase and reinstall OS X, your **Home** directory will remain safely tucked away on another drive.

While it is safe to move your **Home** directory, do not move the **Applications**, **Library**, or **System** folders. Moving any of these other three folders is a very bad idea. OS X expects these folders to reside on the start up drive.

First note that you must have multiple internal drives before attempting to move your **Home** directory. For example, if you have a MacBook Pro with a single internal drive, moving your Home directory to an external drive will do you no good when you're traveling because you won't have access to the external drive. If you have multiple internal drives (I have two SSDs in my MacBook Pro), you may want to move your Home directory in order to gain more space.

First, it is an excellent idea to ensure that you have a current **Time Machine** back up in case anything goes wrong so you can restore your Mac to good working order. Once you have a good Time Machine backup, you'll copy your **Home** directory to its new location. Be sure to copy and not move your **Home** directory. Once you're sure that your new Home directory is working properly, you can go back later and delete your old Home directory to reclaim its space or archive it to an external drive.

Once you have finished copying your **Home** directory to its new location, open the **Users & Groups** preference pane by launching the System Preferences application and selecting the **Users & Groups** icon or from the Apple menu by selecting > **System Preferences...** > **Users & Groups**. Unlock the preference pane by clicking on the padlock in the lower left-hand corner. Enter your password when prompted.

Find your name in the list of users in the left-hand pane and secondary click on it. Select **Advanced Options...** to reveal a drop-down dialog box.

Look for the **Home directory** field halfway down the dialog box. Click the **Choose...** button to the far right of the **Home directory** field. Navigate to the new location of your Home directory and click the **Open** button to select it. Verify that the correct path to your new home directory is listed in the **Home directory** field. If it is correct, click **OK** and close the preference pane.

Do not change any other items on the Advanced pane other than the Home Directory path. Changing other items can cause major problems that require reinstallation of OS X or restoration from Time Machine to fix.

Restart your Mac and verify that everything is working properly. As an added precaution, I recommend you open the **Disk Utility** application and verify and repair disk permissions just to be safe. If **Verify Disk Permissions** is grayed out, click **Verify Disk**. Once the disk has been verified, click **Repair Disk**, if necessary.

Move a Time Machine Backup to a New Drive

After backing up with **Time Machine** for a while, it is inevitable that you will run out of disk space. While Time Machine will automatically delete old backups to make room for newer data, you will lose old data that you may want to save. When this time comes, and believe me it will come faster than you think, you'll probably buy a larger backup drive and will want to transfer your existing Time Machine backup to your new drive. Doing so, isn't as simple as copying your backup from your old drive to your new one.

Transferring a Time Machine backup is a multi-step process.
1. Connect you new drive to your Mac.
2. If your new drive contains any data, copy it to another drive as you are going to format this drive.
3. Launch **Disk Utility**. You can find the Disk Utility application by searching for it in **Launchpad**.
4. Select the external drive in the left-hand pane. Click on the **Partition** tab at the top of the preference pane. Choose **1 Partition** as the **Partition Layout**. Next, click the **Options** button to reveal a drop-down configuration page.

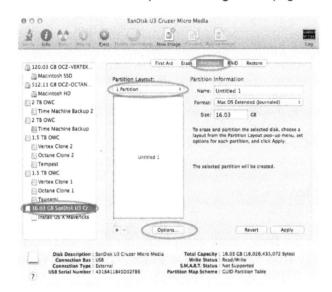

5. From the drop-down configuration menu select **GUID Partition Table**. Click **OK**.

6. On the main Disk Utility window, make sure that **Mac OS Extended (Journaled)** is selected in the **Format** field. Click **Apply**. OS X will partition, format, and prepare your drive.

7. Open **Finder** and secondary click on your new backup drive in Sidebar and select **Get Info** to open the device information pane.

8. Ensure that **Ignore ownership on this volume** under **Sharing & Permissions** is not checked. If it is checked, click the little padlock, enter your password when prompted, and uncheck this check box.

9. Open the **Time Machine** preference pane by launching the System Preferences application and select the **Time Machine** icon or from the Apple menu by selecting **> System Preferences... > Time Machine**.

10. Slide the Time Machine switch to the **Off** position.

11. Open two windows or tabs in **Finder**, one for the old backup drive and the other for your new backup drive.

12. Drag the **Backups.backupdb** folder from your old drive to your new drive. Enter your username and password when prompted. Copying your existing backup will take some time depending on the size of the Backups.backupdb folder.

13. Once the Finder has finished copying the **Backups.backupdb** folder to your new backup drive, open the Time Machine preference pane again.

14. Click **Add or Remove Backup Disk** in the Time Machine preference pane.

15. Highlight your new drive and **Select Disk...**, and click **Use Backup Disk**.

16. Slide the Time Machine switch back to the **On** position.

Kill the Spinning Rainbow Pinwheel of Death

Occasionally **Finder** will crash or get hung and you will experience Apple's spinning rainbow pinwheel of death. Finder will become completely unresponsive as the rainbow pinwheel defiantly spins and mocks you as you twiddle your thumbs hoping it disappears. Sometimes you just have to kill the darn thing.

To kill the pinwheel, relaunch Finder by holding down the ⌥ (option) key and secondary clicking on the Finder icon in the Dock. A contextual menu will appear with the option to **Relaunch** Finder.

Sometimes Finder is so hosed that you will have to switch to another desktop space to make this command work.

An alternate method is to select **> Force Quit...** and choose Finder from the list of applications. Click the **Relaunch** button to kill the spinning pinwheel. You can also display the Force Quit dialog by entering ⌥⌘**esc** (option+command+esc).

Die, rainbow pinwheel, die!

Add a Quit Command

Finder is the one application that you simply can't quit as it is designed to always run. The reason for this is that Finder is responsible for managing the OS X file system. If you check out the **Finder** menu you will not find a **Quit** command. That is because other than relaunching Finder through **Force Quit** or with a **killall Finder** command, Finder must run continuously.

So why would you want to add a **Quit** command to the **Finder** menu? Having a Quit option in the **Finder** menu an easy way to execute the **killall Finder** command.

Open **Terminal** and enter the following commands to add a **Quit** command to Finder's **File** menu.

```
defaults write com.apple.finder QuitMenuItem -bool TRUE
```

```
killall Finder
```

Now you can select **Finder > Quit** or enter ⌘Q to quit Finder. To restart Finder, you will have to click on its icon in the Dock.

To revert back to the OS X default and remove the Quit command from the **Finder** menu, enter the following commands in **Terminal**.

```
defaults delete com.apple.finder QuitMenuItem
```

```
killall Finder
```

13

Window Snapping

There is one feature I miss when switching between my Windows PC at work and my MacBook Pro at home – Microsoft's window snapping feature. Drag a window to the right edge of the screen and it will snap to exactly half the size of your desktop. Drag another window to the left edge and it will snap to the other half. This feature is great when comparing two documents. Another nice feature is the ability to maximize a window by dragging it to the top of the desktop. I know I can maximize a window with the green full screen button, but doing so hides the Menu Bar and the Dock. Often it's more productive to not have to unhide the Menu Bar or the Dock. Luckily there is an application in the Mac App Store that offers window snapping and like everything on a Mac, it is more powerful and more fully featured than Microsoft's implementation.

 BetterSnapTool is a full featured, highly customizable window snapping tool available for $1.99 on the Mac App Store. As I write this sentence, the current version has 111 five-star ratings and 2,198 five-star ratings for all versions. Written by Andreas Hegenberg, BetterSnapTool allows you to instantly change the size of your windows simply by dragging them to the top, left, or right edge, or the 4 corners of your desktop.

Similar to Microsoft's window snapping feature, you can snap a window to the left edge and another to the right edge of your desktop to compare two documents side-by-side. Windows can be maximized by dragging them to the top edge of the desktop. This differs from OS X's maximize function as the Menu Bar and Dock do not hide when using BetterSnapTool.

Everything is just better on a Mac, even window snapping. BetterSnapTool lets you create your own custom Snap Areas anywhere on your desktop and it supports 19 different window resizing and snapping options. It also allows you to create keyboard shortcuts to move and resize windows.

The description on the Mac App Store states that, "BetterSnapTool is very customizable and will change the way you work with your Mac!" I couldn't agree more. I recommend you download it from the Mac App Store now. Buying this productivity tool was probably the best $1.99 I've spent on any application for my Mac.

Enable Snap Areas

By default, BetterSnapTool is pre-configured to snap to 7 locations on your desktop. Snapping a window to the top maximizes it without hiding the Menu Bar and the Dock. Snapping a window to the left or right edge of the desktop, pins the window to the selected edge and resizes it to take up half the desktop. Snapping a window to any of the desktop's four corners pins it to the corner and resizes it to take up a quarter of the desktop.

BetterSnapTool will provide a preview of how the window will resize when the pointer touches the corner or edge of the desktop. Drag and hold a window. Releasing your hold will cause the window to resize. If you don't release your hold, you can drag the window off the edge or corner and release to cancel the resizing.

To open the BetterSnapTool preference pane, click on its Menu Extra in the Menu Bar and select **Preferences**. Click on **General Settings**, if not already highlighted.

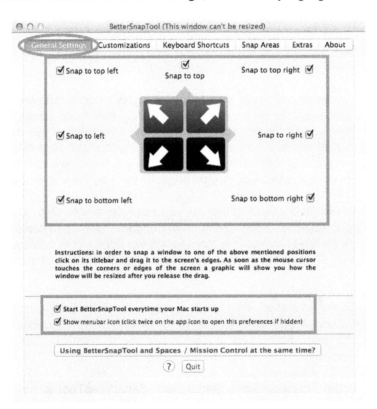

The top part of the preference pane shows the seven snap locations with a check in each check box indicating they are active. Uncheck any check box next to a snap location you do not want to use.

The two check boxes at the bottom of the pane are checked by default. The **Start BetterSnapTool everytime your Mac starts up** ensures that BetterSnapTool is available for you every time you restart your Mac. If you uncheck this box, you'll have to manually launch the application everytime you want to use it.

The check box next to **Show menubar icon** toggles the Menu Extra on and off. This provides easy access to the BetterSnapTool preference pane. Once you have completely configured BetterSnapTool to your liking, you can uncheck this box to remove the Menu Extra, if desired. To access the preferences again, launch BetterSnapTool from Launchpad, Spotlight, or from your Applications folder or stack.

Do not press the **Quit** button at the botton of the preference pane as it quits the application. To close the preference pane, click on the red close button in the upper left.

Clicking the button labeled **Using BetterSnapTool and Spaces / Mission Control at the same time?** opens a window with instructions on how to adjust the drag delay when dragging windows to another desktop space located to the left or right of your active desktop space. The issue here is that too small a delay will interfere with BetterSnapTool's ability to snap to the left or right edge. If the delay is too small, the desktop space will change as OS X assumes you want to move the window to another space. The recommendation is to set the window edge delay between desktop spaces to 2 seconds, giving you sufficient time to drag a window to the left or right edge and release your hold to resize. If you want to drag the window to an adjacent desktop space, simply hold the window along the edge until the window edge delay timer expires and the desktop space changes. BetterSnapTool will preview the window resize, but will not resize the window unless you release your hold. There is an error in the instructions, though. You must enter an additional command for the change to take effect.

To adjust the drag delay between spaces, open Terminal and enter the following commands.

```
defaults write com.apple.dock workspaces-edge-delay -float 2

killall Dock
```

This will adjust the delay timer to 2 seconds. I've used BetterSnapTool for a long time and I've found a 1 second delay works fine for me. You can adjust the time by changing the number after **-float** in the first command to find the right delay that works best for you. Decimals are allowed so you can try 1.5 or 2.5 seconds. Setting the number to 0 completely removes the workspace edge delay and effectively eliminates the edges of your desktop as snap areas for BetterSnapTool.

For more information on the workspace edge delay timer, see the section "Drag an Application Window To Another Space" on page 39.

Customizing the Preview Overlay

When you drag a window to one of the snap locations configured in the **General Settings** tab, BetterSnapTool provides a preview overlay to show you what the window will look like when resized. If you don't like the default of a white border and gray background, you can change these settings as well as the border width, corners, and animation.

Select **Preferences** from the BetterSnapTool Menu Extra in the Menu Bar. If you chose to not show the Menu Extra, launch BetterSnapTool from Launchpad, Spotlight, or from your Applications folder or App Stack. Click on **Customizations** if it is not already highlighted.

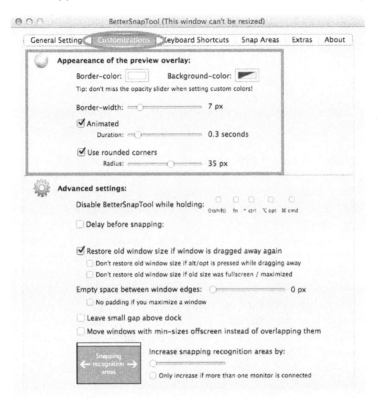

Clicking the white box next to **Border-color** launches a color wheel allowing you to change the color of the border around the preview overlay. To change the preview overlay background from the default, click the black/gray box next to **Background-color**. Similarly, you will be presented with a color wheel to select your desired background color.

You can customize the width of the preview overlay border using the slider next to **Border-width**. Valid widths are from 0 to 50 pixels with the default being 7 pixels. You can also click on **7 px** to directly enter the width in the box provided.

The corners of the preview overlay border are rounded with a default radius of 35 pixels. You can use the slider next to **Use rounded corners** to change the radius to any value between 0 and 60 pixels. Similar to the border width, you can click on **35 px** to directly enter the width in the box provided. Unchecking the check box changes the preview overlay corners to 90-degree angles.

The preview overlay's animation duration can be adjusted from 0 to 2 seconds with the default being 0.3 seconds. The duration is how long it takes the preview overlay to expand to show you how the window will resize. Unchecking the check box next to **Animation** disables the preview overlay animation. In this case, BetterSnapTool will instantly show you how the window will resize when you drag a window to a snap location.

Temporarily Disable Window Snapping

You can configure a modifier key or combination of modifier keys to temporarily disable BetterSnapTool. This is handy if you intend to drag a window to another desktop space and don't want BetterSnapTool to engage. You can choose any one or a combination of the following modifier keys: ⇧ **fn** ^ ⌥ ⌘ (shift, function, control, option, command).

To configure modifier keys to temporarily disable BetterSnapTool, open the BetterSnapTool preference pane and click on **Customizations** if not already highlighted. Check the check boxes above your desired modifier keys in the **Advanced settings** section.

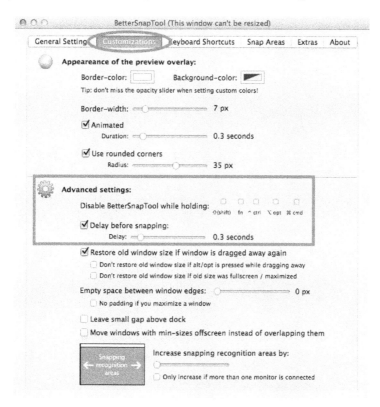

Configure the Snap Delay

By default, BetterSnapTool displays the preview overlay animation the moment your pointer touches a defined Snap Area. If you would like to add a delay before the preview overlay is displayed, open the BetterSnapTool preference pane and click on **Customizations** if not already highlighted. Check the check box next to **Delay before snapping** to reveal a slider that supports values between 0 and 2 seconds. You can also click on the **second** box to directly enter the delay.

Be careful setting this delay timer as it can conflict with the workspace edge delay between desktop spaces. If the workspace edge delay is set to a smaller delay than the snap delay, BetterSnapTool will never display the preview overlay. The workspace edge delay timer will expire and your window will be moved to the adjacent desktop space.

Disable Window Size Restoration

After resizing a window with BetterSnapTool, you can resize it back to its original size by dragging it away from the Snap Area. For example, if you resized a window to occupy half your desktop by dragging it to the right edge, dragging it away will restore it to its original size. This function is enabled by default. However, a notable exception is Microsoft Office (of course), which will not resize back to its original size.

To disable window size restoration, open the BetterSnapTool preference pane and click on **Customizations** if not already highlighted. Uncheck the check box next to **Restore old window size if window is dragged away again.**

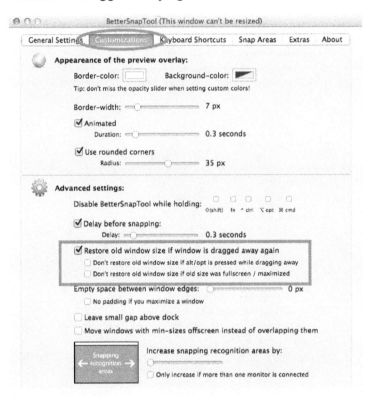

Another option is to disable window size restoration when pressing the ⌥ (option) key. To enable this feature, check the box next to **Don't restore old window size if alt/opt is pressed while dragging away**.

Another available option is to disable window size restoration when the original window size was full screen or maximized. To enable this feature, check the check box next to **Don't restore old window size if old size was fullscreen / maximized**.

Add Padding Around Windows & the Dock

By default, BetterSnapTool leaves no space between the edge of the desktop and the window when resizing. BetterSnapTool allows you to configure the amount of padding around a window after it is resized.

If you would like some padding around a window, open the BetterSnapTool preference pane and click on **Customizations** if not already highlighted. Use the slider next to **Empty space between window edges** to select a value between 0 and 100 pixels. You can click on the **0 px** to directly enter the padding size in the box provided. Note that the padding will be applied around all four sides of the window.

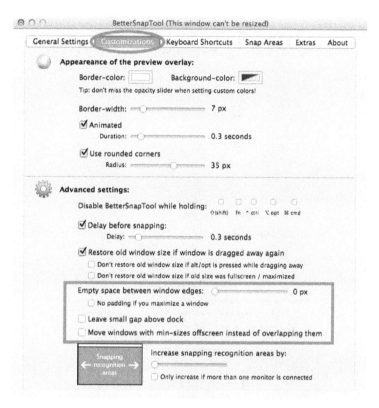

You can check the check box next to **No padding if you maximize a window** to avoid adding padding around maximized windows. If you do not check this option and have padding configured, windows will not fully maximize as they will be surrounded on all sides by the padding configured by the slider.

By default, BetterSnapTool will not resize a window over the Dock. You can increase the separation between the bottom edge of a window and the Dock by checking the box next to **Leave small gap above dock** and moving the slider to your desired gap. Valid entries are 0 to 10 pixels. Similar to other configuration items, you can click the setting and directly enter a value into the configuration box.

A final option is to ensure windows with minimum sizes do not overlap. When this option is enabled, minimum sized windows will be pushed off screen.

Increase the Snap Recognition Area

BetterSnapTool will play the preview overlay animation or resize a window the moment your pointer reaches an active Snap Area. You can increase the snap recognition area up to 100 pixels (the default is 0). The increased snap recognition area means that you will no longer have to move your pointer all the way to the edge of an active Snap Area. You only have to move your pointer near it.

To increase the snap recognition area, open the BetterSnapTool preference pane and click on **Customizations** if not already highlighted. Use the slider next to **Increase snapping recognition areas by** to select a value between 0 and 100 pixels.

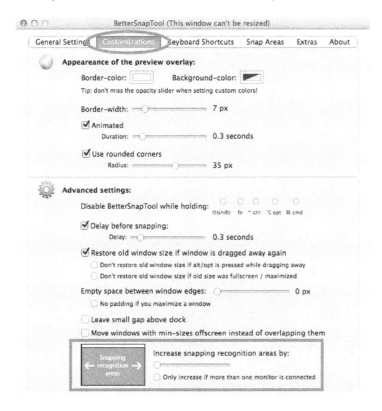

If you have a multiple monitor system, you will have to configure a larger snap recognition area in order for BetterSnapTool to resize windows dragged to the edge of the desktop. In a dual monitor setup, you will notice that only one edge resizes windows. Dragging a window to the opposite edge of the desktop moves the window to the other monitor. By increasing the snap recognition area, BetterSnapTool will resize the window without the pointer actually having to touch the edge of the desktop.

You can configure larger snap recognition areas to enable only when more than one monitor is connected. This is handy if you have a MacBook Pro or MacBook Air and are using it in a dual monitor setup. When docked in dual monitor mode the larger snap recognition area is enabled. When undocked, the larger snap recognition area is disabled. Check the box next to **Only increase if more than one monitor is connected** to enable this option.

Create a Pop-up Window Resizing Menu

BetterSnapTool supports a total of 19 window resizing options. Only 7 of the options are available by dragging a window to a snap recognition area. The additional 12 window resizing options can only be accessed by configuring BetterSnapTool to display its pop-up resizing menu using a keyboard shortcut.

To access the 12 additional resizing options, open the BetterSnapTool preference pane and click on **Keyboard Shortcuts** if not already highlighted. Choose your desired keyboard shortcut in the **Click to record shortcut** box next to **show menu with all selected actions**. You can optionally check the box next to **also duplicate the menubar preferences to this menu**. This option tacks the menu from BetterSnapTool's Menu Extra to the pop-up resizing menu.

To use the pop-up menu to resize a window, hover your pointer over the window you want to resize and enter the keyboard shortcut you configured. The pop-up resizing menu will appear. All you need to do is select your desired resizing choice.

BetterSnapTool lets you configure which resizing options are displayed on the pop-up resizing menu. Uncheck the options you don't want to appear. You can optionally assign keyboard shortcuts to any or all of the resizing options.

Create Custom Snap Areas

If 19 resizing options and 7 Snap Areas aren't enough for you, BetterSnapTool offers virtually limitless resizing and Snap Area options through an advanced feature called **Snap Areas**. This feature allows you to define a specific window size and a customized snap recognition area.

Creating a custom Snap Area is a multi-step process.

1. Resize an arbitrary window to the desired position and size. Make sure this window is the active window.
2. Click on the BetterSnapTool Menu Extra and select **Snap Areas (Advanced Feature)**.
3. Select **Create New Snap Area (Use Active Window As Template)**.
4. BetterSnapTool will enter editing mode. The active window will be grayed out and bordered by a dotted red line. A dialog box will appear in the center of your monitor instructing you to click the box to define a new Snap Area.

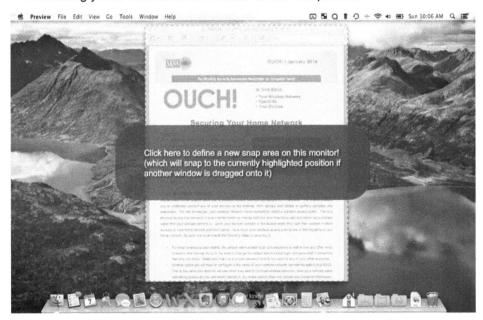

5. The blue Snap Area box shown below will appear on your desktop. Resize it using the resizing handles and move it to the area of your desktop where you want your Snap Area to be located.

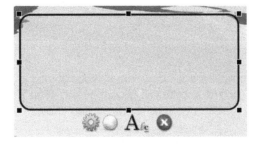

6. There are four tools under the Snap Area. From left to right, the first tool (the one that looks like a gear) allows you to require one or more of the following modifier

keys: ⇧ **fn** ^ ⌥ ⌘ (shift, function, control, option, command) to be held down to show the custom Snap Area. Configuring this option will prevent the Snap Area from displaying every time you move a window. You can also configure BetterSnapTool to display the Snap Area only when a window from a specific application or set of applications are being moved.

7. The color wheel tool allows you to select the background and border colors. You can also configure border type and width and corner radius if you do not like the defaults. There is also an option to make the Snap Area invisible. When invisible, the Snap Area will only appear when you hover over it with your pointer. Finally, the tool lets you configure the length of the preview overlay animation.

8. You can add custom text to your Snap Area with the text tool.

9. Clicking the **X** in the last tool will delete the Snap Area and exit edit mode without creating your custom Snap Area.

10. Once you have finished configuring the Snap Area options, enter ⌘**W** (command+W) or click the gray box in the center of your desktop to exit edit mode. Your custom Snap Area is now ready to use.

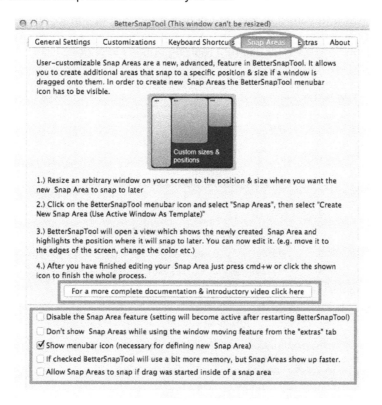

To access a video showing how to create a custom Snap Area, open the BetterSnapTool preference pane and click on **Snap Areas** if not already highlighted. Click the introductory video button. Your default browser will open and will navigate to the page containing the video. There are also 5 additional configuration options at the bottom of this tab.

The Snap Areas feature does have some limitations. Snap Areas only work on the display where they were created, although they will work on any desktop space defined on that display. That means if you create a Snap Area on an external display at work, your external display at home won't show the Snap Area. The Snap Area will only work on your monitor at work. If your MacBook Pro or MacBook Air is connected to an external monitor and you create a Snap Area on your external display, it will not work on your MacBook's internal display. Snap Areas will not work on both monitors in a dual monitor system. You will have to create separate Snap Areas for each monitor.

Edit or Delete a Custom Snap Area

To edit or delete a previously configured custom Snap Area, click the BetterSnapTool Menu Extra and select **Snap Areas (Advanced Feature) > Edit Snap Areas**. Click on the custom Snap Area you want to edit and make your desired changes. To delete a Snap Area, click the **X** and confirm you want to delete. When finished enter ⌘**W** (command+W) or click the gray box in the center of your desktop to exit edit mode.

Define the Window Control Buttons

BetterSnapTool has a feature that lets you define a resizing option for the window control buttons in the upper left of a window when you secondary click on them or use a mouse with a middle button. You have 22 different resizing options to choose from.

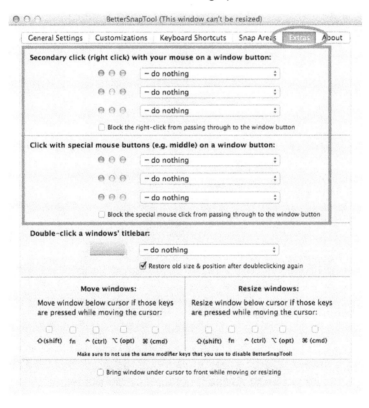

To define resizing options for the window control buttons, open the BetterSnapTool preference pane and click on **Extras** if not already highlighted. Select options for each window control for a secondary click, or middle button if your mouse has one. You will need to check the check box next to **Block the right-click from passing through to the window button**. If you fail to do so, you will be disappointed. BetterSnapTool will execute the resize command and immediately afterward OS X will execute the command associated with the window control.

Resize by Double-Clicking the Title Bar

You can configure BetterSnapTool to resize a window when you double-click on the window's title bar. Similar to the window controls, you have 22 different resizing options from which to choose.

To configure resizing by double-clicking the title bar, open the BetterSnapTool preference pane and click on **Extras** if not already highlighted. Choose the desired resizing action. If you have already configured OS X to minimize a window by double-clicking the title bar, a dialog box will warn you of the conflict. You can choose to **Cancel** or have BetterSnapTool open the **Dock** preference pane so you can clear the conflict.

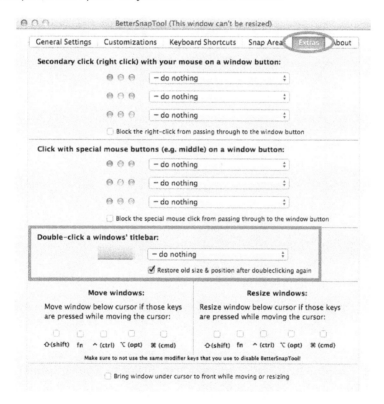

Check the box next to **Restore old size & position after doubleclicking again** if you want a second double-click on the title bar to restore the window's original size and location.

Move & Resize Windows with a Modifier Key

The OS X default is that a window must be active for you to move or resize it. Not with BetterSnapTool. All you have to do is hover your pointer over the window you want to move or resize, hold down the configured modifier key, and move your pointer to move or resize it. It doesn't matter if the window is active or not.

To configure modifier keys to move and resize a window, open the BetterSnapTool preference pane and click on **Extras** if not already highlighted. Select the desired modifier keys for each action. Optionally, you can configure BetterSnapTool to make the window active while moving or resizing it. Check the check box next to **Bring window under cursor to front while moving or resizing** to configure this option.

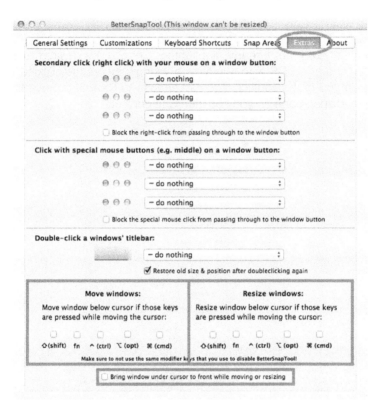

Change App Specific Settings

BetterSnapTool allows you to change the size of the standard resize areas on a per application basis. App specific settings only change the horizontal width of the window when resizing to the left or right edges or the left or right corners of the desktop. Click the BetterSnapTool Menu Extra and select **Specific Settings For Current Application**. Use the sliders to change the horizontal width or type the desired setting directly in the % box.

14

Safari

Safari Preferences

For most users, **Safari** requires little customization and can be operated in an "Out-of-the-box" mode. However, there is a tremendous amount of customization that can be done to fine tune Safari, change its appearance, and make it perform a little better. First, let's explore the Safari preferences.

General Preferences

Launch Safari and select **Safari > Preferences...** or enter ⌘, (command+,) to bring up the Safari preference pane. Click the **General** icon at the top of the pane if it is not already selected.

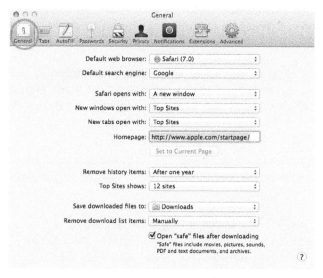

The first item on the General pane is the **Default web browser**. By default, this is set to **Safari**. The default web browser is the browser that is used when you click on a link in an e-mail or another application. While it may seem odd, Apple allows you to choose another browser installed on your Mac as the default. If you want to change the **Default web browser**, use the drop-down menu.

The **Default search engine** is configured for **Google**. Apple allows you to choose between Google, Yahoo, or Bing as the **Default search engine** from the drop-down menu.

The next attribute, **Safari opens with**, lets you to choose whether you want to start a new browsing session or resume your last session when you open Safari.

Safari allows you a number of choices with which to open new windows. The drop down menu next to **New windows open with** allows you to choose from **Top Sites**, a **Homepage** of your choosing, an **Empty Page**, the **Same Page** which you most recently viewed, with all of the **Tabs** from your **Favorites Bar**, or a set of tabs using a bookmark folder of your choosing. By default Safari will open with the Top Sites, a selection of 6, 12, or 24 of your most frequently visited websites.

The drop down menu next to **New tabs open with** allows you to choose from **Top Sites**, a **Homepage** of your choosing, an **Empty Page**, or the **Same Page** which you most recently viewed. By default, Safari opens new tabs with the Top Sites.

Homepage allows you to select a webpage that will open if **Homepage** is selected in either the **New windows open with** or **New tabs open with** setting.

By default, Safari will **Remove history items** after one year. Safari allows you to **Remove history items** after one day, one week, two weeks, one month, one year, or manually.

Top Sites are configured to show 12 sites by default. The drop-down menu allows you to choose either 6, 12, or 24 sites.

You can choose where to **Save downloaded files to**. By default, Safari saves downloaded files to the **Downloads** folder. If you would like to save to a different folder, use the drop-down menu to navigate to the folder where you would like to save downloaded items.

Safari maintains a list of all downloaded items. Using the **Remove download list items** drop-down menu, you can choose to remove download list items **Manually**, **When Safari quits**, or **Upon Successful Download**. Manually is configured by default.

Tabs Preferences

Click on the **Tab** icon to access the Tab pane, which is used to set options for using Safari tabs.

By default, Safari will **Open Pages in tabs instead of windows**. The drop-down menu next to this attribute allows you to turn this feature off by choosing **Never**. The default is **Automatically**. If you choose the **Always** option, Safari will create a new tab even if a website requests a window of a particular size.

By default, holding down the ⌘ (command) key while clicking on a link opens a new tab. To turn this feature off uncheck the check box next to ⌘-**click opens a new link in a new tab**.

You can choose to make a new tab or window active when it opens by checking the check box next to **When a new tab or window opens, make it active**. This feature is off by default.

Autofill Preferences

The **Autofill** preferences pane allows you to automatically fill web forms with your contact info, username and password, credit card information, or saved information entered on webpage forms. All four of the options are checked by default. Any option can be turned off by unchecking the check box next to it. The **Edit** buttons allow you to edit information specific to each category.

Safari can complete web forms with information from your contacts card. This information consists of your name, address, city, state, zip code and phone number. This feature is handy when filling out shipping information when purchasing from websites. To edit your contact information information, click the **Edit** button next to **Using info from my Contacts card**.

Safari can securely save your usernames and passwords used on websites and will automatically enter this information when you revisit the same website. To edit your username and password information, click the **Edit** button next to **User names and passwords**.

Safari also can securely save your credit card number, expiration date, and cardholder name and will automatically enter this information when needed to complete a purchase. To edit your credit card information, click the **Edit** button next to **Credit cards**. You can also add or remove saved credit cards using the **Edit** button.

The **Other forms** attribute allows Safari to save information entered on webpage forms and automatically enter the information when you revisit the same webpage. To view or edit, click the **Edit** button next to **Other forms**.

Passwords Preferences

The **Passwords** preferences pane allows you to view or edit usernames and passwords saved for various websites.

The search field allows you to search for website addresses, usernames, or passwords in the list.

The check box next to **AutoFill usernames and passwords** allows Safari to securely save usernames and passwords entered on webpages and automatically enter this information when you revisit the same webpage. Every time you enter your username or password on a webpage that you have not visited previously, Safari will ask you if you want to save your information. Unchecking the check box next to **AutoFill usernames and passwords** turns off this feature. If you uncheck the check box, Safari will never again ask you to save your username and password for websites.

A check box at the bottom of the pane allows you to **Show passwords for selected websites** so you can see what your password is for a particular website in the list. Another check box labeled, **Allow AutoFill even for websites that request passwords not be saved**, allows you to override requests from specific websites to not save your login credentials to your browser.

Finally, you can remove any websites from the list by highlighting them and clicking the **Remove** button.

Security Preferences

Safari's **Security** preference pane blocks or allows certain types of web content and can turn security warnings on or off. All four options on this preference pane are turned on by default.

Safari will warn you if you visit a website that has been reported as fraudulent when the check box next to **Warn when visiting a fraudulent website** is checked.

The **Enable JavaScript** allows JavaScript, which is used for certain types of web content. Some websites will not work properly if you disable JavaScript.

Safari blocks annoying pop-up windows by default. However, some websites use pop-up windows to display essential content. You can uncheck the **Block pop-up windows** check box when you want to view pop-up windows from certain websites.

The **Allow Plug-ins** attribute allows you to block certain plug-ins from websites that you have visited.

Privacy Preferences

Safari's **Privacy** preference pane is used to remove and block data that websites use to track you. These include cookies, location services, and other website data that can be used to track your browsing behavior.

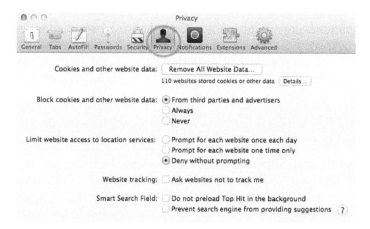

You can remove all cookies and other website data by clicking the **Remove All Website Data...** button at the top of the preference pane. Safari will confirm that you want to remove this data. Click **Remove Now** or **Cancel** on the next drop-down. Clicking the **Details...** button allows you to see which websites have stored cookies and other information on your Mac. You can also remove store data for individual websites or for all of them.

Safari provides three options to **Block cookies and other website data**. By default, Safari allows cookies and other website data **From third parties and advertisers**. This attribute will reject cookies and other data from websites other than those you have visited and will prevent advertisers from storing cookies and other data on your Mac. You can **Always** block cookies and other data, but that may prevent you from using some websites. The **Never** option allows all websites, third parties, and advertisers store cookies and other data on your Mac.

Safari can be configured to **Limit website access to location services**. Websites can use information about your location to provide various services and features. If you don't want to be asked if a website can use your location information, click the radio button next to **Deny without prompting**. The other two choices allow a website to prompt you either once a day or a single time for your location information.

Safari can be configured to ask websites to not track you by checking the check box next to **Ask websites not to track me**. Each time you visit a website, Safari will send a request not to track you.

By default, Safari will preload the website best matching your search entry in the address and search field. Preloading a website will make it appear faster if you select it from the search suggestions list. To turn off this feature, check the check box next to **Do not preload Top Hit in the background**.

As you enter words in the Safari address and search field, Safari sends them to your chosen search engine so it can suggest results for searches similar to yours. If you would prefer to keep your search words private, check the check box next to **Prevent search engine from providing suggestions**.

Notifications Preferences

The Safari **Notifications** preference pane allows you to view, change, or remove push notifications from websites that have previously asked for permission to show alerts in Notification Center. You can selectively allow or deny push notifications from the websites in the list or remove any or all of the websites that have asked for permission to send you push notifications.

Extensions Preferences

Extensions are small applications created by third-party developers to customize and enhance your web browsing experience. The Safari Extensions preferences pane allows you to turn all third-party extensions on or off, selectively enable or disable them, or uninstall them. Unless you have installed Safari Extensions, this preference pane will be empty. My Extensions pane, shown below, lists four extensions I have installed – Evernote Web Clipper, Add to Amazon Wish List, 1-ClickWeather, and a Reload button that can be moved anywhere on the Safari Toolbar.

The on/off switch at the top of the pane turns all extensions on or off. Changes do not take effect for some extensions until you browse to a new page.

The Extensions list shows which extensions are installed on your Mac. You can select an extension to show any available settings or to uninstall it.

The **Updates** button at the bottom of the left-hand pane is used to control automatic updates. Apple recommends that automatic updates be turned on so that you do not have to manually check and install updates and your extensions are kept up-to-date with the latest release.

The **Get Extensions** button at the lower right opens the **Safari Extension Gallery** website, where you can browse and add extensions which add new features to Safari. Extensions can be installed with one click and there is no need to restart Safari.

Customize the Safari Toolbar

The **Safari Toolbar**, located at the top of the Safari window, provides a number of tools to enhance your web browsing experience. The picture below shows the default Safari Toolbar in OS X Mavericks.

Let's take a closer look at the default tools before we customize the toolset.

The forward and back buttons are located at the left end of the Safari Toolbar. Next is the **iCloud Tabs** tool, which will display the open Safari tabs on all of your iOS and OS X devices. This handy feature allows you to browse to a page you started to read on another device. The **Share** tool allows you to add the currently displayed webpage to the Reading List, add it as a Bookmark, or share it using Mail, Messages, AirDrop, Twitter, Facebook, or LinkedIn. The **+** next to the left of the **Address and Search** field lets you bookmark the current page.

At the end of the Address and Search field is a **Reload** tool. It will reload the currently displayed web page to update its content. While a page is loading, this tool will change to an **X**, which allows you to stop a webpage from continuing to load. The **Reader** tool allows you to view web content in a format that is optimized for easier reading. Reader stitches together content that is broken up over multiple pages and removes advertising for a better reading experience. It also features a tool to increase or decrease the font. The Reader tool will be grayed out if a webpage cannot be converted to the Reader format. Finally, the **Download List** tool lists all downloads that are in progress or completed. Clicking on a downloaded item in the list launches it.

The Toolbar's second row contains three tools and the Favorites Bar. The **Bookmarks** tool toggles the display of the Bookmarks, Reading List, and Shared Links pane, which is located on the left-hand side of the main Safari window. The **Top Sites** tool is next. It displays the Top Sites in the main Safari window. The **New Tab** tool is located at far right and is used to create a new tab.

OS X allows you to customize the Safari **Toolbar**, adding, removing, and rearranging tools as you see fit. Secondary click in any open area of the Toolbar to reveal a contextual menu with a single option to **Customize Toolbar...**, which reveals a drop-down tools palette with the entire selection of tools available. Unlike the Finder Toolbar, the only option is to customize the Toolbar. Safari does not allow you to choose how the tools appear.

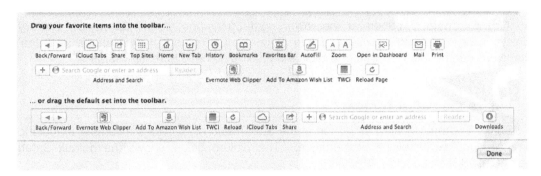

The Safari tools palette allows you to add additional tools to the Toolbar by dragging them off the palette and onto the Toolbar. Tools can be dragged off the Toolbar and onto the palette to remove them. In addition, any tool can be removed from the Toolbar at any time by holding down the ⌘ (command) key and dragging it off. Tools can be rearranged at any time by holding down the ⌘ (command) key and dragging.

The additional tools available on the Safari tools palette include a **Home** button, which will take you to the home page you configured in the Safari preferences. The **New Tab** button does the same thing as the **New Tab** tool located at the far right of the toolbar, but allows you to place the tool in a more convenient location. The **History** tool will display your browsing history organized chronologically. The **Bookmarks** tool toggles the display of the Bookmarks, Reading List, and Shared Links pane at the left of the main Safari window. The **Favorites Bar** tool toggles the Favorites Bar on and off. The **AutoFill** tool automatically enters information configured in the Safari AutoFill preferences.

The **Zoom** tool increases and decreases the font size on a webpage. Similar to the **Share** tool but more limited, the **Mail** tool allows you to share a webpage via the Mail application. The **Print** tool allows you to send the current webpage to a printer or create a PDF file. At the bottom of the Safari tools palette is the default set of tools. If you want to start over, simply drag the default set onto the toolbar. Click the **Done** button when you are finished customizing your Safari toolbar.

You probably noticed I skipped three tools – Evernote Web Clipper, Add to Amazon Wish List, TWCi and Reload Page. These tools are extensions, small applications created by third-party developers to customize and enhance your web browsing experience. The Evernote Web Clipper allows me to clip a webpage and save it to Evernote, a popular cross-platform note taking application for OS X, iOS, Android, and Windows. The Add to Amazon Wish List does what you would it expect it to do. TWCi immediately takes me to the Weather Channel page with my location pre-configured. Finally, the Reload Page tool does the same thing as the Reload tool located at the far right of the Address and Search field, but allows you to place the tool in a more convenient location. I'll cover how to add Extensions to Safari in the next section.

Here is my Safari toolbar customized with the tools I frequently use.

Tools located on the toolbar can be moved without having to use the drop-down tools palette. To move a tool, hold the ⌘ (command) key down while dragging the tool to its new location. You can also use the ⌘ (command) key to remove a tool. Hold down ⌘ (command) while dragging the tool off the toolbar. The tool will disappear in a puff of smoke.

To revert back to the default set of tools, drag the default set onto the Finder toolbar to replace the existing toolset. Note that any installed extensions will appear in the default toolset.

Add Safari Extensions

Safari **Extensions** are small applications created by third-party developers to customize and enhance your web browsing experience. You can search for, download, and install extensions from the **Safari Extensions Gallery** located on the Apple website at https://extensions.apple.com.

Extensions are organized in the Safari Extensions Gallery by various categories such as the most popular, most recent, email, entertainment, news, photos, and social networking, to name a few of the categories. You can search for, download, and install extensions directly from the Safari Extensions Gallery. Extensions are automatically placed on the right side of your Safari toolbar just past the Address and Search field.

Safari Extensions are controlled and updated using the Safari **Extensions** preferences pane accessible from **Safari > Preferences...** or by entering ⌘, (command+,) and clicking on the **Extensions** icon at the top of the preferences pane. The Safari Extensions pane allows you to turn all third-party extensions on or off, selectively enable or disable them, or uninstall them. This preferences pane also controls Extension behavior including how they are updated. Please refer to the Extensions Preferences section a few pages back for more information.

Create a Shortcut to Update Shared Links

With OS X Mavericks, Apple added a Twitter and LinkedIn client called **Shared Links** to Safari. Unfortunately, Shared Links is lacking an auto refresh capability and there seems to be no key combination to update the feed. Given that both of these social network feeds are always updating, the lack of an auto refresh capability is a severe limitation. The only way to update the feed is by selecting **View > Update Shared Links**. Oddly, Apple chose not to include a keyboard shortcut to update the Shared Links. You can fix this limitation by creating your own keyboard shortcut.

To create a custom keyboard shortcut to Update Shared Links, open the **Keyboard** preference pane by launching the System Preferences application and selecting the **Keyboard** icon or from the Apple menu by selecting > **System Preferences... > Keyboard**.

Click on the **Shortcuts** tab and then **App Shortcuts** in the left-hand pane. Next, click the **+** button to to reveal the drop-down configuration menu that will allow you to add a new shortcut.

From the drop down menu next to **Application**, choose **Safari**. In the **Menu Title** field enter **Update Shared Links** exactly as it appears in the Safari **View** menu. Next choose your shortcut key combination. Click the **Add** button to add your custom shortcut to Safari. You can now close the Keyboard preference pane. Check out the View menu in Safari to see your new keyboard shortcut.

Rename a Favorites Bar Bookmark

Sometimes your favorite websites will use incredibly long names for their bookmark. For example, try adding Amazon.com to your **Favorites Bar**. The bookmark is **Amazon.com: Online Shopping for Electronics, Apparel, Computers, Books, DVDs & more**, which is a little large for the limited real estate available on the Favorites Bar. Safari shortens these long bookmarks by truncating them, so Amazon's bookmark is truncated to **Amazon.com... Ds & more**. That still takes up too much space.

To rename a bookmark in the Favorites Bar, click and hold the bookmark until the name becomes highlighted. This is similar to how you rename a folder in Finder. Rename the bookmark to something shorter and more meaningful.

Bookmarks in Safari's Favorites Bar can be rearranged by dragging them to a new location on the Favorites Bar. To remove a bookmark, drag it off the Favorites Bar and it will disappear in a puff of smoke.

15

Mail

Mail Preferences

 Other than configuration of mail accounts, **Mail** requires little customization and can be operated in an "Out-of-the-box" mode for most users. However, there is a large amount of customization that can be done to fine tune Mail, change its appearance, and make it perform a little better. First, let's explore the Mail preferences.

General Preferences

Launch **Mail** and select **Mail > Preferences...** or enter ⌘, (command+,) to bring up the Mail preferences pane. Click the **General** icon at the top of the pane if it is not already selected.

The first item on the General pane is the **Default email reader**. By default, this is set to **Mail**. While it may seem odd, Apple allows you to choose another application to serve as the default email reader. If you want to change the **Default email reader**, use the drop-down menu.

The **Check for new messages** attribute determines how often Mail downloads new messages from the mail server. The default is **Automatically**, however, the drop-down menu allows you to configure the Mail application to check for new mail every 5, 15, 30, or 60 minutes or manually.

The **New messages sound** allows you to select from a number of sounds to play when a new message arrives. Mail can also be configured to make no sound. Use the drop-down menu to make your desired selection.

The **Mail** icon in the **Dock** displays a red badge showing the number of unread messages. The unread message count can be limited to only those messages in the inbox, unread messages received today, or all unread messages across all mailboxes.

New message notifications will display a notification when a message arrives in the mailbox specified in the drop-down menu. The Mail alert style must be set to either Banners or Alerts in the Notifications preference pane for new message notifications to work properly.

You can choose whether to **Add invitations to Calendar** automatically or never.

The location of downloaded items is configured using the drop-down next to the **Downloads folder**. **Remove unedited downloads** determines when attachments temporarily saved in the Mail Downloads folder are deleted. By default, an attachment is deleted when you delete the e-mail containing it.

If an outgoing server is unavailable for any reason, you can configure Mail to try another server or to try sending your e-mail later.

When searching mailboxes, you can choose to include results from the **Trash**, **Junk**, or **Encrypted Messages**. By default, only search results from the Trash are included.

Accounts Preferences

Clicking on the **Accounts** icon presents three tabs – **Account Information**, **Mailbox Behaviors**, and **Advanced**. We will customize only Mailbox Behaviors as the other two tabs are automatically configured when Mail sets up a new account.

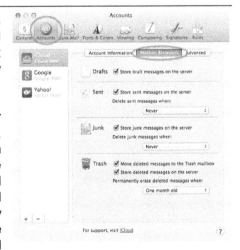

The Mailbox Behaviors tab is divided into four sections to control how **Drafts**, **Sent** mail, **Junk**, and the **Trash** are handled. **Draft** messages can be stored on the mail server so that they are available to use when you access your mail account on other devices. **Sent**, **Junk**, and deleted e-mail is also stored on the mail server by default. Deleted messages are moved to the **Trash** mailbox. If you turn off this option, deleted e-mail will remain in your inbox or other mailbox, but will be dimmed or hidden. Mail can be configured to delete **Sent**, **Junk**, and **Trash** e-mail after one day, one week, one month, when you quit the Mail app, or never. The option to store messages on the server is available for IMAP and Exchange accounts only and is turned on by default.

Junk Preferences

The **Junk** preferences pane controls how e-mail suspected as being junk is handled.

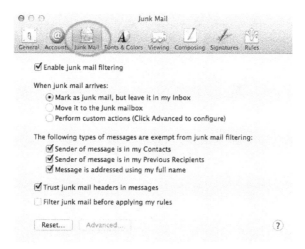

Junk mail filtering is enabled and e-mail suspected as being junk is marked as junk and left in your inbox. You can choose to move junk e-mail to a special junk mailbox or configure Mail to perform custom actions against e-mail suspected as junk. **Choosing Perform custom actions** allows you to click the **Advanced** button to access a drop-down panel to further refine your junk mail filters.

The next section contains three check boxes which exempt e-mail from being considered as junk. These include if the sender is in Contacts, the sender is a Previous Recipient, or the e-mail is addressed to your full name.

Trust junk mail header in messages is turned on by default and uses any junk mail detection already present in e-mail you receive.

You have the option of filtering out junk mail before applying any other mail filtering rules. Doing so, ensures that all e-mail is first evaluated by the junk mail filter.

Finally, a **Reset** button allows you to restore the default junk mail configuration.

Fonts & Colors Preferences

The **Fonts & Colors** preferences pane allows you to select the fonts for messages, the message list, and the color of quoted text.

Viewing Preferences

The **Viewing** preferences pane allows you to configure options when viewing e-mail.

The top portion of the **Viewing** preferences pane controls the layout of the **Preview Pane**, whether you want the To/cc label shown, whether you want contact photos, and how many lines of the message will be displayed in the message list.

The next section is used to configure how message **Headers** are shown. By default, the date and subject are shown. If you want more fields displayed, choose **Custom** from the drop-down menu. Displaying unread messages with a bold font helps you to distinguish them from read messages. Displaying remote images in HTML messages retrieves images from a remote server, however it can reveal information about your Mac. While Apple recommends turning this feature off, your e-mail with be devoid of any images. **Smart Addresses** display only the recipients' names and not their e-mail addresses if a recipient is in **Contacts** or in the **Previous Recipients** list.

By default, messages in a conversation that is not grouped will be highlighted with the color shown in the preferences pane. Mail will include Messages from other mailboxes that are related to a conversation that you are viewing. You can choose to mark all messages in a conversation as read when you open a conversation. By default, Mail displays the most recent message at the top of the messages list. By turning this feature off, the order is reversed in the oldest message will appear at the top of the list.

Composing Preferences

The **Composing** preferences pane is used to configure the options for messages that you create. The preferences pane is organized into three sections – **Composing**, **Addressing**, and **Responding**.

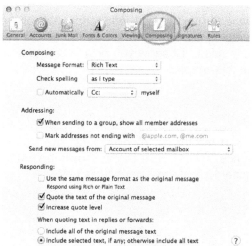

You can choose to compose your outgoing messages using the default of **Rich Text** or **Plain Text**. By default, Mail checks the spelling of your outgoing e-mail as you type it. You can choose to have Mail check your spelling when you click **Send** or **never** check your spelling. You can optionally choose to have Mail copy or blind copy you.

Mail will show the e-mail addresses of members of a group instead of showing the group name. The next option, **Mark addresses not ending with**, allows you to enter specific domains. Mail will turn e-mail addresses red if they are not within the listed domains. For example, if the domain of your company is listed under **Mark addresses not ending with**, Mail will turn the e-mail addresses of people outside your company red. This helps prevent you from sending e-mail to unintended recipients. If you have multiple Mail accounts configured, new messages are sent from the account of the selected mailbox by default. If you want your mail to originate from a specific Mail account, select it from the drop-down menu.

The **Responding** section controls the behavior of messages when replying and forwarding. You can choose to utilize the same message format as the original e-mail, either **Rich** or **Plain Text**. Mail will quote the text of the original message when replying or forwarding. By default, Mail will indent any text included from the original e-mail when replying or forwarding. To turn this feature off, uncheck the check box next to **Increase quote level**. You can choose to include all the text of the original e-mail or selected text when replying or forwarding.

Signature Preferences

The **Signature** preferences pane allows you to create signatures for each of your Mail accounts. Mail automatically adds the signature configured in the preference pane to messages you send. Mail allows you to have multiple signatures for each mail account and the preference pane allows you to add and remove signatures for each account.

Rules Preferences

The **Rules** preferences pane is used to add, edit, copy, activate, deactivate, and remove mail handling rules for incoming e-mail. A drop-down mail rule panel guides you through the creation of mail handling rules. I'll show you how to create a mail rule to play a sound when e-mail arrives later in this chapter.

Customize the Mail Toolbar

The **Mail Toolbar**, located at the top of the Mail window, provides a number of tools to enhance your Mail experience. The picture below shows the default Mail Toolbar in OS X Mavericks. Let's take a closer look at the default tools before we customize the toolset.

Reviewing the tools from left to right, the **Get Mail** tool does exactly what you expect it to do. It gets new mail for each of your mail accounts from the server. The function of the **New Message** tool is also pretty obvious. You use it to create a new e-mail. The **Delete** message tool is used to move messages to the mail trash. The **Junk** tool is used to mark incoming e-mail as junk mail. The next set of three tools are used to Reply, Reply All, or Forward e-mail. Finally, the **Flag** tool is used to assign a colored flag to e-mail messages.

OS X allows you to customize the **Mail Toolbar**, adding, removing, and rearranging tools as you see fit. Secondary click in any open area of the Toolbar to reveal a contextual menu. This menu allows you to choose how the tools appear. Tools can be displayed using both their **Icon and Text**, **Icon Only**, or **Text Only**. An option to completely hide the toolbar is also available. The final option, **Customize Toolbar...** allows you to add, rearrange, and remove tools using the drop-down tools palette with the entire selection of tools available.

✓ Icon and Text
  Icon Only
  Text Only
  Hide Toolbar

Customize Toolbar...

Let's review what each tool on the palette does. The first question you might ask is, "Why are their two sets of **Delete/Junk** tools?" The first set is combined into a single tool that accomplishes both functions. In the second set, the tools are separated allowing you to separate and place them anywhere on the Toolbar.

The **Archive** tool archives the current message to an archive folder if your mail service allows archiving. Next similar to the Delete/Junk tool, you'll see two sets of **Reply**, **Reply All**, and **Forward** tools. The first set is combined into a single tool accomplishing all three functions, while the second set are individual tools which can be placed anywhere on the Toolbar.

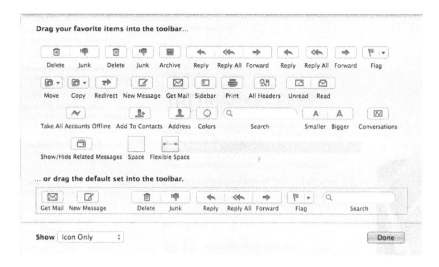

If you have multiple folders configured in your mail account you can use the **Move** and **Copy** tools to move or copy the currently selected message to one of the folders.

The **Redirect** tool performs a function similar to Forward, but does not quote the original message. The original message is redirected to an e-mail address you specify in the **To** field.

The **Sidebar** tool toggles the Sidebar on and off. The **Print** tool is used to print the currently selected e-mail message. The **All Headers** tool shows full message headers of the currently selected e-mail message and does the exact same thing as clicking the **Details** link shown in the upper right corner under the date of each e-mail message. To turn off full headers for any e-mail message click the **Hide Details** link in the upper right corner of the message.

The **Unread/Read** tool is used to mark the currently selected e-mail message as unread or read.

The **Take All Accounts Offline** tool is used when you want to disconnect the **Mail** client from the mail servers. An individual mail account can be taken off-line by secondary clicking on it and choosing to take it off-line.

The sender's contact information can be added to Contacts by clicking the **Add To Contacts** tool. The **Address** tool brings up a Contacts window of e-mail addresses.

The **Smaller/Bigger** tool decreases and increases the font size.

The **Conversations** tool is used to toggle the feature to organize messages by conversation off and on. The **Show/Hide Related Messages** tool will toggle the display or hiding of messages that are part of a thread.

Here is my Mail Toolbar customized with the tools I frequently use.

Tools located on the toolbar can be moved without having to use the drop-down tools palette. To move a tool, hold the ⌘ (command) key down while dragging the tool to its new location. You can also use the ⌘ (command) key to remove a tool. Hold down ⌘ (command) while dragging the tool off the toolbar. The tool will disappear in a puff of smoke.

To revert back to the default set of tools, drag the default set onto the Finder toolbar to replace the existing toolset.

Add Emoji

Emoji are those cute little emoticons that originated in Japan in the late 1990s and have spread around the world. You can reveal the OS X emoji set in almost any application by pressing the **^⌘ space** keys (control+command+space). Not only will you have access to the emoji, but other special character sets are available. Click the icons at the bottom of the window to display the other character sets. Click on an emoji or special character to insert it into your document.

Create a VIP Mailbox

Not all e-mail messages are created equal. You may want to prioritize e-mail messages received from certain people into a special mailbox. This feature is called the VIP mailbox.

To add someone to the VIP list, first find an e-mail message from them.  Click the empty star next to their name in the e-mail or secondary click on their name and select **Add to VIPs**. Once you have added one person to your VIP list, a new VIP mailbox will appear in the Sidebar and in your Favorites Bar.

To remove someone from the VIP list, find an e-mail message from them and click on the star next to their name or secondary click on their name and select **Remove from VIPs**.

Customize the Favorites Bar

Directly below the Toolbar is the **Favorites Bar**, another customizable component of the Mail window. At the extreme left is the **Hide** button, which you can use to toggle the **Sidebar** from **Show** to **Hide** and vice versa. The space to the right of the separator line is completely customizable.

To customize your Mail **Favorites** bar, drag any item from the **Sidebar** on to the Favorites bar. You can drag individual mailboxes, section headings (i.e., **On My Mac**, **VIPs**, **Flagged**), a mail account, or a single flag. Practically anything in the Sidebar can be dragged on to the Favorites bar. Clicking on any item in the Favorites bar will change the Mail window to the selected view and the button will turn a darker shade of grey to denote that it has been selected.

If an item has sub-items, a small triangle will appear to its right. In this case, the button will both toggle the view on and off as well as displaying a drop-down menu. For example, clicking on **VIPs** in the picture above will display all the messages from everyone you have designated as a VIP. If you click the triangle to the right of the **VIPs** button, a drop-down menu will appear allowing you to select a specific VIP.

Click and drag any item to rearrange it. To remove an item from your Favorites bar, click and drag it off until a puff of smoke appears and release.

Create a Mail Rule to Play a Sound

Not all e-mail messages are created equal. While you can configure Mail to play a sound when new e-mail arrives, you may want Mail to play a different sound to notify you when mail arrives from a particular person, VIP, or with a particular subject. Configuring this feature requires setting up a mail rule.

To set up a mail rule, select **Mail > Preferences...** or enter ⌘, (command+comma) to bring up the Mail preferences pane. Select **Rules** if not already selected, and click on the **Add Rule** button.

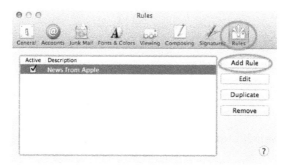

A drop-down dialog box will appear. Enter a descriptive name in the **Description** field. For this example we will set up a rule to play sound and bounce the Mail icon in the Dock when an e-mail message is received from a VIP. In the conditions section, choose **Sender is VIP** from the drop-down menu. In the **Perform the following actions** section, choose **Play Sound** from the drop-down menu and choose whatever sound you like from the next drop-down. Next, click the **+** button next to the first action. This will bring up another line. Select **Bounce Icon in Dock** from the drop-down menu. Click **OK** to finish and click **Apply** on the next dialog box.

Rules can be edited to refine or change them. To edit an existing rule, open the Mail preferences pane, select **Rules**, highlight the rule you want to change, and click the **Edit** button. The **Rules** configuration drop-down will appear to allow you to make the requisite changes. You can also Duplicate existing rules from the **Rules** preference pane by highlighting the rules you want to duplicate and clicking the **Duplicate** button. The **Rules** configuration drop-down will appear to allow you to make any changes.

To remove a rule, open the Mail preferences pane, select **Rules**, highlight the rule you want to remove, and click **Remove** button.

Embed Links in Email Messages

An embedded link allows the recipient of an e-mail message to click on a link embedded within the message and go directly to a website, start a chat in Messages, or start a FaceTime call.

To embed a link into an e-mail message, enter **⌘ K** (command+K). A drop-down dialog box will appear asking you to **Enter the Internet address (URL) for this link**.

To embed a link to a website, enter the following followed immediately by the website's URL.

`http://`

To embed a link that will allow the recipient to start a chat session with you in **Messages**, enter the following followed immediately by your ten-digit phone number or e-mail address.

imessage://

To embed a link that will allow the recipient to start a FaceTime call with you, enter the following followed immediately by your ten-digit phone number or e-mail address.

facetime://

Any link embedded in an e-mail message can be dragged and dropped on the Desktop or into a Finder window to create an Internet Location file. An Internet Location file is a small file containing the embedded link, that when double-clicked, will execute the action called for by the embedded link.

Links can also be embedded in other types of files, such as Word or Pages documents or Powerpoint or Keynote presentations, using ⌘ **K** (command+K).

16

Applications

Change the Font & Background in Messages

 The OS X **Messages** application allows you to set both the background color and font of your own messages as well as the background color, font, and font color of messages received from others.

To configure the font and color of messages, open the Messages application, select **Messages > Preferences...** or enter ⌘, (command+,) to launch the Messages preference pane. Select **Viewing** at the top of the preference pane if not selected already.

There are two sections to the **Viewing** preferences. The top section is used to configure the background color, font color, and font of your outgoing messages. Use the three drop-down menus to configure how you want your messages to appear when sending messages to others. The second section is used to configure the background color, font color, and font of incoming messages you receive. Use the three drop-down menus to configure how you want received messages to appear. The preview area at the top of the preference pane shows you how messages you send in receive will look. Note that messages received by your friends may look different based on the settings they have configured.

The two check boxes at the bottom allow you to set a keyboard shortcut to bring the Messages application to the front and to highlight your name when it is mentioned in an incoming message.

Make Help Center Behave

The OS X **Help Center** has a rather obnoxious habit. Help Center refuses to act like other windows because it refuses to go to the background when it is not the active window. It stubbornly stays on top of all other windows whether or not it is active. This tweak changes that rather obnoxious behavior and forces Help Center to act like all other OS X windows.

First, close the Help Center window if it is open. Enter the following command in **Terminal**. The change takes effect immediately.

```
defaults write com.apple.helpviewer DevMode -bool TRUE
```

The next time you open Help Center you'll notice its more polite behavior. It no longer blocks other windows when it is not the active window.

To revert back to the Help Center's default obnoxious behavior, enter the following command in **Terminal**.

```
delete com.apple.helpviewer DevMode
```

Stop Closed Windows from Opening

Some more obnoxious behavior you may have noticed is that OS X will reopen files that were open the last time you quit an app. While this is occasionally useful if you're working on a single document over a long period of time, it is annoying most of the time because you have to close the old document to continue your new work. Those switching from a Windows PC may find this behavior particularly annoying since Windows does not exhibit this odd quirk.

This behavior is easy to correct. Open the **General** preference pane by launching the System Preferences application and selecting the **General** icon or from the Apple menu by selecting > **System Preferences... > General**. Check the check box next to **Close windows when quitting an application** and OS X will no longer open previous documents when you launch an application.

Turn Key Repeat On

Another odd behavior you may wish to correct is how key repeat behaves. By default, holding down a key in OS X does not activate key repeat as expected. Instead, a contextual menu appears, which allows you to choose to insert accented and other non-English characters. If you're not in the habit of writing in a foreign language or using accented or other non-English characters, you can make key repeat operate as you expect it to when you hold down a key.

To turn on key repeat, open **Terminal** and enter the following command. You'll have to log out and log back in for the change to take effect.

```
defaults write -g ApplePressAndHoldEnabled -bool FALSE
```

To revert back to the OS X default where a contextual menu appears displaying accented and foreign characters, launch **Terminal** and enter the following command. You will have to log out and log back in for the change to take effect.

```
defaults delete -g ApplePressAndHoldEnabled
```

Turn Off iCloud as the Default Save Location

OS X save dialog boxes default to iCloud. If you prefer to save your documents locally, you can change the default save location.

To change the default save location from iCloud, first quit all applications. Next, launch **Terminal** and enter the following command.

```
defaults write -g NSDocumentSaveNewDocumentsToCloud -bool FALSE
```

You will have to log out and log back in for the change to take effect. Note that this tweak only affects the save dialog box. The Open dialog box automatically defaults to the last location used, either **iCloud** or **On My Mac**.

To revert back to the OS X default of iCloud as the save location for documents, first quit all applications. Then enter the following command in **Terminal**.

```
defaults delete -g NSDocumentSaveNewDocumentsToCloud
```

Log out and log back in for the change to take effect.

Turn On Dictation

 Dictation is my absolute favorite feature of OS X. In fact, most of this book was written using the OS X dictation feature. Dictation is extremely useful, allowing you to quickly turn your thoughts into large blocks of text whether you're writing a term paper, an email, posting to Facebook, or tweeting your followers.

Dictation is system-wide. You can dictate in any application anywhere text can be entered. This includes not only the usual suspects like Microsoft Office, Apple's iWork productivity suite, or Mail, but other time savers like the address bar in Safari, the search box in Google or Amazon, or in a web form. You can dictate text practically anywhere you're able to type it! Dictation is perfect for when you need to pull an all nighter to finish a term paper or project for work while avoiding getting grease from your extra pepperoni pizza on your keyboard.

To turn Dictation on, open the **Dictation & Speech** preference pane by launching the System Preferences application and selecting the **Dictation & Speech** icon or from the Apple menu by selecting > **System Preferences... > Dictation & Speech**. Click on the **Dictation** tab if not already selected.

Click the **On** radio button next to **Dictation** to turn the feature on. The default shortcut to start dictation is to press the **fn** key twice. Press the **fn** key once when finished dictating. You can change that using the drop-down menu next to **Shortcut**.

You'll be able to dictate up to 30 seconds as the Dictation feature has to send your speech to Apple to convert it to text. Therefore, you are required to be connected to the Internet for Dictation to work. In OS X Mavericks, Apple introduced **Enhanced Dictation**, which downloads a file onto your Mac so you are no longer required to be connect to the Internet nor are limited to 30 seconds of dictation.

Enhanced Dictation

Enhanced Dictation no longer requires you be connected to the Internet to convert text to speech. When you first turn on Enhanced Dictation, your Mac will download and install a 785 MB Enhanced Dictation file. This file not only allows you to dictate without using the Internet, it also removes the 30-second limitation on dictated text. Additionally, you receive immediate feedback as text appears while you're dictating. You can go back and correct text or move your cursor to another location all without having to exit Enhance Dictation.

To turn Enhanced Dictation on, open the **Dictation & Speech** preference pane by launching the System Preferences application and selecting the **Dictation & Speech** icon or from the Apple menu by selecting **⌘**
> System Preferences... > Dictation & Speech. Click on the **Dictation** tab if not already selected.

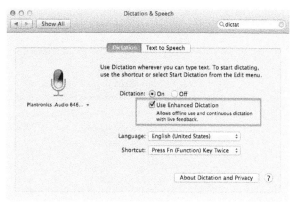

Check the check box next to **Use Enhanced Dictation** to turn the feature on. Your Mac will immediately begin downloading a 785 MB Enhanced Dictation file. You will be able to use enhanced dictation once the file has completely downloaded and installed itself.

Hit the **fn** key twice to start dictating. Your Mac will beep and the Dictation icon will appear to let you know OS X is ready to listen to you dictate.

It's cool to see your text appear immediately. You can also edit your text live without having to stop Dictation as you were required in Mountain Lion. Move your cursor or highlight the text you want to correct and dictate your corrections or use the keyboard to make corrections. You don't have to stop Dictation to edit your text.

Press the **fn** key again when finished dictating.

Change the Text to Speech Voice

OS X includes a number of voice for text to speech applications, such as reading an iBook to you. The default voice is a male voice named Alex. OS X allows you to change the voice, download new voices, and change the rate of speech in the **Dictation & Speech** preference pane.

To change the voice OS X uses in text to speech applications, open the **Dictation & Speech** preference pane by launching the System Preferences application and selecting the **Dictation & Speech** icon or from the Apple menu by selecting **⌘ > System Preferences... > Dictation & Speech**. Click on the **Text to Speech** tab if not already selected.

Use the drop down menu next to **System Voice** to change the voice or select **Customize...** to download other voices. For you iPhone and iPad users who like Siri's voice, choose **Customize...** from the drop-down menu and download Samantha's voice. You can change the speaking rate using the slider below **System Voice**.

The voice you selected will be utilized when your Mac reads iBooks to you. If you check the check box next to **Speak selected text when the key is pressed**, you will be able to highlight any text and have it read to you by pressing **⌥esc** (option+escape). You can change this keyboard shortcut by clicking the **Change Key...** button in the Dictation & Speech preference pane.

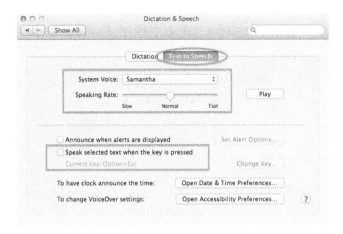

QuickTime Autoplay

QuickTime will not start playing a movie until you click the **Play** button. Use this tweak if you would like to turn on the **QuickTime Autoplay** feature, which will start playing a movie immediately after you open it.

First quit QuickTime and then launch **Terminal**. Enter the following command. Note that both lines are a single command. Do not press **return** until you have entered the complete command.

```
defaults write com.apple.QuickTimePlayerX MGPlayMovieOnOpen -bool
TRUE
```

To revert back to the OS X default of having to press the **Play** button to start a QuickTime movie, enter the following command in **Terminal**.

```
defaults delete com.apple.QuickTimePlayerX MGPlayMovieOnOpen
```

Remove the QuickTime Title Bar

At the top of the **QuickTime** window is a Title Bar with the name of the movie currently loaded. Use this tweak if you would like to remove the Title Bar.

First quit QuickTime and then launch **Terminal**. Enter the following command. Note that both lines are a single command. Do not press **return** until you have entered the complete command. Note that there is a space at the end of the first line.

```
defaults write com.apple.QuickTimePlayerX
MGCinematicWindowDebugForceNoTitlebar 1
```

To revert back to the OS X default, enter the following command in **Terminal**. Note that both lines are a single command. Do not press **return** until you have entered the complete command. Note that there is a space at the end of the first line.

```
defaults write com.apple.QuickTimePlayerX
MGCinematicWindowDebugForceNoTitlebar 0
```

Square Off QuickTime

Steve Jobs loved rounded corners. But if you think you are missing a little bit of your movie with those rounded corners, OS X allows you to square them off so you won't miss even one pixel.

To make the corners in **QuickTime** square, quit QuickTime and launch **Terminal**. Enter the following command. Note that both lines are a single command. Do not press **return** until you have entered the entire command.

```
defaults write com.apple.QuickTimePlayerX
MGCinematicWindowDebugForceNoRoundedCorners -bool TRUE
```

To revert back to the OS X default, quit QuickTime, and enter the following command in **Terminal**. Note that both lines are a single command. Do not press **return** until you have entered the entire command.

```
defaults delete com.apple.QuickTimePlayerX
MGCinematicWindowDebugForceNoRoundedCorners
```

Keep the Controls Around a Little Longer

The **QuickTime** controls appear when you move the pointer inside a QuickTime window. If you move the pointer outside the window, the controls disappear almost immediately. You can configure OS X to keep the QuickTime controls around a little longer after moving the pointer outside the window.

To keep the controls around longer, quit QuickTime and launch **Terminal**. Enter the following command. Note that both lines are a single command. Do not press **return** until you have entered the entire command.

```
defaults write com.apple.QuickTimePlayerX
MGUIVisibilityNeverAutohide -bool TRUE
```

To revert back to the OS X default, quit QuickTime, and enter the following command in **Terminal**. Note that both lines are a single command. Do not press **return** until you have entered the entire command.

```
defaults delete com.apple.QuickTimePlayerX
MGUIVisibilityNeverAutohide
```

Automatically Start Closed Captioning

If your movie has subtitles or is closed captioned, you can start closed captioning by selecting **View > Show Closed Captioning** or by entering ⌥⌘T (option+command+T). OS X allows you to configure **QuickTime** to play closed captioning automatically.

To configure QuickTime to play closed captioning automatically, quit QuickTime and launch **Terminal**. Enter the following command. Note that both lines are a single command. Do not press **return** until you have entered the entire command. Note that there is a space at the end of the first line.

```
defaults write com.apple.QuickTimePlayerX
MGEnableCCAndSubtitlesOnOpen -bool TRUE
```

To revert back to the OS X default, quit QuickTime, and enter the following command in **Terminal**. Note that both lines are a single command. Do not press **return** until you have entered the entire command. Note that there is a space at the end of the first line.

```
defaults delete com.apple.QuickTimePlayerX
MGEnableCCAndSubtitlesOnOpen
```

Remove Shadows from Screenshots

OS X inserts a gray shadow around an image captured by a screenshot. If you would like to remove the shadow, launch **Terminal** and enter the following commands.

```
defaults write com.apple.screencapture disable-shadow -bool TRUE
```

```
killall SystemUIServer
```

To revert back to the OS X default, open **Terminal** and enter the following commands.

```
defaults write com.apple.screencapture disable-shadow -bool FALSE
```

```
killall SystemUIServer
```

Change the Screenshot File Format

OS X saves screenshots in Portable Network Graphics (PNG) format, an open extensible image format supporting lossless data compression. PNG was created as an improved, non-patented replacement for Graphic Interchange Format (GIF). OS X supports the ability to save screenshots in other formats.

If you would prefer to save your screenshots in **jpg** format, launch **Terminal** and enter the following commands.

```
defaults write com.apple.screencapture type jpg
```

```
killall SystemUIServer
```

OS X also supports **tiff**, **pdf**, **bmp**, and **pict** formats.

To change the default file save format for screenshots to one of these formats, replace **jpg** in the above command with your desired format.

To revert back to the OS X default, enter the following commands.

```
defaults write com.apple.screencapture type png
```

```
killall SystemUIServer
```

Change the Screenshot Destination Folder

By default, OS X saves screenshots to the **Desktop** folder. If you are taking a lot of screenshots, your Desktop can quickly fill up with clutter. OS X allows you to change the default destination folder to something other than the Desktop.

First, determine where you want to save your screenshots. For this example, I'll save screenshots to a folder called **Screenshots** located in my **Documents** folder. The path I need to enter in the command to change the destination folder is:

```
~/Documents/Screenshots/
```

To change the default destination for screenshots this folder, launch **Terminal** and enter the following commands. Note that the first two lines are one command. Do not press the **return** key until you have entered the entire command.

```
defaults write com.apple.screencapture location
~/Documents/Screenshots/
```

```
killall SystemUIServer
```

To revert back to the OS X default of saving screenshots to the Desktop folder, enter the following commands in **Terminal**.

```
defaults write com.apple.screencapture location ~/Desktop/
```

```
killall SystemUIServer
```

Use Multiple Libraries in iTunes & iPhoto

When **iTunes** launches, it opens its default library file, iTunes Library.itl, which is located in **Music > iTunes**. But what if you have only one Mac in the family and each family member wants to synchronize their own music and applications with their own iOS devices? Separate users, each with their own login is one solution. But what if you prefer a single login? Or what if you use a small capacity iPod when exercising and do not want to spend a lot of time sorting through your main music library to pick content to synchronize on this iPod? The solution is the create multiple iTunes libraries.

To create a new iTunes library, first ensure iTunes is closed. Next, hold down the ⌥ (option) key when launching iTunes. A dialog box will ask you to choose an iTunes library or create a new one. Select **Create Library...**, enter the library name, tags, and save location on the next dialog and click **Save**. OS X will create a new folder in your save location using the name you entered in the **Save As** field.

The next time you launch iTunes, it will default to the last opened library. To switch iTunes libraries, launch iTunes while holding down the ⌥ (option) key, click **Choose Library...**, and select the iTunes library you want to open. This trick also works for iPhoto as well.

Add Facebook Events to Calendar

 The **Calendar** application is able to synchronize calendars between a number of email services as well as Facebook. It only takes a couple of steps to configure your Facebook calendar to synchronize with the OS X Calendar application. To add Facebook events to your Calendar, launch the Calendar application. Select **Calendar > Add Account...** to reveal a drop-down sheet. Click the radio button next to Facebook and enter your Facebook username and password when prompted.

To change how often Calendar synchronizes with Facebook or any of your accounts, select **Calendar > Preferences...** or enter ⌘, (command+,) to launch the Calendar preference pane. Select the account in the left-hand pane and click **Account Information** at the top of the pane. You have the choice of synchronizing every 1, 5, 15, or 30 minutes, every hour, or manually. Close the Calendar preference pane when finished.

Create a Save As PDF Keyboard Shortcut

Everyone who knows me knows I hate paper. Yet it is handy and often necessary to print copies of receipts and other important documents. OS X has a nifty feature that allows you to save any printable document in Portable Document Format, more commonly known as a PDF. PDFs can be viewed using the OS X **Preview** application, Adobe Acrobat Reader, or Adobe Acrobat and are portable between OS X, Windows, Linux, iOS, and Android operating systems.

Creating a PDF in OS X is a three-step process. First, you must select **File > Print...** or press ⌘P (command+P) to launch the Print dialog box. Next, you will use the PDF drop-down menu located at the lower left corner of the Print dialog box to select **Save as PDF...** to reveal the Save as PDF dialog box. Finally, you enter a filename and save location in the Save as PDF dialog box. You can eliminate two of these steps by creating a keyboard shortcut to save a document as a PDF.

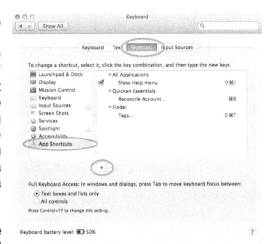

To create a keyboard shortcut for the **Save as PDF...** feature, open the **Keyboard**

preference pane by launching the System Preferences application and selecting the **Keyboard** icon or from the Apple menu by selecting > **System Preferences... > Keyboard**. Click the **Shortcuts** tab at the top of the pane if it is not already selected.

Click on **App Shortcuts** in the left-hand pane, then click the **+** button to add a new shortcut. A drop-down dialog box will appear. Ensure **All Applications** is selected for the **Application**. Type **Save as PDF...** into the **Menu Title** field exactly as shown. Enter a shortcut of your choosing in the **Keyboard Shortcut Field**. I used ⇧⌘S (shift+command+S). Click the **Add** button when finished.

Add Favorite Locations to the PDF Drop-Down Menu

When you select the PDF drop-down menu from the lower left corner of the Print dialog box, did you notice you can **Add PDF to iBooks**, **Mail PDF**, **Save PDF to Web Receipts Folder**, or **Send PDF via Messages**? These are pre-configured printing workflows that allow you to send or save your PDF.

Open PDF in Preview
Save as PDF...   ⇧⌘S
Save as PostScript...

Add PDF to iBooks
Mail PDF
Save PDF to Web Receipts Folder
Send PDF via Messages

Edit Menu...

OS X allows you to add your own favorite locations to this drop-down menu as a printing workflow. To add your own favorite locations to the **Save as PDF** drop-down menu, select **Edit Menu...** to reveal the **Printing Workflows** dialog box. Click on the **+** and navigate to the location you wish to add. Continue clicking the **+** until you have added all of your favorite locations. Your favorite locations will appear on the Save as PDF drop-down menu below **Send PDF via Messages**.

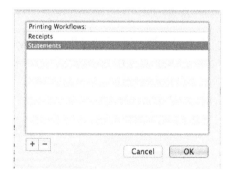

To remove a favorite location, first highlight the location and then click the **–** button.

A Better Way to Add Favorite Locations

While the **Edit Menu...** feature works well, the limitation is that your favorite locations appear at the end of the menu regardless of where they should appear alphabetically. Additionally, you may have absolutely no need for one or more of the existing printing workflows.

A better way to customize the printing workflows shown in the Save as PDF drop-down menu is to add or remove them from the **PDF Services** folder in the **Library**. To open the PDF Services folder, launch **Finder** and enter ⇧⌘G (shift+command+G) to bring up the **Go to folder** dialog box. Enter the following path and click **Go**.

/Library/PDF Services/

You will find the four printing workflows listed on the Save as PDF drop-down menu in the **PDF Services** folder. If you have no need for one or more of the workflows, drag them to the Trash or to another folder in your Home directory if you want to save them just in case you may need them later. Any change to the PDF Services folder requires you to authenticate using your administrator password. Enter your password when prompted.

To add a favorite location, enter ⌘T (command+T) to open another Finder tab. Navigate to the folder containing the folder you wish to add. Create an alias of the folder you want to add as a favorite by secondary clicking on it and choosing **Make Alias**. I suggest you rename the alias by adding "Save PDF to" or "Send PDF to" at the beginning of the alias name. Drag your alias into the PDF Services folder and enter your administrator password when prompted.

To remove a favorite location from the PDF Services folder, simply drag it to the Trash. Enter your administrator password when prompted.

Automatically Accept FaceTime Calls

FaceTime can be configured to automatically accept incoming calls. This allows you to use your Mac as a low-end security system to see what is going on at home by initiating a FaceTime call from your iPhone or iPad. To enable automatic connection of FaceTime calls, quit FaceTime, open **Terminal** and enter the following commands.

defaults write com.apple.FaceTime AutoAcceptInvites –bool TRUE

To revert back to the OS X default of not automatically accepting FaceTime calls, quit FaceTime and enter the following commands in Terminal.

```
defaults write com.apple.FaceTime AutoAcceptInvites -bool FALSE
```

17

Security

Have iCloud Keychain Suggest Strong Passwords

 A new feature in OS X Mavericks is **iCloud Keychain**, which allows you to save encrypted usernames and passwords in iCloud for use on any of your Apple devices. A handy feature is a password generator which suggests strong passwords for you to use and automatically enters them into the password field of a website.

To turn on iCloud Keychain and its password generator, open the **iCloud** preference pane by launching the System Preferences application and selecting the **iCloud** icon or from the Apple menu by selecting > **System Preferences... > iCloud**.

Check the Keychain box in the list in the right-hand panel of the iCloud preference pane. Enter your Apple ID and password when prompted. Safari will now suggest strong passwords when a website asks you to enter a new password. To use Safari's suggested

password click on **Use Safari suggested password,** which will appear below a website's password input field. Don't worry, you won't have to remember this monster. Passwords are automatically saved to the **Keychain Access** application.

Create Strong Passwords with Keychain Access

 Keychain Access is the OS X application that handles certificates, stores passwords from Safari, and allows you to create strong passwords and store other data in an encrypted format. If you're unfamiliar with Keychain Access, it is probably because it is a little hard to find. It is not found in the default OS X Dock. Keychain Access is tucked away in the **Utilities** folder.

I highly recommend that you use a unique password for each website or application you access. This ensures that if one of your passwords is compromised, it cannot be used to break into all of the other sites where you have accounts. Never reuse passwords among websites. I recommend utilizing strong passwords that you change every six months. Keychain Access in combination with Safari can be used to automate the creation, storage, and retrieval of your passwords.

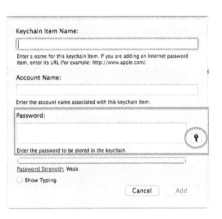

The advantage of using the OS X Keychain Access app is that you can configure it to synchronize passwords over iCloud to make them available across all of your Apple devices.

Keychain Access can be found in **Applications > Utilities** or by searching for it using **Launchpad** or **Spotlight**. To create a new password select **File > New Password Item** or enter ⌘N (command+N). Enter the **Keychain Item Name** and **Account Name**. Next, click the **Key** button to the far right of the **Password** field, which will launch **Password Assistant**.

Password Assistant will launch in a separate window. Using the drop-down menu next to **Type**, select the type of password you would like to create. You have several choices: **Memorable**, **Letters & Numbers**, **Numbers Only**, **Random**, or **FIPS-18 compliant**. Password Assistant will suggest a password of 12 characters, which is a little too short. I

recommend you use the longest password supported by the website or application. Use the **Length** slider to increase the number of characters. As the number of characters increase, you'll notice the **Quality** turns to green as the password become stronger. When finished, click the red close button in the upper left corner and your password will be automatically placed in the password field of the new password item in Keychain Access. Click the **Add** button to save your password to your keychain.

When you want to use your password, launch **Keychain Access** and search for the item by name using the search field in the upper right. Secondary click on the item and enter your password when prompted. Your password has been saved the the clipboard and you can paste it into the website or application. If you are using Safari, you will be asked if you would like to save the username and password. Doing so avoids having to launch Keychain Access and search for your password each time you need it on that particular website.

Lock Your Mac Using the Keychain Access Menu Extra

In addition to securely storing your passwords, **Keychain Access** can be used to lock your Mac using its Menu Extra in the Menu Bar.

First, launch **Keychain Access** through Finder by navigating to **Applications > Utilities** or by searching using **Launchpad** or **Spotlight**. Next, select **Keychain Access > Preferences...** or by entering ⌘, (command+,) to launch its preference pane. Click on the **General** tab if not already selected. Next, check the check box next to **Show keychain status in menu bar**.

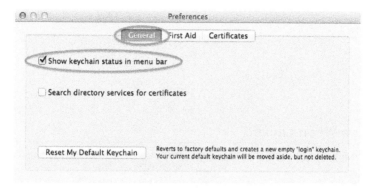

OS X will add the Keychain Access Menu Extra, which will look like an open padlock, to the Menu Bar. The drop-down menu offers an option to **Lock Screen**. In addition, you can use the Menu Extra to **Lock Keychain** when it is no longer in use. **Open Security Preferences...** will launch the **Security & Privacy** preference pane. **Open Keychain Access...** does what you'd expect it to do, open the Keychain Access application. The Menu Extra will remain on the Menu Bar even if Keychain Access is not open.

Require a Password to Wake the Display

For security reasons, it is highly recommended that you require a password to wake your computer from sleep, from displaying the screen saver, or when the display is asleep. To configure your Mac to require a password, open the **Security & Privacy** preference pane by launching the **System Preferences** application and selecting the **Security & Privacy** pane or from the Apple menu by selecting > **System Preferences... > Security & Privacy**. If not already selected, click the **General** tab.

To configure your Mac to require a password, check the **Require password** check box as shown in the next picture. OS X offers you the option of requiring a password immediately or after 5 seconds, after 1, 5, or 15 minutes, or after 1 or 4 hours after the display went to sleep or the screen saver began. Selecting the 5 seconds or 1 minute options, will avoid requiring you to enter a password when the display inadvertently goes to sleep or the screen saver becomes active while you are still working.

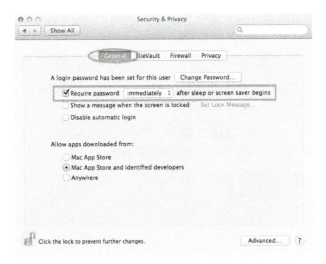

Show a Message When Locked

OS X lets you configure your Mac to show a message when the screen is locked. Open the **Security & Privacy** preference pane by launching the **System Preferences** application and selecting the **Security & Privacy** pane or from the Apple menu by selecting > **System Preferences... > Security & Privacy**. If not already selected, click the **General** tab.

Check the check box next to **Show a message when the screen is locked**. If this option is grayed, check the padlock in the

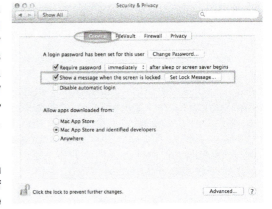

lower left corner of the preference pane to ensure the pane is unlocked. If the padlock is closed, it indicates the preference pane is locked. Click on the padlock and enter your password when prompted.

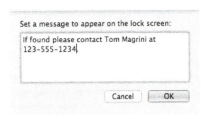

Check the check box and click the **Set Lock Message...** button. Enter your message in the dialog box that drops from the top of the pane and click **OK**.

Disable Automatic Login

With automatic login enabled anyone can access your Mac simply by restarting it. They will be logged in as you with access to all of your files, Mail, Messages, etc. I highly recommend that you disable automatic login, which can be enabled for a specific user from the **Users & Groups** preference pane by clicking on **Login Options** at the bottom of the left-hand pane and turning on **Automatic login** from the drop-down menu.

To disable automatic login, open the **Security & Privacy** preference pane by launching the **System Preferences** application and selecting the **Security & Privacy** icon or from the Apple menu by selecting > **System Preferences...** > **Security & Privacy**.

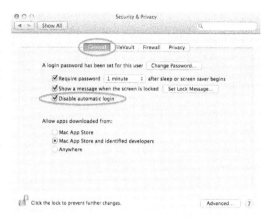

Select the **General** tab if not already selected. Next, check the check box next to **Disable automatic login**. The change takes effect immediately and will also be reflected in the **Users & Groups** preference pane. Your Mac will ask for a username and password when it starts.

Encrypt Time Machine Backups

Hands down, Apple's **Time Machine** is the easiest backup application I have ever used. Its simple "set it and forget it" interface quietly backs up all of my critical data regularly without any intervention on my part. And the best part of Time Machine is that it can quickly and easily restore one file or your entire Mac.

Since Time Machine contains a copy of all of your files, including any data you would like to stay private, I highly recommend you encrypt your Time Machine back up to ensure your files stay private and secure if someone were to get ahold of your backup disk.

To encrypt your Time Machine backups, open the **Time Machine** preference pane by launching the System Preferences application and selecting the **Time Machine** icon or from the Apple menu by selecting > **System Preferences...** > **Time Machine**.

Next, click **Add or Remove Backup Disk...** to reveal a drop-down configuration pane that will allow you to add and remove disks and turn on encryption.

Select the disk drive you would like to add under **Available Disks** and check the check box next to **Encrypt backups** to turn on encryption. Next, click the **Use Disk** button and you are all set. Time Machine is a set it and forget it back up app and it will begin backing up and encrypting your backups.

Make Gatekeeper Less Restrictive

Gatekeeper stops applications that are not digitally signed with an Apple Developer ID from being installed on your Mac. Gatekeeper helps to protect your Mac from malware in applications downloaded from the Internet. Apple's App Store is the safest and most reliable place to download and install applications because Apple reviews each app before they allow it into the App Store. Apple can also remove an application if a problem is discovered later.

If you attempt to install an application downloaded from a place other than the App Store, Gatekeeper checks to see if the app is signed with a unique Apple developer ID. If it is not digitally signed or the digital signature has been tampered with, Gatekeeper will block the application from being installed.

If you want to install an unsigned application that you know is safe, Gatekeeper will block it unless you change the **Security & Privacy** configuration.

Open the **Security & Privacy** preference pane by launching the **System Preferences** application and selecting the **Security & Privacy** pane or from the Apple menu by selecting > **System Preferences... > Security & Privacy**. If not already selected, click the **General** tab. Ensure the padlock in the lower left corner is unlocked. If not, click it and enter your password when prompted.

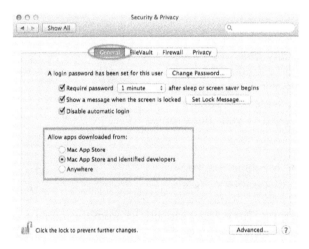

Click the radio button, next to **Anywhere** to tell Gatekeeper to allow apps to be installed even if they lack a digital signature from an Apple Developer ID. I highly recommend that you change this setting only when you want to install a known safe application and then return it to its default setting.

To revert to the OS X default setting, open the Security & Privacy preference pane and click the radio button next to **Mac App Store and identified developers.** Clicking **Mac App Store** adds a layer of protection as Gatekeeper will only allow apps downloaded from the App Store to be installed on your Mac.

Turn Off File Quarantine

Another feature of **Gatekeeper** is download quarantine, where your Mac will warn you when you first open an application downloaded from the Internet. OS X provides file quarantine in applications that are capable of downloading files from the Internet such as Safari, Mail, and Messages. OS X will quarantine a file if it was downloaded by one of these quarantine-aware applications. When you try to open a quarantined file, OS X will warn you that the file came from the Internet and ask, "are you sure you want to open it?" If you have any doubts about the safety of the file, click the **Cancel** button. If you are sure the file is safe, click the **Open** button.

If you would like to turn off the OS X file quarantine feature, open **Terminal** and enter the following command. You will have to log out and log back in for the change to take effect.

```
defaults write com.apple.LaunchServices LSQuarantine -bool FALSE
```

To revert back to the OS X default and turn file-quarantine back on, enter the following command in **Terminal**. You will have to log out and log back in for the change to take effect.

```
defaults delete com.apple.LaunchServices LSQuarantine
```

Encrypt Your Disk Drive

 Encrypting your disk drive is a good idea to protect your data in case your Mac is stolen. Encryption combined with the other security customization covered in this chapter makes it more difficult for a thief to access your data. OS X Mavericks **FileVault 2** can encrypt your entire disk drive with XTS-AES 128 encryption.

Open the **Security & Privacy** preference pane by launching the **System Preferences** application and selecting the **Security & Privacy** pane or from the Apple menu by selecting > **System Preferences... > Security & Privacy**. If not already selected, click the **FileVault** tab. Ensure the padlock in the lower left corner is unlocked. If not, click it and enter your password when prompted.

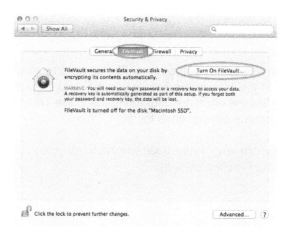

Click the **Turn On FileVault...** button. You'll be asked to identify the specific users who are allowed to unlock the encrypted drive if there is more than one account configured on your Mac. Each user is required to enter their password in order to have the ability to unlock FileVault. After selecting users you'll be shown the recovery key. Make a copy of this key and store it in a safe place. The recovery key is a backup unlock method in case you forget your password. If you lose both your password and the recovery key, you will not be able to access any of the data on your disk drive.

It is a bad idea to keep the copy of your recovery key on your Mac. If you forget your password you will not be able to access any of the data on your Mac including the recovery key, which serves as your backup method to unlock the encrypted drive. Store your recovery key in a safe, external location.

You can store your recovery key with Apple. Choose **Store the recovery key with Apple** on the next dialog box and click the **Continue** button. You'll need to choose and provide the answers to three security questions which Apple will use to verify your identity in the event that you lose your password and need the recovery key. Click the **Continue** button when finished. You will be asked to click **Restart** in the next dialog box to restart your Mac and begin the encryption process. This is your last opportunity to **Cancel**.

Help! My Trash Won't Empty!

Sometimes the **Trash** simply refuses to empty. Often Finder displays an error message claiming a file is in use. Even quitting every application does not help. Finder stubbornly insists a file is still in use. A trick that often clears this error is holding down the ⌘ (command) key to securely empty the Trash. If that doesn't work, another option is to empty the Trash using a command in **Terminal**.

To force the Trash to empty, launch **Terminal** and enter the following command.

```
cd ~/.Trash
```

Next, type the following command but **do not** press the **return key**.

```
sudo rm –R
```

Add a space to the end of the command. **This is very important.**

Next, click the Trash can in the Dock to open a Finder window displaying the contents of the Trash. Highlight all of the files in the Finder window and drag and drop them into the Terminal window. This adds the paths to all of the items in the Trash to the command. The resulting command will become several lines long.

Now you can press the **return** key. Enter your administrator password when prompted and OS X will empty the Trash. Problem solved!

Securely Erase an Old Disk Drive

If you have an old disk drive that you want to get rid of either by trashing it, giving it to charity, or giving it to a friend or relative, I highly recommend you securely erase the drive prior to handing it over. The OS X Disk Utility can securely erase it drive by writing random ones and zeros over multiple passes.

To securely erase an old disk drive, launch **Disk Utility** through Finder by navigating to **Applications > Utilities** or by searching for it using **Launchpad** or **Spotlight**.

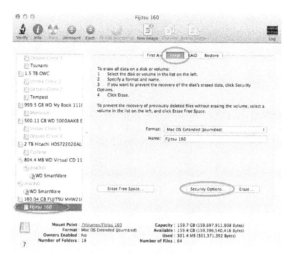

Click on the disk drive in the left hand pane that you want to erase. Click the **Erase** tab at the top of the Disk Utility window. Next, click the **Security Options...** button to reveal the **Secure Erase Options** configuration dialog. The large slider in the middle controls the number of passes Disk Utility will make when writing random ones and zeros to the drive.

The fastest option is the least secure and does not securely erase the files on the drive. A disk recovery application may still be able to recover your files if you use this method.

Drag the slider to the right to preview each of the other options. The first option writes a single pass of zeros over the entire disk. The next option does two passes of random data followed by another pass of no data over the entire disk. The most secure option meets the US Department of Defense (DOD) 5220-22M standard for securely erasing magnetic media. It erases the disk drive by writing random data over seven passes. Note that It takes seven times as long as a single pass to erase a drive using this method.

Once you've selected the method to securely erase your drive, click the **OK** button. Then click the **Erase** button and confirm on the next dialog box. Now sit back and relax because securely erasing a large drive can take many hours, but is well worth it to protect your sensitive data.

18

Some Final Tweaks

Create a Bootable Mavericks USB Flash Drive Installer

 If you own multiple Macs that you want to upgrade to OS X Mavericks, you are facing a lot of downloading from the App Store. A better option is to create a bootable USB flash drive installer. You'll need a copy of the OS X Mavericks installer on your Mac and a USB flash drive of at least 8 GB capacity. Be sure there is nothing important on the flash drive as it will be erased as part of the creation of the installer.

Creating a bootable USB flash drive installer is a multi-step process.
1. Download OS X Mavericks from the **App Store**.
2. While Mavericks is downloading, connect your USB flash drive to your Mac and launch **Disk Utility**. You can find the Disk Utility application by searching for it in **Launchpad**.
3. Select the external drive in the left-hand pane. Click on the **Partition** tab at the top of the preference pane. Choose **1 Partition** as the **Partition Layout**. Next, select **Mac OS Extended (Journaled)** as the **Format**.

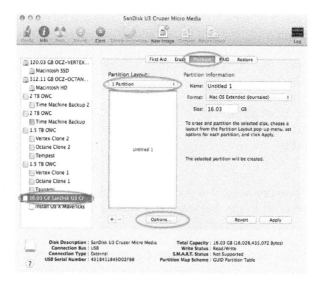

4. Click the **Options** button to reveal a drop-down configuration sheet. Select **GUID Partition Table** from the drop-down. This will allow you to use the flash drive as a start up disk. Click **OK** and then **Apply** on the main Disk Utility window. OS X will partition, format, and prepare your flash drive as a start up disk.

5. When Mavericks finishes downloading, you will see a window asking you to click continue to set up the installation of OS X Mavericks. **STOP HERE!** Exit the installation by quitting the installer.

6. Open Terminal and enter the following command. All four lines are a single command. **Do not** press the **return** key until you have entered the entire command. Be sure to replace "**Untitled**" with the exact name of your USB flash drive. Because this command uses sudo, you will need to enter your admin password when prompted. Don't worry if nothing appears in **Terminal** as you type your password. This is a security feature.

```
sudo /Applications/Install\ OS\ X\
Mavericks.app/Contents/Resources/createinstallmedia --volume
/Volumes/Untitled --applicationpath /Applications/Install\
OS\ X\ Mavericks.app --nointeraction
```

7. Terminal will display a progress indicator and the process will run for several minutes. The process is automated so there is nothing for you to do but wait until Terminal tells you it is done. This is what you will see in Terminal as your installer disk is being created.

```
Erasing Disk: 0%... 10%... 20%... 30%...100%...
Copying installer files to disk...
Copy complete.
Making disk bootable...
Copying boot files...
Copy complete.
Done.
```

8. You can quit Terminal when it is done creating the installer disk. Open Finder and check the Device list in the Sidebar. You should see a device called **Install OS X Mavericks**.

You are now finished with the creation of your OS X Mavericks USB flash drive installer. To use your flash drive to install Mavericks, insert your USB flash drive into your Mac and restart. Hold down the ⌥ (option) key while restarting to bring up the startup disk menu.

From the start of disc menu select your USB installer flash drive to continue booting the Mac directly into the Mavericks installer. Follow the on-screen commands to install Mavericks. It should take about 45 minutes to complete the installation.

Configure Background Updates

Mavericks can be configured to automatically download and install updates in the background. If you would like to manually review the updates OS X plans to make to your Mac before they are installed, OS X offers a number of configuration options.

To configure background updates, open the **App Store** preference pane by launching the System Preferences application and selecting the **App Store** icon or from the Apple menu by selecting > **System Preferences... > App Store**.

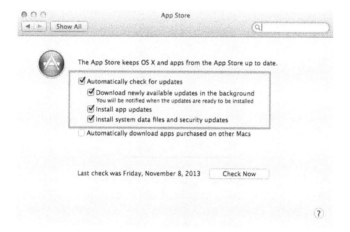

You have several configuration options to control various aspects of the update process. If you uncheck the check box next to **Automatically check for updates**, OS X will no longer check or notify you of the availability of any updates. You will have to manually check for updates using the App Store application.

If you leave the check box next to **Automatically check for updates** checked, you can control how updates are downloaded and installed with the next three check boxes. If the check box next to **Download newly available updates in the background** is checked, OS X will automatically download updates without asking you for permission but will install them based on how the next two check boxes are configured. These control whether downloaded updates are installed automatically or not. The check box next to **Install app updates** controls how OS X installs updates to applications. If this box is checked, OS X will automatically update applications without asking for your permission. Uncheck it to turn off automated application updates. The check box next to **Install system data files and security updates** controls how system files and security updates are applied. If this box is checked OS X will automatically install system files and security updates without asking you for permission. Uncheck it to turn off this feature.

Create Shortcuts to Share using Facebook, Twitter, & LinkedIn

If you click on the **Share** button in any application, you'll find there are no shortcuts to share content using Facebook, Twitter, or LinkedIn. You can easily create a keyboard shortcut for each social network using the **Keyboard** preference pane.

To create shortcuts to share content on social networks, open the **Keyboard** preference pane by launching the System Preferences application and selecting the **Keyboard** icon or from the Apple menu by selecting > **System Preferences... > Keyboard**. Click the **Shortcuts** tab at the top of the pane if it is not already selected.

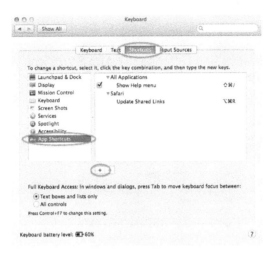

Click on **App Shortcuts** in the left-hand pane, then click the **+** button to add a new shortcut. A drop-down configuration dialog box will appear. Ensure **All Applications** is selected for the **Application**. Type **Facebook** into the **Menu Title** field exactly as shown. Enter a shortcut of your choosing in the **Keyboard Shortcut Field**. I decided to use ⌥⌘F (option+command+F) for Facebook. Click the **Add** button when finished.

Repeat the same process to create shortcuts for **Twitter** and **LinkedIn**. Be sure to spell them exactly as shown in the Share menu otherwise the shortcut will not work. The entry in the **Menu Title** field must exactly match the command shown in the **Share** menu. Once you have created your shortcuts, you are able to see them under the **Share** menu in applications that support sharing of content.

To remove a shortcut, go back to the **Keyboard** preference pane, highlight the shortcut you want to remove, and click the **−** button.

Turn Off App Nap for Specific Apps

App Nap is a new feature in OS X Mavericks that helps save power when you have multiple applications open at the same time. If an app is completely hidden by other windows and isn't currently doing something like iTunes playing music or Mail checking for new email, App Nap will power down the app to conserve battery power. When you begin to use the app again, OS X instantly shifts the app back to full power. App Nap can increase the amount of time you can work on your MacBook Pro or MacBook Air you have to recharge the battery. App Nap can be turned off on an application by application basis.

If you want to turn off App Nap for a specific application, open the **Applications** folder and secondary click on the application icon and choose **Get Info**. You can also open the Get Info window by highlighting the application and entering ⌘I (command+i). Check the check box next to **Prevent App Nap** to turn off App Nap.

Copying Quotes and Citations from iBooks

Mavericks added a new application, iBooks, which contains this neat little feature for students who need to copy quotes and citations from iBooks. Simply select some text that you wish to quote and choose **Copy** from the contextual menu. Next, paste the quote into any word processing application and OS X will format it by adding quotation marks and a citation line.

Selecting **More** will reveal a contextual menu with options to look up the definition of a highlighted word, search the book, search Web or Wikipedia for a highlighted word or phrase, or share using Facebook, Twitter, Messages, or Mail. iBooks can even read a highlighted section to you if you choose **More > Start Speaking**.

Change the Behavior of Print & Save Dialogs

When printing or saving a document, a print or save dialog box will slowly slide downwards from the window's Title Bar. If you would prefer to see print and save dialog boxes appear immediately, launch **Terminal** and enter the following command. You will have to log out and log back in for the change to take effect.

```
defaults write -g NSWindowResizeTime -float 0.01
```

To revert back to the OS X default, enter the following command into **Terminal**. You will have to log out and log back in for the change to take effect.

```
defaults delete -g NSWindowResizeTime
```

Change Your Profile Picture

It's easy to change your profile picture. You do not have to accept Apple's defaults as you can use any picture.

To change your profile picture, open the **Users & Groups** preference pane by launching the System Preferences application and selecting the **Users & Groups** icon or from the Apple menu by selecting > **System Preferences... > Users & Groups**. Click the **Password** tab if it is not already selected. Click on your account in the left-hand pane. You'll see your current profile picture at the top of the right-hand pane.

Apple provides a number of default pictures you can utilize. If you don't like the defaults you can choose a picture from iCloud, Faces in iPhoto, a folder on your Mac, or you can take a picture using your Mac's camera.

To use a picture located in a folder on your Mac, open Finder, find the picture, and drag it onto your current profile picture in the **Users & Groups** preference pane.

Turn Keyboard Backlight Off When Idle

One of the great features of a MacBook Pro and MacBook Air is keyboard backlighting is standard on all models. Anyone who has fumbled around in dim light on a PC keyboard knows the value of keyboard backlighting. Keyboard backlight is on by default and does not turn off even if your Mac is idle.

If you would like to dim your keyboard lighting after your Mac has been idle for a period of time, open the **Keyboard** preference pane by launching the System Preferences application and selecting the **Keyboard** icon or from the Apple menu by selecting > **System Preferences... > Keyboard**. Click the **Keyboard** tab if not selected already.

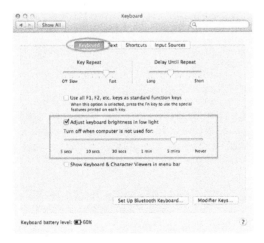

Check the check box next to **Adjust keyboard brightness in low light**. Adjust the amount of time you want your Mac to be idle before the keyboard backlight is dimmed.

Put Disk Drives to Sleep Faster

If you own a MacBook Pro or MacBook Air, you can conserve battery power by putting your disk drive to sleep when not in use. For example, if you are simply browsing the Internet with your Mac, your disk drive is simply wasting precious battery power. OS X allows you to put your disk drive to sleep when it has been idle for a period of time.

To put your disk drive to sleep to save power, open the **Energy Saver** preference pane by launching the System Preferences application and selecting the **Energy Saver** icon or from the Apple menu by selecting **> System Preferences... > Energy Saver**.

Check the check box next to **Put hard disks to sleep when possible**. OS X will put your disk drive to sleep if it has been idle for 10 minutes.

The idle time can be adjusted to be more aggressive in order to save more battery power. To shorten the idle time, open **Terminal** and enter the following command.

```
systemsetup –setharddisksleep 5
```

This command will put your disk drives to sleep if they have been idle for five minutes.

To revert back to the OS X default, enter the following command in **Terminal**.

```
systemsetup –setharddisksleep 10
```

Turn Off Drag-and-Drop

Drag-and-drop is a feature that allows you to drag and drop text within applications. Instead of using the cut and paste method to move text, you can simply highlight text and then drag it to its new location in the document. If you find this feature bothersome because you often accidentally move text that you did not intend to move, you can turn it off using a command in Terminal.

To turn off the drag-and-drop feature, open **Terminal** and enter the following command. You will have to log out and log back in for the change to take effect. This command effectively turns off the drag-and-drop feature in all applications in which it is supported.

```
defaults write –g NSDragAndDropTextDelay –int –1
```

To restore the drag-and-drop feature, enter the following command in Terminal. You'll have to log out and log back in for the change to take effect.

```
defaults delete –g NSDragAndDropTextDelay
```

Enable Sticky Keys

If you have trouble holding down two or more modifier keys simultaneously, the OS X **Sticky Keys** feature allows modifier keys to be set without having to hold them down. The following modifier keys can be enabled as sticky: ⇧ ^ ⌥ ⌘ (shift, control, option, command). When the Sticky Keys feature is enabled, pressing a modifier key will hold it down. The "stuck" key will display in the upper right of the screen to let you know it was pressed. To "unstick" the key, press it again.

To enable Sticky Keys, open the **Accessibility** preference pane by launching the System Preferences application and selecting the **Accessibility** icon or from the Apple menu by selecting > **System Preferences... > Accessibility**.

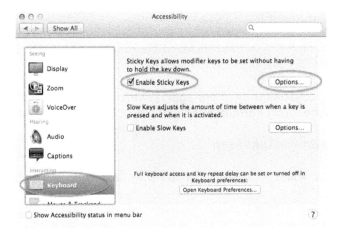

Select **Keyboard** in the left-hand pane and check the check box next to **Enable Sticky Keys** to enable this feature. Click the **Options...** button to configure sound and display options. By default, OS X will beep and display the key in the top right of the screen when a modifier key is set.

Zoom the Entire Display

OS X allows you to zoom the entire display using a keyboard shortcut or scroll gesture. To enable the display zoom feature, open the **Accessibility** preference pane by launching the System Preferences application and selecting the **Accessibility** icon or from the Apple menu by selecting > **System Preferences... > Accessibility**.

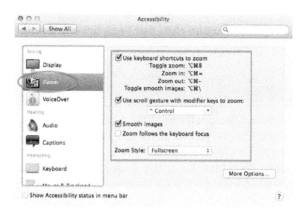

Select **Zoom** in the left-hand pane and check the check boxes next to **Use keyboard shortcuts to zoom** or **Use scroll gesture with modifier keys to zoom**. The keyboard shortcuts are listed in the Accessibility preference pane. The scroll gesture is a two finger drag while holding down the modifier key chosen in the Accessibility preference pane. Be sure to check the check box next to **Smooth images** so the images won't pixelate as they become larger.

The **More Options...** button offers additional settings to configure the maximum and minimum zoom, show a preview rectangle when zoomed out, and to control the screen image as you move the pointer around the screen.

Set Visual Alerts

Sometimes you have to quiet your Mac. If you're working in a quiet office environment the cool alert sound you found may not be appreciated by your office mates. However, you still want to be alerted when a new message or e-mail arrives. Instead of using an audible alert, OS X can flash the screen to alert you.

To turn on visual alerts, open the **Accessibility** preference pane by launching the System Preferences application and selecting the **Accessibility** icon or from the Apple menu by selecting > **System Preferences... > Accessibility**.

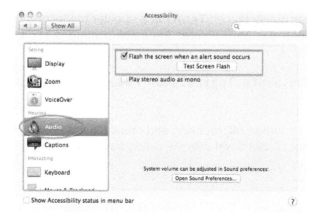

Select **Audio** in the left-hand pane and check the check box next to **Flash the screen when an alert sound occurs**. You can click the **Test Screen Flash** button to see what a visual alert looks like.

Caffeinate Your Mac

If you would like to leave your Mac unattended for a period of time but do not want it to go into sleep mode, you can caffeinate your Mac by turning off idle sleep mode for a period of time or until you turn it back on. Idle sleep mode is a process that is used to detect if you haven't done anything with your Mac for a while, so OS X can put your Mac into sleep mode.

To caffeinate your Mac for specific period of time, open **Terminal** and enter the following command.

```
caffeinate -dt 3600
```

The number at the end of the command represents the number of seconds that idle sleep mode will be turned off. In the example above, idle sleep mode will be off for one hour as there are 3,600 seconds in an hour. To prematurely end your Mac's caffeination, enter **^C** (control+C), otherwise it will remain caffeinated until the timer expires.

If you would like your Mac to be caffeinated indefinitely until you enter **^C** (control+C), launch **Terminal** and enter the following command.

```
caffeinate -di
```

Your Mac will remain caffeinated as long as the Terminal window remains open and the command is still running. To prematurely end your Mac's caffeination, enter **^C** (control+C).

Disable Power Button Sleep

You can put your Mac to sleep immediately by pressing and releasing its power button. OS X allows you to turn off this feature if you have no need for it.

To disable power button sleep, launch **Terminal** and enter the following command. Do not press the **return** key until you have entered the entire command. Log out and log back in for this change take effect.

```
defaults write com.apple.loginwindow PowerButtonSleepsSystem -bool
FALSE
```

With power button sleep turned off, pressing and releasing the power button will cause OS X to verify that you want to shut down with the dialog box shown on the next page.

Shut Down Immediately without Confirmation

When shutting down, OS X will confirm whether you really want to shut down. A dialog box will ask, "Are you sure you want to shut down your computer now?" You are presented with a choice of **Shut Down** or **Cancel** or waiting until the timer expires.

If you want to shut down immediately without OS X confirming your intention, hold down the ⌥ (option) key while selecting > **Shut Down**.

Another method is the hold down the ⌃⌥⌘ keys (control+option+command) while pressing the **eject** button to force your Mac to shutdown immediately.

About the Author

Tom Magrini is the author of 3 books in the Customizing OS X series, which teaches Mac users to completely customize their OS X experience with hundreds of tweaks, hacks, secret commands, and hidden features. His books teach Mac users how to customize OS X Mountain Lion, Mavericks, and Yosemite to give their Macs their own unique and personal look and feel.

Tom is an information technology professional with over 30 years experience as an engineer and senior manager. He has used Macs since 1984 and still fondly remembers his first Apple Macintosh computer with its 8 MHz Motorola 68000 processor, 9-inch 512 x 342 pixel black-and-white screen, 128 kB of RAM, and built-in 400 kB 3½ inch floppy drive. Tom also worked with NeXT computers and the NeXTStep operating system, the forerunner to Apple's OS X.

During the work week, Tom is a busy IT manager, leading a team of IT professionals who maintain two data centers and the network, telephony, servers, storage, security, and desktop computing infrastructure for a large city. Tom has taught programming, operating systems, Cisco Networking Academy, and wireless technology courses as a professor at two colleges.

When Tom isn't working on his MacBook Pro or hanging out with his family and dogs, he enjoys reading, movies, writing, and the beautiful Arizona weather with its 300 days of sunshine.

Please subscribe to Tom's Flipboard magazine, *Mac OS X Yosemite*, where he keeps you up-to-date on the latest OS X Yosemite and Apple news, features, tips, and tricks.

Books by Tom Magrini

Customizing OS X – Yosemite Edition – Fantastic Tricks, Tweaks, Hacks, Secret Commands, & Hidden Features to Customize Your OS X User Experience

Catch the Wave: Customizing OS X Mavericks – Fantastic Tricks, Tweaks, Hacks, Secret Commands, & Hidden Features to Customize Your OS X User Experience

Taming the Pride: Customizing OS X Mountain Lion – Fantastic Tricks, Tweaks, Hacks, Secret Commands, & Hidden Features to Customize Your OS X User Experience

www.ingramcontent.com/pod-product-compliance
Lightning Source LLC
Chambersburg PA
CBHW080359060326
40689CB00019B/4072